MW00851091

Charlie Gould
Memories of a Cowboy

Copyright 2018 Ed Ashurst
First Edition August 2018

ISBN-13: 978-0-9898676-9-6

Printed in the United States

Published by:
Ed Ashurst Publishing Company
azgabbyashurst@gmail.com
(520) 508-2846

All rights reserved. No part of this book may be reprinted, reproduced, stored in a retrieval system, or transmitted in any form or by any means, electronic, mechanical, photocopying, recording or otherwise without prior written permission.

Charlie Gould
Memories of a Cowboy

Written by Ed Ashurst
Illustrated by Mike Capron

Ed Ashurst Publishing Company
Douglas, Arizona

Other Books By Ed Ashurst

Non Fiction

Miracle or Coincidence

Real Cowboys

Wagon Boss

Mavericks

The Life and Times of Warner Glenn

Alligators in the Moat

Fiction

Stealin' From the Neighbors

"Cowards never lasted long enough to be real cowboys."
Charles Goodnight

For Cole, Sam, and Jake

Foreword

In the foreword to Ed Ashurst's book Wagon Boss, Charlie Gould wrote, "I am not now nor have I ever been a good cowboy." Ha! Arguable as that statement is, I don't know how Charlie arrived at that, but I reckon what he is tryin' to say is that he's never stopped learnin', and no matter how many years he's been at it, he's still trying to be better. In other words, in Charlie's mind there is never a point or plateau when a feller can say he's "good." It keeps a man humble.

I think it's fair to say that Charlie is a student of "cowboyology" (I made that up). He has punched cows or hunted from the border of Mexico to Canada and most places in between.

Charlie holds no prejudices or preconceived notions about where a person hails from, whether he is called cowpuncher, buckaroo or cowboy. Makes no difference to him whether his outfit is a center-fire or double rig saddle, whether his rope is tied hard and fast or he dallies with a sixty foot reata. You'll find that Charlie holds in high regard anyone who "makes a hand" regardless of what he's called, what kind of outfit he has, or what culture he's a product of. Texan, buckaroo, cowpuncher or rough country wild cowman, no matter, Charlie can tell you stories about the ones he's worked with.

Ed has latched on to this and will take you on the trail of Charlie's adventures. You're in for a history lesson on cow outfits and the men that work them. You'll meet many of the best (and some of the worst) but at any rate many memorable characters along the way.

I personally love history, characters and circumstances that come together to make it. Ed has done a great job in bringing out the "character" of the cowpunchers and others who helped shape and influence Charlie's life.

I worked with both Charlie and Ed when they first broke their home ties and started out on the cowboy trail and then again in later years when they both had families. If I sound partial, that I am, for I have known both for over fifty years and value them both for their good and loyal friendship all these many years.

Now, I'll say it—they are both good hands, anywhere, anytime.

Sit back and enjoy the trip, and be like Charlie and never stop learnin'.

I can hear the rain hitting the tin roof so I'm gonna stop now and pray that this is the start of the end of the 2018 drought.

Thanks be to God for the Western way of life He has blessed us with.

Mike McFarland.

Order of Chapters

A Runaway Kid

Sand and tumbleweeds were blowing sideways, and the eternal dust made visibility little better than guesswork at any distance of more than fifty yards. The sun was about a half hour before disappearing behind the sandy mesa out on the western horizon when a 1927 Dodge pickup pulled into the gas station on the outskirts of Las Cruces, New Mexico. The truck was connected to a homemade single-axle trailer that was fashioned out of pieces of iron found in a scrap pile, and a bumper of unknown origin. The whole affair was dusty and dried-out looking, the effects of the sun and wind that are ever present in the American Southwest.

Captured inside the homemade trailer was a rather large horse, at least he looked large, a result, no doubt, of the fact that the trailer was small. The horse wore a cowboy's saddle complete with several Navajo blankets underneath it and a homemade leather halter on his head which hung out over the front of the cage on wheels that held him confined. In the truck were several large bedrolls protected by heavy canvas tarps and rolled up and tied with pieces of rope. There was also a trunk or two and boxes that held a camp outfit, dutch ovens, coffee pot and skillet, and somewhere in the midst of this plunder was a crate that had a portion of flour, baking powder, salt, coffee and a slab of bacon.

When the outfit came to a stop in close proximity to the gas pump, two healthy looking men stepped out and stretched their arms and legs and pulled their cowboy hats down a little tighter on their heads making sure the wind didn't catch their hat brims and then carry them off to some distant sand dune. The man who stepped out of the passenger side of the automobile was tall, about six two, and was ruggedly handsome in a Western sort of way, complete with a mouthful of teeth that were impossible to ignore when he grinned or laughed, which was often. He strode toward the door of the building with the intention of entering therein to pay cash money for some gasoline, and as he walked he noticed a young boy sitting on a rustic bench that sat up against the side of the building. Tucked under the bench and behind the boy's feet was a small cardboard suitcase, and rolled up in his fists, the boy held what looked like an old coat.

The big man was walking in a southwesterly direction which faced the gusty wind, and although he was generally a man who held his head up and looked straight ahead, he was now looking downward avoiding the gusts of dirty air. Under his hat brim he noticed the boy whose body was protected from the wind by the building he was sitting against. Their eyes met but nothing was said.

The man's name was Everett Bowman. He entered the establishment and laid three dollars on the counter and told the lady who stood behind it that he wished to pay for ten gallons of gasoline that his brother Skeet was going to pump and then deposit into their vehicle. He also purchased two sacks of Bull Durham smoking tobacco and two candy bars. He was polite and smiled at the woman as she counted out sixty-two cents in change. "Thank you, ma'am."

Everett Bowman turned and walked to the door and stepped outside. The door was on the north side of the building, and because the wind was coming from the southwest, he was now somewhat protected from the gusts. He stopped after taking one step and looked down at the boy who was still sitting on the bench, which was to his left. They stared at each other momentarily, pondering from different angles. Everett spoke, "You've run away from home, haven't you, kid?"

"Yes," came a simple reply.

Everett stared off into the distance and the dust and tumbleweeds that were blowing over San Augustine Pass and on

"Get in kid. We're going to Arizona."

toward Alamogordo. He tore open the paper wrapper that held the chocolate candy bar. He broke off a piece and put it in his mouth, and for a moment he stared at the dust, and then turned and handed the boy the rest of the candy bar. "Come on, you can come with us. We're goin' back to Arizona." He proceeded toward the car and horse trailer, and after four steps he stopped and turned facing the wind.

The boy sat on the bench looking at him in defiance. "I'm looking for a job on a real cattle ranch where I can work hard and get paid for it," the boy answered.

Everett Bowman threw his head back and laughed out loud. "Ha ha! You're in luck, kid, at least on the first two accounts. We got a real cow outfit and lots of hard work; but you're gonna be disappointed in the pay!" He walked toward the car and horse trailer, and when he got halfway there, the twelve-year-old boy picked up the cardboard suitcase and followed him.

It was 1929, not long before the stock market crash and the beginning of the great depression. The boy's name was John Gould, and he had left his home and family in Riverside, Illinois, several weeks earlier and had been making his way west hitchhiking, hopping onto trains and sometimes walking. His destination was anywhere in Arizona. His family were good middle-class people who were quite content with a suburban Midwest lifestyle, but John, the boy, had been ruined several years earlier when his father had pulled up stakes and moved to Arizona. That move changed John forever. He saw cowboys and wild, wide-open spaces and fell in love with the idea of being a real cowboy, although he really knew little about it. Arizona didn't suit anyone else in the Gould family, and after a year or so they migrated back to Illinois. But John was miserable. He hated Illinois, especially the cities, and he hated the lifestyle; and he was determined to go back to Arizona. He snuck away with a small amount of cash and a couple changes of clothes. The clothes were dirty and the cash was gone when Everett Bowman found him at the foot of the mountain on Highway 70 out east of Las Cruces a couple of miles.

The gas pump was comprised of a metal cylinder two-foot in diameter and about four-foot high. On top of that was a cylinder glass storage that would hold ten gallons of liquid and was painted with marks on its side that would show how much it was holding: one, two, three and on up to ten gallons. Near the bottom of the metal platform that held the glass storage, there was a long metal handle a yard in length that was in an upright position a few inches away from the metal platform and parallel in its position. The handle was connected at the bottom by a steel pin that was part of the pump mechanism. An individual wanting to pump gas up into the glass container moved the metal handle back and forth, a foot one way and then a foot the other way, and the movement worked the pump that pulled gasoline from an underground tank and pushed it up into the glass tank. As you pumped, you watched the marks on the tank and stopped pumping whenever you had pumped the desired amount. About the time Everett reached the car with John Gould in tow, Skeet had pumped ten gallons into the glass container. He took the rubber hose that was plumbed into the bottom of the glass storage and stuck the end of it into the car's gas tank. He then opened a valve and let the gasoline flow via gravity into the car.

"This kid here has run away from home. Says he wants to work on a real cow outfit."

Skeet put the hose back in its proper place when his ten gallons had been transferred into the car. "Howdy! They call me Skeet. What's your name?"

"John Gould."

"Nice to meet you, John."

Everett looked at John and stuck out his hand. "I'm Skeet's brother Everett. Everett Bowman. That's our last name, Bowman." He handed Skeet the other candy bar, and Skeet broke it in half and gave half to John. "Get in, kid, we're goin' to Arizona!"

The Bowman brothers were on their way back home from a rodeo in Madison Square Garden in New York. They were among professional rodeo's elite for that day in time as was their oldest brother, Ed, although he wasn't present on this trip. Everett would be the one out of the Bowman brothers who would eventually gain the most notoriety as a rodeo hand. He would be crowned the World Champion Cowboy in 1935 and 1937, which was before records and statistics began to be kept in any official capacity by the Cowboys' Turtle Association. The Turtles, as it was commonly called, was pro rodeos first organization controlled and made up of the contestants themselves. Prior to the formation of the Turtles, several major rodeos would crown the winners of their various events "world champions," and Everett won at least eleven of those titles also. When the Cowboys' Turtle Association was formed in 1936, Everett was elected as its president and served in that capacity until 1944 when the association evolved into the Rodeo Cowboys Association. It was at that time that Everett retired from rodeo competition.

Everett and Skeet made an impression on their peers in more ways than one. Five years before they picked up runaway John Gould during a southern New Mexico dust storm, the two brothers made the history books by pulling the first horse trailer across several states to a major rodeo event. In 1924 they wanted to enter the Cheyenne Frontier Days Rodeo because of the large purses that could be won there. But they did not own a truck large or powerful enough to haul two rope horses that far, so their brother Dick suggested they haul one in a trailer pulled behind their Dodge pickup in which they could load the other. Dick was the most mechanically inclined of the six brothers, and he offered to make Everett and Skeet the trailer. The manufacturing process took one afternoon. The trip from Safford, Arizona, to Cheyenne, Wyoming, took the better part of a week, and when they pulled into the Cheyenne rodeo grounds with a horse loaded in the homemade trailer, people laughed. They didn't laugh long because Everett and Skeet cleaned house, winning far more than their share of the prize money. The first sighting of the "Bowman" trailer started a trend that has grown far greater than anyone could have imagined at the time.

Everett and Skeet, with John Gould riding in back, drove west through the dust and tumbleweeds toward Safford, Arizona, and then forty miles farther toward their A Dart Ranch near Stanley Butte. The forty miles mentioned would be miles in a straight line on a map, by road it was much farther; but it didn't matter much because the road wasn't good enough to take the pickup and trailer anyway. The truck and trailer were left at their brother Ed's ranch which was known as the Hook and Line; and Everett, Skeet and John would have to make the last fifteen miles to Stanley Butte on the back of a horse or mule. Everett and Skeet built a road all the way to the A Dart using a mule-drawn, iron-wheeled grader several years after John Gould moved in with them.

One of the best cowboy books ever written is *Lost Pony Tracks* by Ross Santee. In the book the author relates many stories about the cow country surrounding Globe in Gila County. One of the well-documented stories is about Ed Bowman, and I will include it here as an excerpt from Mr. Santee's book:

> Old-timers will tell you the Gila doesn't roll any more as it did before Coolidge Dam was built. In the old days, before the river was bridged, there were often days, sometimes weeks, when the Gila could not be crossed unless a man walked the railroad trestle, and not many had stomach for that.
>
> Ed was courting Louise Graham, the girl he later married. The Gila was booming and no one had crossed for days. Never one to travel afoot, Ed rode a bronc across the railroad trestle. They were

about halfway when Ed saw the approaching train. He got down and pushed his bronc off the trestle into the river. Then Ed hooked his big hands about a railroad tie and hung above the swirling water until the freight had passed. Then he climbed up again and ran to catch his bronc. The pony swam out the way he had come. Ed caught him as the pony crawled out of the water and mounted again. This time they crossed the trestle without incident since they didn't meet a train.

Ed, the oldest of the six brothers, was the first to own a ranch in that area. Sometime between 1910 and 1914, Ed took over as manager at the Hook and Line Ranch working for his father in-law, George Graham. The ranch headquarters was at the confluence of the Gila River and Hawk Canyon, six miles below present day Coolidge Dam which was completed in 1928. There was no road into the ranch when Ed moved in there, and everything that was used at the ranch had to be packed in on the back of a mule. The nearest supplies of any kind were at Rupkey's store at old San Carlos fifteen miles away, and the trail crossed the Gila River, which could be very dangerous when it was at flood stage. Under Ed's leadership nobody ever lost their life crossing the Gila, although one cowboy working for him almost drowned. The cowboy panicked and quit his horse while swimming across the river at flood stage, and the cowboy's head kept bobbing up and down like a cork in the rough water with Ed running along the shore attempting to rope him. Ed finally threw his lasso at the man's head and pulled it up tight around his neck and drug him up on dry land. He had a severe rope burn around his neck as a result of Ed's effort and was mad at Ed for some time. Ed laughed at him thinking perhaps he would have been happier dead. Eventually Ed and his wife Louise bought out George Graham and became sole owners of the Hook and Line, and one of the first improvements they made was the construction of a crude road built with equipment that was pulled by mules.

In the early days of professional rodeo, Ed Bowman was a very successful competitor and was known for riding good horses. He had a calf roping horse he called Pete that was famous for backing up and keeping the rope tight while Ed was down flanking and tying the calf. Ed would holler at the horse saying, "Backup, Pete," and the horse would obey his commands and work perfectly. The horse became a star and was known as Backup Pete.

Ed traveled to and was successful at places like Madison Square Garden, Chicago, Cheyenne, Calgary and Prescott. He was innovative and not afraid to try new things. Backup Pete was famous for working a rope, which was uncommon in that era, though a common and accepted practice in modern times. Ed was the first man to dismount from his calf horse on the right side, which he would do in situations when the calves were small enough, although in that day most of the calves roped at big rodeos were huge and were "legged down" instead of flanked. He rode fast horses and used a shorter rope than most cowboys and would wear Keds tennis shoes while competing so he could run fast.

In 1926 the bulldogging steers at the Calgary Stampede weighed over 1300 pounds, and nobody could throw them. So after the first day the Stampede's promoters changed the event to a steer decorating contest where a man was supposed to slip a red ribbon attached to a rubber band over the steer's left horn. In a hotel room the night before his run, Ed practiced for hours slipping one of his wife's garters over a brass bed post. He won the event.

For many years the big Prescott Frontier Days Rodeo had a relay race they called the Strap and Cinch Relay. Each contestant was supposed to ride a horse a quarter mile and then change his saddle to a new horse, doing this four times at each quarter of the mile long, oval race track. Ed would always use Backup Pete on the first leg of the race. Ed Bowman won the race nine times in a row and retired from the event undefeated.

In 1949 Ed and Skeet Bowman matched Hugh and Ralph Bennett to a ten head team tying contest. The Bennett's were famous rodeo hands themselves, and Hugh Bennett and Everett Bowman were married to sisters. The match was well publicized and the Bowman's won by a narrow margin.

In 1927 Ed won the All Around award at the Prescott Frontier Days Rodeo. At the age of forty-one, he roped and tied three very big calves in an average of 18.3 seconds over a sixty-foot score. That set a record that was never beaten until the score was shortened by 50 percent to thirty feet. For the All Around win, he was given a silver cup known as the Hoot Gibson Trophy. There is a famous picture of Ed holding the trophy that stands two and a half feet tall and weighs twenty-five pounds. He's riding Backup Pete and wearing heavy batwing chaps and is posing in the rocky roping arena at the Hook and Line Ranch. Ed, Everett and Skeet built the arena out in the front of the ranch house where a mesquite thicket had thrived when Ed moved to the ranch. They pulled the mesquite stumps out of the ground with a team of mules and became champions practicing in the rocky arena riding good horses that Ed raised. They were good because they punched cows on them first and rodeoed on them second.

Ed competed in roping events until he was sixty-four years old and then took up training cutting horses. He moved from the Hook and Line on the Gila River to a ranch near Peyton, Colorado, and started raising registered Hereford cattle and training cutting horses. When he was sixty-seven years old he won the American Quarter Horse Association cutting contest riding a horse he raised and trained named Sunny Boy. Altogether in one year he and Sunny Boy won the Western States, Pacific Coast, and National Cutting Horse Association titles. The younger men couldn't beat the old man who would tell them, "Sunny Boy can cut the soda out of a biscuit!" Everett's brother-in-law, Hugh Bennett, who is honored in the American Quarter Horse Hall of Fame, National Cowboy Hall of Fame, and the Pro Rodeo Hall of Fame said, "When Ed and Sunny Boy are at their best, they're unbeatable!"

Skeet Bowman was the baby in the family and was born on September 27, 1902, at Hope, New Mexico. He came along with his family to Safford, Arizona, when he was a small boy. He grew up cowboying with his brother Everett on ranches around Safford and Clifton. They both worked for the famous Chiricahua Cattle Company as young men. At age twenty he and Everett drove a large herd of cattle to a ranch near Ely, Nevada, a distance of over 900 miles. The pair stayed for a year working on the big ranch that had purchased that herd. The brothers tired of the climate in that northern country saying there were only two seasons near Ely, Nevada, late fall and winter. They returned to Arizona and took up professional rodeoing and established their A Dart Ranch near Stanley Butte with their winnings.

On September 4, 1928, Skeet married Jewel Sorensen Claridge. On his wedding day he left the Hook and Line, with brothers Ed and Everett, riding toward Safford some forty plus miles away. Between the ranch and town, they roped eight maverick bulls and tied them to trees. The wedding went on as planned, and when the cowboys, along with Jewel, rode back to the ranch, they led the wild bulls with them. On his fiftieth wedding anniversary, Skeet roped and tied a wild cow to a tree, laughing as he told several friends who were with him, "I've been doing this for over fifty years and I'm still enjoying it." Later that day he had a heart attack, and doctors performed surgery on him and put in a pacemaker to keep his heart beating in rhythm. He kept on cowboying for several more years after that.

Skeet competed at rodeos during the '20s and '30s traveling with Everett and was considered by some, including his brothers, to be the best roper in the family. He was especially successful as a calf roper and won many championships at the big shows. His first love was cattle ranching, and as the 1930s wore on, he slowed down as a rodeo competitor, traveling to far away places like Madison Square Garden less, although he roped calves at Arizona rodeos up into the 1940s.

In 1940 Skeet hired on as a deputy sheriff for Graham County. In 1944 he ran for the sheriff's position and won the election and served until 1952. He ran again in 1956 and won and served until 1969, becoming the longest serving sheriff in Graham County history.

In 1967 a fight broke out in the Arizona Lodge in Safford between two well-known local men. The fight ended when one of the two pulled a pistol and shot and killed the other. The shootist was very well liked locally, and witnesses claimed the dead man had instigated the fight in the first place. When the resulting trial went to court, the shootist ended up being convicted and was subsequently sentenced to serve one year at the federal penitentiary at Florence. The guilty man never showed up at Florence, but instead Skeet took him out to his ranch at Stanley Butte and let him work out his sentence there. No one, including authorities, said anything about the unusual procedure, and the guilty man finished out his sentence at the ranch.

Skeet eventually bought out Everett's interest in the A Dart and was the sole owner. And then the federal government kicked all cattle ranchers off of that part of Arizona, which was known as the Mineral Strip, and Skeet, like many others, had to leave and see his ranch given to the Apache Tribe. He fought long and hard to have the government mandate overturned but was unsuccessful.

Everett and Skeet fixed John Gould up with a cowboy outfit: a bed, saddle, chaps, and everything else a young cowboy might need. None of it was new or fancy, but it was functional and got him started. They taught him the rudiments of how to gather and work cattle in the rough country where the Stanley Butte ranch was located. A lot of learning the cowboy trade comes from experience, in other words, learning from one's mistakes. Like everyone else, John made mistakes, but he loved the life, and he took to it handily and was soon trustworthy enough to be left alone at the ranch while the Bowmans went off to rodeos, sometimes more than a thousand miles away. When they would get back home, things would be taken care of, and they would find John happy in his work.

About the only thing that bothered John was his lack of education. He wanted to be an Arizona cowboy but also wanted to be able to read and acquire knowledge. He wanted to be able to run an outfit someday and be a top hand like the Bowmans. While living alone at the A Dart Ranch, he began practicing something that would endure to the end of his life. He read everything he could get his hands on. He would read old newspapers, Sears and Roebuck catalogs, cookbooks, even the writing on cans of food like peaches or canned tomatoes. If there were printed words, he would read them. He began a lifelong pursuit of educating himself and collecting books that he could afford. He set his sights on being a self-educated man.

John Gould stayed at Everett and Skeet's A Dart Ranch at Stanley Butte for several years. At times by himself while the two Bowmans would be off rodeoing, but most of the time one of the Bowmans would be at the ranch. As the decade of the '30s wore on, Skeet traveled to the big rodeos less frequently than Everett, so John, without a doubt, spent a considerable amount of time with him at the ranch.

Sometime before 1935 John struck out for new territory, although his leaving his employment with the Bowmans was not because of any bad relationship or negative conduct. This fact is proven by letters and other communications that were written after John moved on. Actually he would work for Everett again.

At some point in the mid-1930s, probably '33 or '34, John worked for a while at the J. W. Smith Ranch near Willcox. In a letter written to John and postmarked October 20, 1936, Mrs. J. W. Smith relates events that had just happened during the fall roundup at the Smith Ranch and towards the end of the letter she writes, "Jim says to tell you he appreciates all the hard work you did."

Sometime during this timeframe, John also worked at the Chiricahua Cattle Company at San Carlos and for the Little Boquillas at Fairbank in Cochise County.

In late summer of 1936, John went back to Riverside, Illinois, to see his family, and he met Margaret Bradberry, a beautiful girl who was from the area. They soon married and John wanted to stay involved in the livestock industry so he got a job at the famous Chicago Stockyards tying bulls to the sides of railroad cars to keep them from fighting and killing each other. When the railroad cars would get loaded, John would climb through a small manhole located up high at the end of the cars. When he had got himself inside carrying a bunch of pieces of rope, he would get astraddle of a bull, riding on his back, and lean over and tie a piece of rope around his neck; and then by prodding and pushing he would get the bull near the side of the car and tie the other end of the rope to the edge of the car, similar to the way an Arizona cowboy would neck a wild cow to a tree. When he got the bull tied he would climb aboard another and repeat the process, doing it time and again until all the bulls were tied. There would be twelve or fourteen big bulls in each car, and he would be able to do three or four cars each shift. It was very dangerous work.

This was about the time that Everett and Skeet Bowman dissolved their partnership at the Stanley Butte ranch, and Everett bought a ranch south of Hillside in Yavapai County.

Everett's wife Lois wrote John a letter postmarked Fort Worth, Texas, March 19, 1938, and addressed to Mr. John W. Gould, % of Gable Apartments, Riverside, Illinois. Among other things in the five page letter she writes, "Guess you knew our Everett won the 1937 Champion Cowboy. He got the champion calf roping and steer roping. Besides the $700, he got the keenest silver-mounted saddle. It's all black leather. It's a beauty!" She closes the letter saying, "Let us hear from you more often! We are always glad to hear from you. Tell your sweetheart and family hello for us. We both send our best regards. Love to you, Lois and Everett."

On June 19, 1939, Lois Bowman wrote a letter to "Dear John and Margaret" and mailed it to Riverside, Illinois. The return address on the letter was Hillside, Arizona, so Everett and Lois had moved to the Hillside ranch sometime before then. The letter was type-written on stationary with the Cowboy's Turtle Association letterhead and logo on the top. The officers and directors are also listed at the top alongside the logo. The names are Everett Bowman, Herman Linder, Rusty McGinty, Hugh Bennet, Paul Carney, Eddie Curtis, Huey Long, James Minotto, and Everett Shaw. Lois mentions in the letter that Everett was not feeling real healthy (due to a rodeo accident?) but was going to head out on the rodeo trail on the Fourth of July weekend. The first planned stop was Reno. She also writes that Everett said he couldn't afford to stay at home, insinuating that Everett viewed rodeoing as a prosperous enterprise. She mentions toward the end of the letter that they would meet at the Bowman Ranch at Hillside in the fall so perhaps John had made an agreement with Everett to move out and go to work that summer or fall.

John and Margaret were definitely working for Everett at Hillside in the fall of 1941. Everett wrote them on October 11 on stationary from the Belvedere Hotel in New York City. And then two weeks later, October 25, he wrote another saying he had won about $900 at Madison Square Garden. Average annual per capita income in the United States was $8478. On October 30 Everett and Lois were in Boston competing at the big rodeo there. Everett wrote the Goulds on hotel stationary and closed the letter with the question, "How many calves have you branded?"

Sometime between 1941 and '46, John went to work for the 7 Vs north of Prescott. In those days the 7 V took in some of the country that became the Spider Ranch and the Cross U. One day while working for the 7 Vs, John found some initials carved in a rock in Horsewash Canyon near a water hole. This was south of Tailholt Mesa. The initials were EKM for Elton K. Mills who was a legendary cowboy in Yavapai County for six decades. Whistle (Elton) would end his career as wagon boss on the O RO outfit and was working and making a hand up into his late seventies. John hobbled his horse and carved his initials, JWG, next to Whistle's, and the year, 1942. This spot is a couple canyons north of a place known as Fair Oaks. While working for the 7 Vs, John and Margaret's oldest child, a girl named Carolyn, was born.

John also worked for awhile at the Yolo near Camp Wood in the mid-forties. And then in 1946 John took a job running a ranch north of Marathon, Texas, for a man named Leonard Hess. He stayed at the Hess Ranch for seven years. A rough old mountain known as Leonard Mountain was right in the middle of the ranch, and it was a tough piece of desert country.

While at the Hess Ranch, John hired a runaway fifteen-year-old boy from Kansas named Mike Landis. Mike had grown tired of his life on his family's farm where his strict religious father ruled with an iron hand. Mike dreamed of being a cowboy and went south to Texas, and when he got to Marathon he ran out of money, and John found him (much like Everett Bowman had found John) and gave him a job. Mike knew nothing except he wanted to be a cowboy. A Western cowboy. He picked up on every nuance of cowboy lore and culture he heard about or saw. He took to smoking cigars and Bull Durham cigarettes. One evening while sitting on the porch of John and Margaret's house at the Hess Ranch headquarters, he was puffing on a cigar, its end being real hot, and then took it in his hand; and while wildly gesticulating telling a cowboy story, he slung his hand with the cigar and slammed the fiery stick into Skeet Gould's forehead. Skeet was John and Margaret's second child, and the cigar burned his head considerable. Mike Landis' career as a storyteller and acquaintance of the Gould family was just getting started.

Mike wasn't real keen on bathing. One day he was riding a colt in the picket corral at the ranch when a pretty teenage girl showed up to visit John and Margaret. Mike was desperate to impress her with his accomplishments as a horseman and was whipping the bronc he was on around and around the picket corral as the pretty girl watched. As he passed close by, a snag sticking out from a picket caught hold of his Levis and ripped a large hole in them exposing a very large portion of Mike's leg from his thigh to the middle of his calf. The exposed leg was very dirty, not having been washed with water or soap in a good while. The girl was shocked at both the leg and the soil welded to it. She walked off. Her leaving didn't bother Mike, he figured bathing was not a virtue recognized by good cowhands.

John had been working hard since he worked for the Bowmans at educating himself. He bought and read books, he read newspapers and livestock publications and was interested in progressive management. While managing the Hess Ranch, he won several awards for his conservation efforts and range management. The ranch's owner, Mr. Hess, promised John a bonus if he could improve weaning weights and the calf crop. Over a year's time after Mr. Hess's promise was given, the weaning weight of the calves topped over 400 pounds for the first time in the ranch's history, and the calf crop's percentage improved substantially, even though the year had been drier than usual. In spite of all the improvement that he delivered, John did not receive the promised bonus. Mr. Hess claimed he just couldn't afford to come through with what had been promised, so John quit after six years as the Hess Ranch manager and headed back to Arizona.

Charlie Bradbury Gould was born not long after John and Margaret's return to Yavapai County. Now there were three Gould children all born in Prescott: Carolyn in 1941, Skeet in 1944, and Charlie in 1953.

A Prisoner In Town

In 1955 John and Margaret were in Colorado working on a ranch where the cows were gentle and the haystacks high, and one night while sitting around the house, John picked up his shotgun chaps that were laying on the living room floor. He pondered the chaps and the fact that there was very little use for them on the ranch where he was working. Leather hay bibs to protect your legs from grass stems might be necessary, but heavy Arizona chaps were sort of out of place. He stuck his hand down into the pocket of the left chap leg and felt something. He pinched it with his fingers and pulled it out, and it turned out to be a couple juniper berries and twigs from an Arizona juniper tree. He crushed the berries and held them up to his nose and smelled them. For a moment he sat and stared off into space and then announced, "We're going back to Arizona. In the morning!" They owned a 1950 International pickup, and at sunup they started loading everything they owned onto the truck. When it was finally loaded, they drove south, John, Margaret, Carolyn, Skeet, and Charlie who was four years old.

When they got to Holbrook they turned south and drove down through Showlow and by the Cibecue turnoff and descended down into the Salt River Canyon. About the time they crossed the bridge over Salt River, Margaret remarked, "Man, I would hate to think I was going to live in this place!" They drove on and went to Milton Forman's home in Globe. Milton Forman was a well-known cowboy and had worked on alot of the San Carlos cattle

country and had run outfits, but at the time the Goulds moved
from Colorado, he was working as a Gila County sheriff's deputy.
John and Milton were old friends so Margaret and Carolyn, Skeet
and Charlie stayed with the Formans, and John went to work for
the San Carlos Tribe helping several associations gather and ship
cattle at the Calva Stockyards.

The San Carlos Reservation encompassed 2910 square miles
of land, all of it rough, mountainous terrain and covered with a
great deal of brush and trees. The ranch was divided into different
ranches known as associations. The various associations were
managed by white cowboys employed by the San Carlos Tribe
to oversee the various herds of cattle. The truth is no one knew
how many cattle were running on the reservation. The official
count according to records was over 30,000 head of grown cattle,
but that number was unreliable. Mack Hughes was probably the
most well-known white cowboy who ever worked for the San
Carlos Tribe, and he ran two of the associations: first the Ash
Creek Association and later the IDT. Several books have been
written about Mack. About the time John Gould moved back
to Arizona from Colorado, in one 2-year-period Mack gathered
and branded over 1200 mavericks (unbranded cattle) on the Ash
Creek Association. Mack did not claim to have all of the cattle
accounted for. The fact is there was lots of work for a cowboy
at San Carlos in those days, and John Gould found employment
there in the fall of 1955.

About the time all the San Carlos cattle were shipped and the
fall roundup was completed, John got word that there was an
opening on the White River Apache Reservation. The White River
Reservation bordered the San Carlos across on the north side of
the Salt and Black rivers. The White River Apaches needed to hire a
stockman for the Grasshopper Association which ran from the Salt
River north to a ranch known as Grasshopper some fourteen miles
west of Cibecue. Grasshopper, as the association was commonly
referred to, ran in excess of 2500 mother cows on over 400 square
miles of rough mountainous terrain. It was some of the roughest in
Arizona. The camp where John would need to move his family lay
in the bottom of Salt River Canyon about twenty miles downstream

from the bridge where Highway 60 crosses over the Salt River. This bridge is where Margaret had made the comment, "Man, I would hate to think I was going to live in this place."

The cow camp was known as Medicine, and John timed it so they made their move at night so Margaret couldn't see where she was being taken. Medicine consisted of a house for the stockman to live in that was decent enough for that day in time, consisting of several rooms and large enough for a small family; but it was not a mansion by anybody's standards. Down the canyon several hundred yards was a smaller and less spacious affair where the stockman's right-hand man lived. In this case that man was Victor Beatty and his wife Irene who were both Cibecue Apaches. Victor had the reputation of being a very good cowboy, and he and John Gould would become good friends who respected each other. There was also a small barn and corrals at Medicine that were typical of an Arizona rough-country ranch. It was all very basic and nothing fancy. In time Margaret learned to love living at Medicine in spite of the fact that John was gone a great deal of the time, and he had tricked her by moving at night.

When they arrived at Medicine there was one animal in the horse corral, a mule; and after unloading what furniture and supplies they had brought with them, John caught the mule and saddled it and proceeded to wrangle the horses he could see grazing on the canyon walls in the horse pasture. Everything was higher than the house and corrals which sat in the bottom of the rough canyon, and trails led upward into the rough horse pasture or the huge cow pasture which lay north of the camp. He rode the mile up onto the steep canyon walls and got behind the horse herd and began following them downhill toward the corral, and the mule blew up and bucked John off as well as the saddle. Charlie watched as his dad came walking back into camp packing his saddle. John caught the mule a second time and saddled the mule, but this time he stole a britchen off of a pack saddle that was in the saddle house, and he whipped the mule down a hind leg and proceeded to finish the horse wrangling job; and when the mule tried to buck John off a second time, he didn't get it done.

...and he whipped the mule down a hind leg.

Irene Beatty was an old-time Indian. She wore a squaw dress and moccasins and had old-time ways. Charlie had been told by his mother to not go down and get in the horse corral without permission, but he would sneak down there when she wasn't looking. One of the saddle horses had a very severe wire cut on one of his front legs, and Irene Beatty took it upon herself to doctor the horse who had the reputation of not being very gentle. One day when Charlie snuck down to the corral, Irene was in the process of doctoring the horse. The horse was standing in the corral, and Irene had a bucket of water and a rag and was sitting under the horse's belly washing the cut leg with the rag and some recipe of herbs that she had concocted and mixed into the water. As she dipped the rag into the home remedy and then massaged the severe wound with the wet rag, she would softly sing some Indian chant. Charlie slowly walked up close to Irene and the horse and watched as she patiently ministered to him. The horse was supposed to be a kicker, but he stood there allowing the Indian woman to sit almost underneath him without attempting to move away or hurt her. She chanted and washed the wound. After a while she looked at Charlie who watched from a few feet away and said in broken English, "Charlie, if you want them to be gentle, you have to treat them gentle." Irene Beatty was a granddaughter of the famous Apache scout Peaches.

Peaches' Apache name was Tso-ay or Tsoe, depending on whose opinion of correct spelling you choose to believe. According to legend he was nicknamed Peaches by US Army soldiers because of his unusually fair and smooth complexion. He wore the nickname for the rest of his life. Peaches was born in 1853 into the Canyon Creek Clan of Cibecue Apaches. As a young man he took two wives who were members of the Warm Springs Clan under Chief Loco. Chief Loco and his followers were relocated to San Carlos by the US government, and Peaches and his wives were part of that relocation.

Not long after this forced relocation, Chief Loco's clan and many others at San Carlos suffered near starvation when the local Indian agent, a government contractor, stole and sold the tribe's government-allocated rations. Trouble boiled to the surface, and on September 30, 1881, three-fourths of the Apaches held in captivity at San Carlos broke out and fled the confines of the reservation; included in the Apaches who left were a renowned chief named Juh and Geronimo. Chief Loco and many others opposed the breakout fearing the fate that would surely befall them when the US Army caught up to them. So Peaches stayed with Chief Loco, but then on the morning of April 19, 1882, the outlaw Indians snuck back onto the reservation and roused Chief Loco and his band, including Peaches, and forced them to march south into Mexico and the Sierra Madre.

The US Army pursued them with a vengeance and several battles took place between the US soldiers and Apaches in Sonora and Chihuahua Mexico. Finally a famous Mexican Indian fighter named Colonel Lorenzo Garcia ambushed the Apaches near Janos, Chihuahua, and Peaches was severely wounded. Both of his wives were killed. In the battle at least seventy-five Apaches lost their lives, and several dozen women and children were captured by Colonel Garcia's men who undoubtedly sold them into slavery.

What was left of the Indian party fled back into the mountains to lick their wounds. Chief Loco and Peaches had never wanted to join this marauding band of outlaws, and as time went on, Peaches was treated with disdain. They did not recognize him as being a true Chiracahua Apache, and he was little more than a slave with no friends or allies.

The party at some point joined in with the outlaw Apache named Chato and his crew. They returned north back into Arizona and made an attack against whites near Fort Huachuca. They were desperate to acquire ammunition for their rifles and fought savagely against anyone they came upon. Chief Chato was famous for his cruelty.

Some reports say that about this time Chato and his band met up with Geronimo, Juh, and Naiche while in route to Southwest New Mexico, but that is unclear. It is certain, however, that Chato was present when Apaches attacked Judge H.S. McComas a few miles south of Silver City, New Mexico. The judge had rented a horse and buggy and was traveling south toward Lordsburg with his wife and six-year-old son, Charlie. They had stopped and were eating a picnic lunch under a tree when the Indians attacked. The judge's family made it to the wagon, and he returned fire while whipping the team into a dead run, but he was finally shot from an Apache's rifle. His wife grabbed the lines and continued to flog the horses with the ends of her lines until one of the horses was shot and went down. She was brutally clubbed in the head and killed. Little Charlie was taken, and no trace of him was ever found. Every major newspaper in the nation ran a story about the McComases' murders and kidnapping, and fear of the Apaches grew to epidemic proportions.

Lieutenant Britton Davis, one of the commanding officers at the San Carlos Agency, has been quoted extensively about the next move the renegades under Chato made. Brigadier General George

Crook, the commanding officer of the Army's Department of Arizona sent a message through the telegraph wire to Lieutenant Davis at San Carlos warning him of an impending attack on all the whites at San Carlos. Crook's telegram was based on intelligence received about Chato and his band's movements. Davis is quoted as saying the massacre of all the whites at the agency was not at all improbable.

In the middle of the night of March 30, 1883, someone snuck into Lieutenant Davis's room at San Carlos, and in doing so came close to getting shot. It turned out to be an Indian with important news that he whispered to Lieutenant Davis who lay in bed with a gun pointed at the bearer of intelligence, Tar-gar-de-chuse. The Indian said quietly, "Chiricahua come." Chato and his outlaws were camped about a dozen miles up the San Carlos River from San Carlos Agency.

Lieutenant Davis quickly assembled three dozen Apache volunteers and marched all night to Chato's camp. At dawn they had the camp surrounded and moved in for the capture or kill, whichever developed; but instead they discovered Chato and all of his men had escaped the noose. All except one—Peaches. Davis and his volunteers took custody of Peaches who was not the least concerned about his fate. He probably had deliberately stayed behind and hoped to be taken into custody because of the bad treatment he had received from Chato's crew.

When news of Peaches' capture was sent to General Crook, he instructed Davis to attempt to enlist Peaches' help as a scout and chief guide in an expedition into Mexico and the Sierra Madre with the intent of finding Geronimo, Chato and all the renegade Chiricahuas. Peaches immediately agreed.

The outlaws felt very secure in their various hideouts in the Sierra Madre along the border of Sonora and Chihuahua. They never dreamed Peaches would assist the US Army in an invasion of their turf. They let their guard down. On May 15 Peaches guided an advance column under Captain Emmet Crawford into the camp of Chato and Bonito, and a battle erupted, and nine Indians were killed and five captured. The Indians claimed little Charlie McComas was present in the camp and was killed, but his body was never found. As a result of Peaches' work as guide and the Army's successful invasion into the Apaches' camps, Geronimo, Naiche, Chato, Chihuahua, and Bonito sued for peace. Only Juh refused to surrender, and he remained in Mexico for years, creating havoc and spreading fear among the scattered peoples of the Sierra Madre. On the trail north, back into the United States, Peaches rode at the head of the column with General Crook.

In 1916 Peaches served under General John Pershing as his personal scout in Mexico when the general was in pursuit of the revolutionary Pancho Villa.

Peaches settled down in the country around Cibecue and remarried and had four children. He turned to farming for his livelihood and late in life converted to the Christian faith. He died in 1933.

Victor Beatty was a top Apache cowboy, and he and John Gould worked well together. Also among the crew of Apache cowboys who worked for John while he was at Grasshopper was Calvert Tessay, Joe Cromwell and Charlie Cromwell, all well-known cowboys who shared one thing in common, they had all worked off of the reservation on ranches owned by white men and with crews of white men. They understood how to work cattle the way white men worked them and had a better work ethic than the Apache cowboys who had no experience outside of reservation life.

Medicine, the cow camp where the Goulds lived, was very isolated, and getting three children to school was a problem. For a while Skeet lived away at a boarding school, but Charlie stayed at home, and Margaret taught him using correspondence courses, and he was learning the basic curriculum, but John was worried that Charlie needed a better school atmosphere. He was worried that Charlie would grow up as wild as some of the permanent residents of the reservation. Charlie had an eye for the wild hare in the bush, the hawk on the wing, the wild cow on a steep slope, or an Indian on the warpath, so John decided to go to town and find work and civilized neighbors and public schools.

They packed up and moved down the mountain to Tempe, and John went to work for the Tovrea feedyard where he rode pens doctoring sick steers, sorting fat steers and loading them on trucks to be sent to the packing plant.

The Tovrea feedyard was located on East Washington near 48th Street and for a time was the largest cattle feeding operation in the United States. The feedyard was owned by the Tovrea family who owned and operated five cattle ranches in Arizona and California as well as farms that grew feed for the steers they fed and a packing plant close by to butcher and process the steers when they were finished. The family also opened and operated the famous Stockyards Restaurant known for serving high quality beef, steaks in particular. The Tovrea operation was a complete start to finish beef producer. The packing plant was eventually sold to the Cudahy meat packing company.

The Tovrea family built a three-story castle where they lived in close proximity to the large feedyard. The Tovrea castle sat on a slight rise north of Van Buren and could be seen from a great distance and was a famous landmark.

Close by to the Tovrea feedyard was the Cornelius Livestock Auction, which in the '50s and '60s was the largest livestock marketing facility in Arizona. Thousands of cattle changed hands every week in that part of the valley of the sun. The area was considered to be out in the country.

The foreman over the cowboy crew at the Tovrea feedyard was Sam White, a very well-known and capable cowboy. About two years after John went to work for Sam White at Tovrea's, the company which had become known as T and C Feed Yard, or Tovrea and Christopherson, built a new feedyard at Maricopa south of Tempe some forty miles. John Gould was offered the foreman's job at the new facility. He went down to look at the new Maricopa facility and saw that they had built houses for the cowboy crew. The homes were nice and modern but were also within walking distance to the feedyard. John turned the foreman's job down saying that if he lived that close to the yard the company would own him because he would never escape the work. It probably didn't make much difference because Sam White took the job, and John became the foreman at the old facility, and even though he lived ten miles away, he was dedicated to the job. On holidays, like Thanksgiving and Christmas, while most of the crew took the day off, John worked riding pens and doctoring sick cattle, and his crew would be his family. Charlie grew up working on holidays and eating holiday dinners in the saddle house at the feedyard. His mother would prepare the meal at home and bring it to her family at the yard.

Charlie had spent four years at the Medicine Ranch down in Salt River Canyon in the middle of nowhere with nobody around except his family and a bunch of Apache cowboys. He had learned to ride and keep up with older men as they pursued cattle over some of Arizona's roughest mountains. Before he turned eight years old, most of the companions he had that were similar in age were Apaches. Many of the people he admired were only a generation or two away from the Stone Age. Moving to Tempe was a shock to him, and he never overcame the distinct hatred he had of the place. He never fit in. There were no other cowboy kids in the school he attended, and he was never a good student. The whole time he lived in Tempe he dreamed of going back to the reservation. He hoped that someday he could go to work for the famous cowboy Mack Hughes who was stockman on the big IDT Association at San Carlos.

In the winter months while school was in session, Charlie would work for his dad at the feedyard. Sometimes he would have colts to break for someone and would get paid for it. He always had a horse or two of his own. He learned to rope in a roping arena practicing with Sam White's son-in-law Ralph Vaughn who was a professional level roper. Beginning when he was nine or ten years old he would go and stay with his sister Carolyn or brother Skeet in the summertime.

On one of the first of such trips, he went to stay with Carolyn who was married to a cowboy named Moe Beck, and they were living on a ranch near Verde Hot Springs and Childs, Arizona. Moe Beck was running the ranch that was owned by a man named Amo

Rovey. The outfit had lots of trashy cattle, and when Charlie came for his first visit, they were camped on Houston Creek. Among the crew were Mike Cullen, Jake Moore, Jim Marler, Chili Beach plus Moe and Carolyn. Their camp was in a very remote and primitive place. Chili Beach was a grizzled old-timer who had a wooden leg.

The first night Charlie was staying with the crew, everyone was sitting around a big fire telling stories and listening to the coyotes howl and wild bulls beller off in the brush thickets. Charlie was about nine years old, and he became fascinated with Chile Beach who was by far the oldest member of the crew. He had whiskers, and a sweat-stained cowboy hat, and lines in his face like a Charlie Russel painting or Ross Santee novel. Chili Beach had a large and very sharp pocket knife, and while he sat with the flames creating mysterious shadows on the contours of his visage, he whittled on a stick, and every once in a while he would glance at Charlie who was staring at him. Chili waited until the timing was just right and Charlie was watching. He took the shiny blade of the knife, and with a violent thrust he stabbed himself below the knee, leaving the knife stuck and shaking in the wooden prosthesis. Charlie jumped and stampeded out into the night as the whole crew rolled on the ground laughing while they could hear limbs breaking in the brush thicket that Charlie had ran into in his attempt to escape.

Not many years later, Chili Beach was hauling a load of cattle down out of the Four Peaks toward Roosevelt. He was driving an old bobtail truck with no emergency brake when he stopped to open a gate on a hill. He had stopped the truck thinking it was resting against a rock in the road, and he got out to open the gate. About the time he was getting the gate unlatched, the truck rolled free from the rock and ran into Chile penning him against the gate post. When they found Chili, the truck was still idling, and Chile was dead standing upright with his back to the truck and his chest against the gate post.

One weekend when Charlie was eleven years old, John and Margaret took Charlie and a friend, Sharon Gearhart, to the Casa Grande ruins on a sight-seeing trip. That was a first date, and years later Charlie and Sharon got married.

In the summer of 1966, Charlie went and stayed with Carolyn and her husband in Fallon, Nevada, and spent the summer riding colts, helping his sister and husband train horses, and going to a few rodeos.

In the summer of 1967, Charlie went to stay with his brother Skeet who was working on the Yolo Ranch west of Prescott. The Yolo Ranch was several hundred sections of some of Arizona's roughest country. On the north end of the ranch near the Yolo headquarters, there were mountain peaks close to 7000 feet in elevation. Twenty miles south in the bottom of Scotts Basin, the lowest part of the ranch lay at 3500 feet. The western boundary of the ranch was Burro Creek Canyon and Conger Creek Canyon with vistas similar to Salt River Canyon or tributaries of the Grand Canyon. Several other canyons named Wilder Creek and Boulder Creek dissect the ranch and thus creating long mesas that run like fingers going south with steep rocky cliffs and rim rocks that in most places make passage from one mesa to another nigh onto impossible. A cowboy can be riding his horse on Contreras Mesa and look west to Bozarth Mesa and see cattle that are a mile and a half away but may need to ride half a day or even longer to reach them.

The southeast quarter of the Yolo Ranch took in about half of a magnificent piece of country known as Scotts Basin. The Muleshoe Ranch that lies to the south has the south half of the basin. Scotts Basin is a bowl-shaped piece of country with numerous canyons and ridges descending 500 feet or more to the bottom where Sycamore Creek runs south toward the Santa Maria River. It's a granite country and very brushy. It's known for being one of the best spring countries around if ample rain falls through the winter. In the bottom of the basin on the Yolo side was an old cow camp with corrals built out of granite stones stacked on each other and an old shack that had newspapers from the 1920s glued to the walls for wallpaper and insulation.

The Yolos was a famous old cowboy outfit where most of the old legendary wild-cow-cowboys had worked at one time or another. Men like Travis Heckles, Whistle Mills, Ed Koontz, and Ralph Chapman had all spent time there. When Skeet and Charlie were there, an old cowboy named Gene Smith was running the outfit, also on the crew was Monk Maxwell, Floyd Martin, and Lorrie Smith. Prior to Charlie showing up, Lorrie's brother Brad had been there, and a young boy named Jess Leslie.

Charlie helped the crew brand calves and finish up the spring cow work. The year before the outfit had bought some yearling Charolais bulls but for some reason had not branded them, and so while Charlie was there, they roped and branded the Charolais bulls that by that time had grown to a very great size.

One day while the crew was working out of the Strodjust Camp, Gene Smith, the old cow boss, tied a horse to the horse corral fence and was shoeing him. The horse boogered at something and set back and jerked a big board off of the fence and the board hit Gene in the area of his kidneys on his backside and injured him severely. Monk Maxwell had been Gene's second-in-command so he now took over as boss. Monk had been raised in Yavapai County and had learned to punch cows there using a double rig saddle and typical Arizona costume, but he had decided he wanted to be a center-fire-man and had a new fancy single rig made by a good saddle maker named Chick Logan. One day a colt run Monk's knee into a post in the corral and injured his knee so bad it swelled up like the trunk of a pine tree. His fancy center fire saddle was brand new, and he wanted to get it broke in so he asked Skeet to ride it for him a few times. Skeet was fixing on saddling up a colt that was broncy and bad about falling over, and he told Monk that it wasn't a good idea to put his fancy new saddle on that particular colt, but Monk insisted so Skeet put the center fire on the colt's back, and he fell over backwards and landed on the new saddle three times before he finally settled down. Monk seemed satisfied that the saddle was probably broken in correctly.

The outfit had been in the process of taking a bobtail tally on the cow herd. This was something that was done on outfits where some cattle would get missed and unaccounted for during every roundup. When they cut the tuft of hair off of the end of a cow's tail, it took a few months to grow back, so when they got a bunch of cows in a corral, they cut the ends off of their tails and then got a good count on them when they turned them out the gate. As they went along they would know that any short-tailed cow had been accounted for. At the next roundup, say six months later, they could cut tails off of any long-tailed cows and add them to their count and eventually get somewhat of an accurate count, depending, of course, on how many cattle were not gathered before the tails all grew back out. The usual process was done by crowding cattle into a tight corral and a man walking through the herd, grabbing tails, and cutting the hair with a very sharp pocket knife. It was dangerous work. Sometimes men would ride through the herds and lean over in the saddle and cut the tails while mounted. Even then it was dangerous. When Gene Smith got hurt and ended up in the hospital, Monk started giving the orders, and he announced they were going to team rope every cow to cut her tail for the tally. Charlie got to do a lot of roping that summer.

Skeet stayed on working at the Yolo Ranch the fall of '67 while Charlie went back to high school in Tempe. On December 13, 1967, the snow began to fall all over the northern half of Arizona, and the storm turned out to be one of the worst in Arizona history, even worse than the famous snow of December 1949. Skeet went through lots of trials and tribulations dealing with the deep snow on the Yolo Ranch. Historically cattle ranchers in Arizona have never been well prepared for deep snow and abnormal blizzards: It just doesn't happen that often. After the snow melted, Skeet enrolled in the Graham school in Kansas where students go through an intensive week-long course learning the rudiments of pregnancy testing and artificial insemination. With his diploma in hand he came back to Arizona and went to work for the San Carlos Apaches on their ranch at Arsenic Tub. This is where the Apaches' registered herd was kept, and Skeet was given the job of overseeing the breeding of the registered cow herd by artificial insemination. He was excited to be given the opportunity to use the skills he had acquired at the famous Graham school.

The Apaches in those days were entering the final stage of their evolution into and back out of the cow business. For twenty years the various San Carlos associations had successfully grown their business into well-run ranches with white cowboys like Mack Hughes, Pat Hughes, Nick Stockton, John Gould and others at the helm. But infighting and jealousy was spreading like cancer through the tribal council, and more and more Indians were demanding that the white cattle managers be replaced with Indians. The white bureaucrats from the offices at the Bureau of Indian Affairs made the situation worse because of their lack of knowledge about the cow business or the everyday running of a cattle ranch. The general mood in all of the federal government was drifting toward the Welfare State, especially concerning the affairs of any minority group. Operating in a fiscally responsible manner and turning a profit meant nothing to a government man, including BIA employees. The San Carlos ranches began to suffer because of this trend. Within a few short years all non-Indian cowboys would be gone, and the San Carlos cattle industry would be as good as dead.

Charlie showed up to help Skeet artificially inseminate the registered cowherd which numbered in the hundreds. The two men had no help, but they set about the task to the best of their ability. The corrals where they were told to do the work were falling down to the point they were almost nonexistent. The cows were wild, and finally things got so bad they were roping and dragging cows into the corrals and even into the squeeze chute. It was a wreck but the Indians didn't care. It was almost as if the tribe wanted the work to fail. It did. Late in the summer Skeet and Charlie were told to quit messing with the registered cowherd and spend their time riding a string of broncs.

In the fall Charlie went back home to Tempe and his junior year of high school, and Skeet went to Calva and helped the Indians ship thousands of Apache Hereford cattle. While working at Calva that fall among big crews of cowboys, most of whom were Apaches, there were five men named Skeet, and all had been named after Skeet Bowman.

One of the repeat buyers of San Carlos cattle was a rancher from California named Darrell Zwangh. Skeet went to California to work for Darrell when the fall roundup at San Carlos was over. Skeet Gould and Darrell's daughter Diane met that winter in California, and in May of 1969 they were married.

When school was out in late spring of 1969, Charlie headed north to Mojave County to work for Dale Smith on his huge Diamond Bar Ranch on the north end of the Hualapai Valley. The Diamond Bar took in hundreds of square miles running north from what is known as Red Lake in the middle of the Hualapai Valley all the way to Lake Mead at Pearce Ferry. On the east side it bordered the Hualapai Reservation and the Grand Wash Cliffs. To the west toward the White Hills, it butted up against what was known in those days as the Big Outfit that was owned by Jim Smith, Dale's father. Those two ranches, the Diamond Bar and the Big Outfit, took up all of the country from Red Lake and Dolan Springs going north to Lake Mead, and from the Hualapai Reservation west to the Colorado River and Black Mountains. In time and space it was vast, hot, dry and desolate. But there were cows there. For the most part they were cows with a lot of ear (Brahman influence), and their experiences with men were infrequent. The major waters, whether they were wells or natural springs, had wire corrals built around them and triggers, and the use of those triggers was the main way Dale Smith gathered and worked his cattle. The triggers would be set to allow cattle to enter the corrals in search of water and salt but not allowing them to exit. The calves were branded because of the use of triggers, and also weaned, or old cull cows and bulls captured so they could be sold. Occasionally Dale would take his crew and scatter them out over a piece of country and gather cattle, but the use of triggering cattle was preferred. The cattle by ordinary men's standards would have been considered wild, but then there was never anything ordinary about Mojave County, its men or its livestock.

The headquarters was somewhat of an oasis because of the blessing of a very good spring of fresh water that ran year round, and it sat about thirty miles northeast of Dolan Springs. That summer Dale's wife and family were living there with him at the Diamond Bar, and his wife cooked for the cowboy crew that consisted of Dale's children (occasionally), John Hamilton, an Indian named Curtis Lane, and Charlie. They spent their time branding and gathering yearlings to sell and roping wild trashy cattle that refused to submit to the triggers.

Curtis Lane was a Hualapai in late middle age when Charlie was sixteen. Late middle age to a Hualapai cowboy was probably about forty, but nobody knew for sure how old Curtis was. In his day he was quite well known. He was a small man and a very good cowboy and a better than average bronc rider. He had ridden broncs at Indian rodeos and a few pro rodeos with some success: the success being dependent on how sober he was, which usually wasn't very sober. He had worked on quite a few big white man outfits like the O RO, and the Diamond A at Seligman, and he had spent some time on the big ranches in Northern Nevada. Curtis and Charlie became good friends.

One day Dale, John Hamilton, Charlie, and Curtis were way out on the north end of the ranch near Pearce Ferry pursuing some fast cattle and a big Brahman cow ran off acting like she didn't want to cooperate. They were intending on roping her but she reached the Colorado River right at the edge of Lake Mead before anyone could get close enough to catch her. When she got to the river she bailed off into the water and started swimming toward the Arizona Strip. The water was deep and at least a quarter mile across to the north shore. She swam the distance with the cowboys watching, and when she reached the far side she stood on the water's edge shaking her head at the men in defiance. Charlie and the other men wondered if Dale might order them to bail off into the deep water and try to get her back. Dale could be somewhat domineering when he wanted to be. They all looked at him waiting for his dreaded orders. "Oh, hell with 'er," he said. "I'll let that Mormon @^*@#%^* on the other side have 'er, and I'll steal one from him someday." The Mormon @^*@#%^* on the other side was his brother Kent who owned a ranch across the river.

Not long after that, Dale, Charlie and Curtis were riding near Pearce Ferry, and they jumped a couple wild horses. Dale was always mounted on good, well-bred horses, and he was a world champion roper. He took to one of the horses and run him down and roped him in short order, making it look easy. Charlie took up pursuit of another, and things didn't go as good for him as they had for Dale. He ran him a considerable distance and finally got him caught, but in the process he abused the horse he was riding by running him through the rocks, and the horse was a little lame and had some small cuts on his legs from the rocks, plus he was sweating profusely and had the looks of a gutted jaybird. Dale got mad at Charlie for running a good horse so hard after a worthless mustang. Under Dale's orders, the men tied the mustang down and rolled Charlie's saddle under him, and Dale told him to ride him up. Charlie rode the wild horse back to camp and continued to ride him for days afterward.

After Charlie had been at the Diamond Bar for six weeks or so, Curtis Lane decided to quit; and after lunch one day he told Dale he was leaving and requested a ride to Peach Springs. Depending on what road you took, Peach Springs was a long ways away. If you went down through Dolan Springs, which was the most improved road, it was no less than 130 miles. Straight across country over the top of Music Mountain, it was about seventy miles. Dale told Curtis that he was not going to take him to town, at least not that day. The two of them argued, and Dale would not relent, so finally Curtis said he would just walk. Dale acted like he didn't care what Curtis did. As he walked out of the bunkhouse door he told Charlie, "Hey, Charlie, you make sure he brings me my bed and saddle."

"Okay, Curtis, see you later," Charlie replied, and he watched the Indian walk south. Charlie didn't own a vehicle or he would have taken Curtis to Peach Springs himself.

The next morning Dale announced that he was going to Peach Springs and deliver Curtis's saddle and bedroll and what other plunder he had left at the ranch. He told Charlie to ride along with him, so they took off in Dale's pickup going southwest through Dolan Springs. A short time before noon they pulled up in front of the post office in Peach Springs, and there sat Curtis on the sidewalk with his back leaned up against the post office wall. "Curtis, how in the heck did you make it here so fast? It must be seventy miles across there, maybe farther?" Charlie questioned him.

"Oh, Charlie, I'm an Indian," was all Curtis said.

Charlie quit the Diamond Bar soon after that and found a

job down at Yucca working for Phil Perner who was running La Cienaga Ranch for a fellow named Lyle Trimball. Phil Perner had a rosinjaw sort of drifter working for him who was driving a truck hauling water. Carolyn and JoAnn McDonald were cooking for Phil and the truck driver and Charlie who rounded out the crew.

Down at Yucca there was a notorious beer joint known as the Honolulu Club, and there was always something going on there. The people who owned the bar liked action. They had a very large glass aquarium in the middle of the bar, and they always kept a bunch of live rattlesnakes in it. They would pay anyone who brought one in five dollars a foot for any rattlesnake as long as it was alive. They kept a continuous pot that could be won by anyone who could put the palm of their hand up to the glass and keep it there when a mad snake struck at it from the inside. If you wanted to try your hand at winning the pot, you had to pay a five dollar entry fee that was added to the money already present. There was a fortune in the pot. The rules also said that you had to keep your eyes open and watching your hand as it lay against the glass, but before you put your hand on the glass, the bartender would take a long stick and stir the snakes up with it making them good and mad.

The rosinjaw truck driver would work late at night when it was cool, and one evening Charlie went with him for something to do. As they drove down a sandy ranch road with a load of water for cows to drink, they could see in the headlights a huge rattlesnake crossing the road in front of them. The rosinjaw stopped the truck and set out to catch the snake, which he finally did. The snake was a Western diamondback at least six-foot long.

"Okay, Charlie, you get in and drive, and I'll ride shotgun and hold my snake," the rosinjaw ordered.

"I ain't gettin' in that truck with no rattlesnake! And I'm not a truck driver."

"Okay, you little jackass, I'll drive and you hold the snake." The rosinjaw started to hand Charlie the six-foot long monster.

"I ain't holdin' no rattlesnake!"

"Okay you sorry @#$%^&*. I'll just kick your ass then!"

"Well, you're gonna have a hard time kickin' my ass while you're holdin' that rattlesnake."

The rosinjaw got mad and tossed the snake out into the desert and drove on to their destination, and they unloaded the water. When they got back to camp the rosinjaw quit, and Phil Perner put Charlie to driving the water truck fulltime.

Late in August Charlie quit and went down to Prescott to see his friend Dewey Brown. It was time to go back to school. Charlie had decided that he wasn't going to school but was going to get a job on one of the big ranches in the Prescott area. Then John Gould showed up. "I can't make you come back and finish school, but I'm askin' you as a favor to me to come back and finish high school. Just one more year." Beings his dad asked him like a friend, Charlie said that he would come home and go one more year.

About fourteen years later, Charlie was in Prescott in Matt's Saloon on Whiskey Row. It was summertime and it was raining straight down. He had been in Matt's awhile visiting a friend, and his wife Susan and his two boys were waiting for him in his pickup that was parked a short distance away.

As he stepped out onto the sidewalk, Curtis Lane walked by. He saw Charlie and approached him. He had been on a running drunk for many days, and he was filthy dirty and having a hard time standing up.

"Hey, Charlie, my old friend, glad to see you. How about giving me a ride out to Fort Whipple?" There was a veterans' hospital at Fort Whipple, and Curtis was a veteran. He could stay there. Charlie looked at Curtis and saw how dirty and smelly he was. He thought about his wife and kids in the truck.

"No, Curtis, I guess I can't give you a ride right now. I gotta go."

He left Curtis standing there in the afternoon thundershower and reached his pickup and family and drove off to do some business on the other side of town. He kept thinking of Curtis and how he had left him there, and he made a U-turn and headed back toward Whiskey Row looking for the Indian whom he had left wandering down the street. After driving around for twenty minutes, he finally spied Curtis soaking wet and wandering around down by the depot house. He stopped and got out and walked up to his old friend. "You still need a ride to Whipple, Curtis?"

Curtis stood there drunk but stoic and looking all around as if studying the architecture of the surrounding buildings. He gazed at the sky and finally replied, "Well, it looks like I'm still here, so I guess I still need a ride."

Charlie loaded him in his pickup along with everyone else, and they headed toward Fort Whipple. For a long time Curtis was silent and looked steadily out the passenger-side window. Finally he broke the silence. "You know, I been thinkin'. I thought you and I was friends. Friends don't treat their friends that way."

That was the last time Charlie Gould ever saw Curtis Lane.

Kids on a Cow Ranch

In 1970 if a cowboy said he was going to work for Babbitts he meant he was going to work on their outfit north of Flagstaff. That outfit was actually two large ranches: The C O Bar ran from the Little Colorado River east of Gray Mountain and went west on the north slope of the "mountain" which was what cowboys called the San Francisco Peaks. The W Triangle was west of Highway 64, north of Ashfork, and southwest of the Grand Canyon Village. It took in close to half of the geological phenomenon known as the Cataract Plains. These two ranches were, for all practical purposes, run as one unit by the same man with a crew that would move back and forth from place to place camping and doing the cow work. They were, however, two separate properties with a twenty-mile stretch in between them that was owned by other people. There was a third ranch south of Flagstaff and much smaller that was known as the Hart Ranch, but it was smaller than the C O Bar and W Triangle and was managed by a different man as a separate unit. But in the cowboy cult to say you were working for Babbitts usually meant you were working on the C O Bar and W Triangle, and you would be taking orders from the man Babbitts were paying to run it.

In 1982 Marshal Trimble, who held the title of Arizona's Historian, wrote a book titled *C O Bar*, which is a history of the C O Bar Ranch coupled with a fine collection of Bill Owen art. The book has a foreword written by John G. Babbitt who was president of Babbitt Ranches and universally known as a fine man. In his book, Mr. Trimble states that the C O Bar Ranch had a total of 850,000 acres of land on which cows could graze, and that did not include the W Triangle Ranch, which was about fourteen townships in size. Mr. Trimble's estimate of 850,000 acres was inaccurate. The C O Bar was smaller than that by nearly half, but at any rate it was still a good-sized cow ranch. The C O Bar and W Triangle took in something in the vicinity of 1100 square miles of grazing land and ran about 4500 mother cows. All of the Babbitt calves were weaned in the fall and kept for a year and sold as yearlings, most of them being eighteen months old when they were shipped.

The Hart Ranch south of Flagstaff ran about 750 mother cows, and their calves were kept with the C O Bar and W Triangle calves and shipped at the same time. The steer calves off of all three ranches were branded with a Bar V Bar on the left ribs but the heifers were branded with the iron of the ranch where they were born.

The Babbitt name dominated the business community in Northern Arizona in 1970 and had for eighty years. At that time the two biggest grocery stores in Flagstaff were Babbitt stores. When a lady wanted to purchase an expensive dress, she purchased it at the large Babbitt brothers' department store in the middle of town. There was a Babbitt lumber yard, and next door to it was the Babbitt wholesale hardware. If you wanted a new Ford pickup you bought it at Babbitt Ford which was located a couple blocks east of the department store. From Kingman to the west of Flagstaff 150 miles and to Springerville to the east 180 miles, it was the same: Babbitt grocery stores, Babbitt lumber yards and hardware. The Navajo Indian Reservation had several Babbitt trading posts on it, and the Grand Canyon Village inside the national park boundary had a Babbitt grocery store.

In the early days of Northern Arizona, the original Babbitt brothers, Edward, Charles J., David, George, and William, established a ranching empire comparable to any other in American history. They came to Flagstaff in 1886 from Cincinnati, Ohio, with money and a desire to invest in land and livestock. In Marshall Trimble's book, he states that at the height of its glory

Babbitt's ranching empire ran thousands of cattle on hundreds of thousands of acres of land in three southwestern states. The majority of the Babbitt holdings were always in Northern Arizona on top of the Mogollon Rim in the Little Colorado River Valley and on the Coconino Plateau. Besides the C O Bar, W Triangle and Hart ranches, in the first half of the twentieth century Babbitts owned or were partners in several other large ranching companies including the famous Hashknife Ranch, the Circle S, and the Arizona Cattle Company also known as the A – 1 Outfit.

There is no other cattle ranching enterprise in Arizona history that can compare with the Babbitt operation when it comes to longevity. The Babbitt family and their various ranching companies, the Hashknife, the Pitchfork, the Hart Cattle Company, the A – 1 Cattle Company, C O Bar Livestock, Cataract Livestock, and the Babbitt Brothers' Trading Company have been in the cattle ranching industry in a big way since 1886. They have weathered drought, economic depression, bad cattle prices, and managed to stay in business for over 130 years. Several books could be written about the reasons why they have been successful, but for certain one of the reasons must be their employees. At the top of the list of all the great people that have drawn wages from Babbitt Ranches would be their foremen, or men in charge. The Babbitts have always had a man in charge who was first and foremost a very good cowboy and cowman. Usually those men went by the title of wagon boss which would be the equivalent of a cow boss in buckaroo country, but the job description is the same. The men who made the decisions on their big ranches were working men; in other words, they were out there on a horse running the cow work at the same time they did the managing. Men like Bill Jim Wyrick, Charlie Young, Tom Moore, and Frank Banks, all of whom understood working cattle coupled with a basic knowledge of the economics of their day and an abnormal blessing of common sense. None of those men had a college degree. It's doubtful any of them had a high school diploma, yet they were very successful ranchers. They were not desk men.

Frank Banks worked for Babbitts his entire life. In Stella Hughes' book *Hashknife Cowboy*, one of the best cowboy books ever written, she mentions a young Frank Banks working with Mack Hughes on the Hashknife near Winslow in the 1920s. Frank took over as manager of the W Triangle in 1937, and then in 1940 Babbitts made him manager on both the C O Bar and the W Triangle ranches, a position he held until 1969. He ran the cowboy crew, led the drives, worked the herds, cut the replacement heifers, and culled the cows. He rode a horse daily and worked hard and made million dollar decisions on a regular basis.

Frank was a whiskey drinker and famous for leaving the wagon at sundown and driving on some rocky dirt road for forty miles to a bar along Highway 89 or Tusayan where he would drink Seagram's VO until midnight and return to reach his bedroll at 2:00 a.m. Then at 4:00 a.m. he would get up and crack a raw egg into a porcelain-covered tin coffee cup and drink it and chase it with black coffee. He would be cold sober. His mind was like a steel trap. He stood six foot, five inches and never had a pound of fat on his body. He was fearless but he wasn't mean. Men liked him but very few could keep up with him. The men who tried to keep up with his whiskey-drinking night-time trips to a saloon would after three or four days be walking and riding zombies, but he would keep going, humming on eight cylinders and running a ranch like clockwork. For his day and time, he was a master, a force to deal with. He took the C O Bar and W Triangle from a primitive state of raw land with few water resources and turned it into a ranch with millions of gallons of water storage and hundreds of miles of pipeline and a herd of Hereford cows that had few equals in his day. He was a true character, an individualist, and a leader. When he was old he would tell someone a story, and when he was finished he would say, "Do you believe that?" And of course the listener would always reply, "Sure Frank, I believe that." And then he would say, "What do you believe?" He expected the person to be able to relate the facts of the story he had just heard. If you were around Frank, you better pay attention.

Bill Howell arrived in Flagstaff in October of 1963, with his wife and two very small boys, having driven south from Ekalaka, Montana, looking for a cowboying job on a ranch. Bill had been

"Well, I suppose I can ride any kind you want me to ride."

the foreman on a large ranch in Northeast Utah where an older cowboy who worked for him advised him to go to Northern Arizona where there were some big ranches that would appreciate his skills, especially his ability with a horse and a rope. The old man had mentioned the Diamond A at Seligman and the Babbitt ranches north of Flagstaff.

The Babbitt Ranch office was upstairs in the famous Babbitt building in downtown Flagstaff which housed the Babbitt department store on the ground level. Somebody in the ranch office gave Bill instructions on how to get to the Spider Web Camp thirty-five miles north of town and said he should look for Frank Banks when he got there. Bill left his wife Gloria and sons Vic and Tim at a motel and drove north to Spider Web where Frank's wife Helen gave him instructions to go to Harbison Camp some forty miles to the west. As an afterthought she asked Bill if he would deliver several clean shirts to Frank.

The C O Bar wagon and crew were working cattle in the Harbison area and were camped there. It was almost sundown when Bill got there, and Frank and the crew had just finished catching horses for the next day. Bill approached Frank and asked for a job, and Frank answered him saying that he didn't need anyone at the time, so after a few words Bill turned and walked back to his car, and when he reached it he remembered the clean shirts Helen had asked him to deliver, so he got them and walked back to Frank and handed them to him. He had turned and started back to his car a second time when Frank spoke to him, "What kind of horses can you ride?"

"Well, I suppose I can ride any kind you want me to ride."

"Well, I've got a bunch of broncs here, four-, five- and six-year-olds that are green, and they need rode. They buck."

"I can ride anything you can lead out to me."

"You're hired."

When the roundup was over that fall, Frank moved Bill into the Redlands Camp which as the crow flies is about forty-five miles north of Ashfork or thirty-five miles southwest of Grand Canyon Village. It was a wild and lonely place, eighty-five miles to Flagstaff by the shortest, but not necessarily the best, road. Frank told Bill he needed someone who would make a lot of horse tracks there because he had not had a good, hard working cowboy there for several years.

Another cowboy named Pat Cain was working for Claude Neal on the Willaha Ranch which borders the W Triangle and Redlands to the east. Pat Cain and Frank Banks were friends and were known to drink whiskey together, and one day early in 1964 several months after Frank hired Bill, Frank stopped in to see Pat. While visiting he made the remark, "Well, Pat, I've hired the man who is going to replace me in a couple years. He's staying over at Redlands and his name is Bill Howell."

In essence Bill Howell was the equivalent of the perfect storm: the right man in the right place at the right time. Frank Banks was a hard man to follow, for in his time and place he was a legendary figure. In his mid-fifties he had decided to retire and buy a liquor store and trading post at Fredonia. Dealing in pawn for Navajo blankets and silver jewelry as well as the sale of cheap wine to Indians and whiskey to dry Mormons seemed like a good retirement. But his loyalty to Babbitts required that he find someone worthy to replace him.

Bill Howell had been born in the Sandhills of Nebraska and raised on bucking horses on the windswept, frozen prairies of the Powder River Breaks of Southeastern Montana. His father, Jim, was a very competent cowman and horseman, although never rising above a primitive existence a long way from town, at least in Bill's childhood. As a boy Bill had punched cows on horses that most men would have been afraid to saddle. He had been foreman on a cow ranch when he was nineteen, an NRCA champion team roper at twenty-eight, and somewhere in between an Army paratrooper. When he showed up at Babbitts, Frank Banks had a crew of middle-aged cowboys whose bronc riding days were over, not only because of their years, but their habit of trying to keep up with Frank Banks' drinking habits. While Frank consumed large quantities of alcohol and continued to work with a clear mind, most of his crew couldn't. As a result the Babbitt Ranch was in dire need of a world-class bronc stomper and top hand. Bill was desperate for a job to feed his family, so it was a perfect match. Frank Banks recognized it from the start.

One of the first things Bill did when he took over as manager was fire an old Texas cowboy who was sour over the change in management. In celebration of his sourness the old puncher remained drunk for several weeks, which culminated in his termination. The old Texan recruited the help of one of Northern Arizona's native sons who owned the reputation of being the toughest fist fighter between the Painted Desert and the Mogollon Rim. The showdown came at sundown in the kitchen of the Spider Web bunkhouse. The bad man walked in while Bill was frying steak for the crew and announced that he was there to kick Bill's hind end. Bill was caught between the kitchen table and doorway where the hombre stood like Paul Bunyon. To Bill's right sat a large wood box that held a hickory axe handle. The fighter blocked the door expecting Bill to fall on his knees and beg to be allowed to escape. Instead he grasped the hickory axe handle and prepared to use it. The hombre left and never resurfaced, and Bill stayed for twenty-three years and became a legend.

Bill Howell took over the reins as the Babbitt manager and wagon boss when Frank Banks retired in June of 1969. During the following winter Skeet Gould went to work for Bill, and he and his new bride Diane moved into the Well Camp. The Well, or Cataract Well as it was sometimes called, was a lonely cow camp about twenty-five miles west-southwest of the Grand Canyon Village. It lay on the northern edge of the Cataract Plains. On the north side of camp, the country climbs over a limestone rim and the pine trees become thicker. South and west of camp, the plains stretch for fifty miles being dissected by the Cataract Canyon, which is an abrupt drop off some 1500 feet deep, and the edge being about four miles west of the Well Camp. The Cataract Canyon cannot be seen until you are almost ready to fall off its cliffs, and in most places it is deeper than it is wide. Down in the bottom of the Cataract Canyon and some thirty miles north of the Well Camp is the small Supai village where the Supai Indians have lived longer than anyone knows.

Because of Skeet having a job and therefore being acquainted with Bill Howell, Charlie lined up a job on the outfit, and he and Bill agreed that Charlie would show up at the Babbitt wagon on a certain date, around the middle of May. He went to the Well Camp a few days early and stayed with Skeet and Diane, helping Skeet with whatever work he had to do.

Before Frank Banks had retired, he had hired Pat Cain to move into the Redlands Camp which lay sixteen miles to the south of the Cataract Well. Sixteen miles by the road, that is, but about twelve in a straight line. Pat Cain had been made jigger boss on the W Triangle part of the ranch by Frank Banks, and when Bill took Frank's place, he inherited that situation and was not happy with it. Pat Cain and Bill both had a company checkbook, yet Bill was clearly over Pat in authority and power. They were both good men but held contrasting opinions about how to work cattle, gather a piece of country, and manage a crew. They tolerated each other but that was the extent of it.

The position of the Redlands' camp man and jigger boss was not an easy one. Whoever held that position was responsible for fifty or so miles of pipelines that fed numerous troughs and storages that supplied several thousand head of cattle with drinking water on hundreds of square miles of country. The primary water source for that pipeline was a spring at the Espee Camp forty some miles south of the Cataract Well. In wet times the spring produced four gallons a minute, but in dry times it might drop to two gallons a minute. For the Redlands' man, water was always a critical issue, and then to top that off, he was supposed to be a top cowboy also.

Bill Howell had been the Redlands' man for four years while working for Frank, and he had been successful at fulfilling his duties, but he had little patience for Pat Cain. Pat was casual and laid-back in his behavior while Bill Howell was always focused and hard driven. Pat Cain usually had a leaking grease gun or overturned oil can in the back of his company pickup, but Bill kept his grease and oil confined to a dirty rag and never on his clothes or saddle. Pat Cain's horses would have witches knots in their manes and tails and might be dragging a stick behind, having been snagged in matted tail hair at ground level. When Pat Cain was cutting cattle out of a roundup it was common to see him pause and light his pipe and take a few puffs of Prince Albert while sitting on his horse staring at a cow for five minutes trying to decide whether or not to cut her. Bill Howell never stopped his horse in the middle of a herd in his life, and his decision on whether or not to cut a cow would consume no more than several seconds. The two men were cut from a different cloth.

About five days before Charlie's agreed date of arrival at the C O Bar wagon, Pat Cain stopped by the Well Camp to talk to Skeet. While drinking coffee and visiting, Pat asked Charlie what his plans were, and Charlie answered him saying that he was going to work with the roundup wagon in about five days.

"Well hell, I'm goin' into Flagstaff this afternoon. You just as well throw your bed and saddle in my pickup and I'll drop you off at the wagon."

Charlie considered Pat's comment and weighed the circumstances. On the one hand he remembered that Bill had told him to show up on a certain date, which was still five days in the future. On the other hand he didn't want to disobey an older man's orders or suggestions. Perhaps Bill wouldn't care. He wasn't sure. He followed Pat's order and loaded his bedroll and saddle and chaps and all of his other plunder in the back of the Ford pickup, and he and Pat set out for Flagstaff some ninety miles away.

The C O Bar wagon was camped at Dent and Sayer in the west end of a 150 section pasture and about halfway between the Well Camp and Flagstaff. They pulled into Dent and Sayer which was five or six miles north of the highway that led into Flagstaff. No one except Lem Davis, the cook, was there. Bill and the cowboy crew were out horseback and a long ways away from camp. While Pat drank a cup of coffee and visited with Lem the cook, Charlie unloaded all of his earthly belongings and laid them in a pile up by a corral made out of cedar posts and quaking aspen poles. His bed and saddle and blankets had all been violated by the leaking grease gun and overturned oil can.

When Pat got in his truck and headed into town to an auto parts store and an inevitable stop at the 66 Club on Santa Fe Avenue, Charlie sat against the aspen poles of the corral and waited for an hour until finally horsemen approached in a long trot. When Bill had unsaddled his horse he turned him loose and approached Charlie. They had never met, their only communication having been over the phone.

"Howdy, I'm Bill Howell." They shook hands.

"I'm Charlie Gould."

"I thought you weren't going to show up until next Tuesday."

"Well, I've been over at the Well staying with my brother Skeet. Pat Cain came by today and told me that I should load my stuff in with him, and he would drop me off on his way into town. So here I am."

Bill looked at Charlie and then at all of his belongings laying on the ground. "Oh—that explains the grease all over your outfit."

Actually Charlie didn't have a whole lot, but what he did have was quality stuff. He owned a flower-carved Bill Oliver saddle made in Amarillo. His chaps were made by Eddie Bacon in his saddle shop in Globe, Arizona. His spurs had been made in the Arizona State Prison in Florence by one of the Powers brothers who were a couple of Arizona cowboys who had started making spurs in prison and became famous for it. He owned a pair of custom made Blucher boots to hang the Power's spurs on, and to top all that off, he owned a hackamore with a rawhide bosal made by Luis Ortega and a Blind Bob hair macate. All in all it made up a first-class cowboy outfit, even if it did have motor oil all over it.

The cows on the C O Bar Ranch were wintered on the eastern end of the ranch next to the Little Colorado River and the Navajo Reservation, and some of that country was lower in elevation than 5000 feet. Starting in February the cow herd would be moved west and south climbing in elevation as they went. Part of the cow herd would eventually make it to the southwest corner of the San Francisco Peaks and graze at 8200 feet. Many of the cows would spend the summer in what was known as the Double Knobs and Slate Lake pastures, fifty miles west of the Little Colorado River. Eight hundred yearling heifers would be trailed to Harbison Pasture north of the Double Knobs and graze there from the first of May until mid-October. This great forced migration of cattle would take from February until the first of July to accomplish, with the cowboy crew moving the cows in bunches as big as a thousand head or as small as a hundred. Bill Howell was a master at moving and working large bunches of cattle, especially cows with babies at their sides. Once the cows started calving, the size of the herds that the crew moved up the country would get smaller, and great detail would be observed to keep the cows and calves paired up correctly.

The Dent and Sayer Camp, where Charlie threw in with the wagon crew, was in the Double Knobs Pasture which was 150 square miles in size and was a mixture of shallow ridges and valleys, and about 50 percent of it had juniper and pinion pine growing in it. As you went south you entered Slate Lake Pasture, and the elevation climbed quickly and, the vegetation turned into ponderosa pine. South of Slate Lake was a piece of country known as Wild Bill, most of which was 8000 feet in elevation or higher with thick pine trees and a good number of quaking aspen trees.

For the first week Charlie worked with the Babbitt wagon, the crew stayed busy moving cows west out of a sixty section pasture known as Mesa Butte. They would make a drive and throw a 150 cows or so together and take them west into the Double Knobs Pasture and turn them loose. Bill Howell was a stickler about keeping cow and calves paired up correctly, especially cows with babies. Many men would be satisfied to gather a bunch of cows and calves and move them into a different pasture, and after reaching their destination just hold the herd up for a while in hopes they would all pair up, but Bill would pair each cow and calf up individually. On the surface that sounds time consuming and seems as if he was overreacting, but he had a method. The crew would get the herd moving and strung out and Bill and another top hand would get up on the points of the strung out cattle and let correctly paired-up cows walk or trot by but turn everything that wasn't straight back. The Babbitt cows had been worked in this fashion a lot, and they were broke into the program. It made for a lot of fast riding, ducking and sliding a man's cow pony, and the good hands on the crew liked it. Sometimes when things went right, the Babbitt crew could pair out 150 pairs in less than ten minutes and ride back to camp knowing that every cow knew where her baby was, and there were no dogies (orphans) created by moving and changing pastures.

About a week after Charlie went to work for Bill, the crew threw a herd of 800 cows together at the Dent and Sayer Camp on the west end of the Double Knobs Pasture. When they had the number of cattle Bill wanted, they trailed the cattle south and uphill into the pine trees as far as Slate Lake. That was the first day, a distance of about fourteen miles, and they penned them in the big water lot at Slate Lake. The next day they trucked the horses they were going to ride from Dent and Sayer to Slate Lake and then trailed the 800 cows on up to Kendrick Park, about six miles distance and 8000 feet in elevation.

When they got back to Dent and Sayer, Bill told Charlie and Dewey Brown to trail the remuda of saddle horses, and everyone else helped Bill move the wagon to Kendrick Park. Bill planned on having the crew help Raymond Holt, who was the Wild Bill camp man, scatter the cattle all over the Wild Bill Allotment. In those days the Wild Bill Allotment and the Slate Lake Allotment were one pasture apiece, and Highway 180, that ran through both pastures, was unfenced.

The cowboy crew that spring consisted of Raymond Holt, who would stay at Wild Bill all summer, Jep Stell the Tubs' camp man, Charlie Markham, Barge Markham, Herschel Tipton, Dewey and Charlie. Pat Cain was the Redlands' camp man, Skeet Gould stayed at the Cataract Well, and Eph Fancher took care of the S P Camp. Those three camps were all on the Cataract side north of Ashfork, and those three men were not working with the crew on the C O Bar side.

The second day they were camped at Kendrick Park, a pickup showed up with two hombres wearing big black hats. The hombres were looking for a job. They had been working at the Grand Canyon wrangling dudes for Fred Harvey. When they left their job at the mule barn on the South Rim, they had stolen two large and stiff mattresses out of the mule wranglers' bunkhouse. That was the only bedding they had, no blankets, no bed tarp; nothing a cowboy would traditionally have for a bed. The mattresses were rigid and wouldn't roll up. The whole Babbitt crew laughed at the looks of the two men's beds and other particulars about their appearance. The two fellas names were Larry and Ed. Charlie and Dewey Brown immediately hung the nicknames of Concho and Washout on them. Larry being Washout and Ed being Concho. The names stuck.

The two men asked Bill for a cowboy job to which he replied, "I've got two jobs. One is a cowboy job and the other is a job hooding for the cook." The hood (cook's helper) would also serve as the horse wrangler.

Washout was the first to reply, "Well, I'm way too good a hand to be a hood and horse wrangler."

So Concho quickly followed up with, "Well, I'm in need of a job and I'm not picky. Hoodin' and horse wranglin' don't bother me, I just need a job."

"Okay boys, suits me, unload your stuff," Bill said. And then he looked at the big stiff mattresses and said, "What are we supposed to do with them?" The stolen mattresses were soon discarded, and Concho and Washout had to roll themselves up in their horse blankets.

Concho got on fine with Lem Davis, the cook, and Washout took his place in the crew. That place soon became the last place, the short end of the stick, and the brunt of lots of jokes all rolled into one. Washout wasn't very handy but wasn't humble enough to admit it.

Lem Davis, the cook, wasn't the best roundup cook, or even in the middle of the pack, but he was steady and usually sober. He had a scar on the lobe of his left ear, the remnants of a fight he had been in the fall before with a Texan named Cole Moorhouse. Cole, Bud Watson and Tim Prosser had come back to Spider Web, the C O Bar headquarters, after a night in the honkytonks of Flagstaff. They were oiled up and demanded that Lem cook them some supper, but he refused. A squabble between Cole and Lem ensued, and Lem grabbed a very large butcher knife to defend himself. Cole took ahold of a large metal spatula that was sharp, the result of scraping hundreds of pancakes off of a hot griddle. The two men, Lem and Cole, took to each other, and Lem came out the loser with a badly sliced earlobe. Cole pushed the bleeding cook into a small room off of the kitchen that was used for a commissary, and he locked him inside. Lem had been suffering from a severe case of lower G I trouble and things got messy. Because of the abuse of the cook, Cole ended up having to find work elsewhere and forever was known as the man who earmarked Lem Davis.

But things were quieter now. Lem and Concho got on nicely. Washout was another story. He was having problems. They worked scattering cows around Wild Bill for several days and then moved back to Dent and Sayer twenty miles north and 2000 feet lower in elevation. They started branding calves in the Double

Knobs, branding 150 or 200 head every day.

One day they had a large herd of cattle penned in a corral about 150 feet long and 80 feet wide. There were probably 150 calves to brand. Bill told Washout to rope. He was riding a big Breeze horse that was known to buck. Almost all of the horses that were sired by the stud known as Breeze would buck. They were big heavy-boned horses, most of them weighing close to 1200 pounds but some a lot bigger. Many of them wore a # 3 Diamond shoe. They were incredibly tough horses with tremendous endurance, but they had no cow at all. You could ride one in a trot and lope all morning, and then he would buck you off at noon.

Washout was trying to drag calves on the big Breeze and things weren't going well. He wasn't catching many and he became increasingly frustrated. Bill and the crew were looking on with less patience every minute. Most of the crew were good ropers. Several were expert ropers. They weren't used to standing around doing nothing. It became very evident that Washout was having trouble navigating though the embarrassing dilemma he found himself in. He was, after all, the man who was "way too good a hand to be a hood or horse wrangler."

Finally he gave up. He was all the way on the backside of the corral that was crowded with cows and calves. His rope was tied hard-and-fast to the saddle horn and about thirty-two feet long. He coiled it up as he rode through the tightly packed herd of cows on his way to tell Bill that he better get someone else to rope. When he got close to the edge of the herd, he took his neatly coiled rope and threw it down in embarrassment and disgust, and he exuded a few curse words. The rope, that was still securely attached to the horn, went down between the big bronc's front legs and then between his hind legs as Washout rode on, pouting as he went. He didn't notice the big Hereford cow stick her front foot in his loop. He didn't notice when the loop pulled up tight around the cow's ankle. They say the big bay Breeze horse would have scored a 21 on any bronc judge's score card at a pro rodeo. When the dust settled, the corral had been demolished and the cows were scattered all over the pasture.

Several days later Bill Howell decided to let Concho drag

some calves to the branding fire. Perhaps it was because Concho seemed to be agreeable and easy to get along with regardless what task he was given to do. Bill never suspected that Concho was any kind of a hand and didn't figure he would rope well, but to everyone's surprise he roped very well, perhaps even impressive. "By golly, I've got the wrong man washin' dishes and wranglin' horses," Bill announced. He told Washout that from then on he was going to hood for the cook and wrangle horses and Concho was going to take his place on the cowboy crew. Several days later Washout quit, being insulted having to wash dishes and wrangle. Because Washout quit, Concho quit also because Washout owned the pickup they had showed up in when they came to the ranch.

When the wagon crew finished branding in the Double Knobs Pasture, Bill moved the wagon to Buck Tank, which was on the W Triangle Ranch and some twenty-five miles away. To get to Buck Tank from Dent and Sayer you had to cross the Ten X Ranch that was owned by Rusty and Gregg Gibbons. He gave the chore of moving the remuda of seventy or eighty horses to Charlie and Dewey. They looked at Bill and asked, "How do you get across there from here?"

"Just go north toward Red Butte and turn west when you get there. Go across the highway and keep going west," Bill answered.

"But we've never been across there."

"So what?" Bill looked at them momentarily and then walked away.

Buck Tank sits in the bottom of a wide draw that flows north to south and runs for miles and miles. There is a large dam and dirt tank there, and usually lots of cattle water there. There is always no less than six inches of powdery sand and dirt everywhere, and every cowboy who ever camped there hates the place. It's like Hazen Hole on the Diamond A Ranch, famous for being hot and dirty.

The afternoon they moved the wagon there, Ben Fancher showed up with a couple beds and his saddle in the back of his pickup. He had been at the Tusayan bar twenty-five miles to the northwest, and he was feeling good. Ben was widely considered to be the best cowboy in Northern Arizona, the equivalent of

Clancy, the Australian made famous in the poems written by Banjo Paterson. He was running the Poquette Ranch, which was thirty plus miles to the south. Clay Tyree, who was fourteen years old at the time, was working for him; and Ben and Clay were going to spend the next ten days helping the Babbitt crew brand all the W Triangle calves. Ben had given Clay Tyree the chore of trailing their horses the thirty-some miles from the Poquette Ranch north to Buck Tank. While Clay did that, Ben drove north to Tusayan and drank a few beers. Clay was like Charlie and Dewey, he had never been over the route he was supposed to take. Actually Clay's chore was more severe because at least Charlie and Dewey had traveled between Dent and Sayer and Buck Tank in a pickup and had seen both the beginning and ending of the trail. Clay had never been north of the Poquette Ranch. He also had another handicap: Ben had contracted to break about a dozen colts to ride for the Yolo Ranch west of Prescott, and they were what he and Clay were going to ride. Clay was mounted on a very green Yolo bronc and driving a herd of very unbroke horses over a trail he did not know. He had on a black hat that he had just starched with the old cowboy recipe consisting of lots of sugar mixed with water. It was hot, and the hat was equivalent to wearing a cast iron dutch oven all day. He came driving his herd of broncs into Buck Tank late in the afternoon sweating a mixture of Cataract Plains' dust, sweat and sugar.

Charlie Markham was Bill's jigger boss when the wagon was on the C O Bar Ranch, and then when the wagon moved west to the W Triangle Ranch, Pat Cain took Charlie Markham's place as jigger (second-in-command). Charlie Markham's son Barge was working with the wagon and was about the same age as Charlie Gould and Dewey Brown. Charlie and Dewey were partners, and when Clay Tyree showed up he was accepted as their equal although he was only fourteen. At fourteen he was a better hand than most men twice his age. You could say he had seen a lot in fourteen years. But Barge was considered the odd man out. Barge had a pair of dainty slippers that he would wear around camp in the evenings. Charlie and Dewey considered them to be something less than acceptable attire for real cowboys, and so one night while Barge wasn't looking, they filled the insides of Barge's slippers with honey. The next morning he stepped into the slippers and honey oozed out all over the place and mixed with Buck Tank dust and sand. Barge was pissed but heavily outnumbered.

Pat Cain had a big sorrel horse in his string that was known to buck. He always rode with his stirrups hobbled and had been known as a good bronc rider, but he was in his mid-forties and had acquired somewhat of a belly. He would get on a bucker and ride off seeming like he was totally unaware that he was about to be bucked off. He was what one might call non-confrontational. He was wont to get along with a horse if at all possible.

The first morning they worked at Buck Tank, Pat stepped on the big sorrel and tried to get out of camp without a showdown, but the big horse was having nothing to do with it. He blew up and went to bucking hard and spinning to the right. Skeet Gould had just stepped on a big Breeze horse called Popcorn that was a bucker of the finest order. Skeet spurred Popcorn and deliberately ran into Pat's sorrel hoping to hit him hard enough to make the horse quit bucking because Pat was barely weathering the storm. Instead of stopping, the sorrel bucked harder, and then Popcorn blew up and went to bucking. Popcorn was jumping high and spinning to the left, and the sorrel was jumping high and spinning to the right, and then because they were close to each other, their heads collided in mid-air. The collision almost knocked Pat's sorrel unconscious, and he began to stagger and then fall over backwards. Someone hollered at Pat, "Get off." Pat quickly stepped off as the sorrel fell to the ground. "You don't have to tell me twice," Pat said. Popcorn kept bucking, but Skeet rode him with no trouble. The sorrel horse never bucked again.

The second night the Babbitt crew was camped at Buck Tank, the senior members of the crew loaded up in a pickup and went to the Tusayan Saloon twenty-five miles away. They refused to take the young men along, which meant Clay Tyree, Dewey, Barge and Charlie. About two in the morning, Clay Tyree hollered, "Here they come. If you guys know what's good for you, you'll get outa here." He lit out running for the brush, but Charlie, Dewey and Barge stuck it out and acted like they were asleep in their bedrolls. The elderly gentlemen got out of the green Ford pickup and accosted the young men, pulling them out of their bedrolls and rolling them around in the sand and dirt. Skeet Gould got ahold of Dewey in a wrestler's headlock and proceeded to comb his hair with a steel curry comb. Dewey didn't heal up from the scratch marks on his head for a week.

Fall Roundup on the Babbitt Ranch

The day after Labor Day in 1971, seven cowboys rode out from the Redlands Camp in the middle of the W Triangle Ranch going northwest to the back side of a pasture known as Little Redlands. The pasture ran north on the west side of the Cataract Creek, with the creek making the east side of the pasture, and the boundary fence between the W Triangle and the huge Diamond A Ranch being the west perimeter of the Little Redlands Pasture.

The Redlands Camp, which consisted of a bunkhouse for the cowboy crew and another dwelling in which Pat Cain and his wife Faye lived, lay along the creek side near the bottom on its western banks. There were several other buildings nearby: a barn, saddle house and shop; and several corrals made up of large cedar posts and aspen poles.

The Cataract flows north, and several miles north of camp, the creek bed comes to an abrupt cliff, near a thousand feet in height, and from that point north, the canyon becomes deeper and more spectacular until it finally meets the Colorado River in the bottom of the Grand Canyon about forty miles north of Redlands.

The seven cowboys were Ben Fancher, Mike McFarland, Harvey Howell, Rusty Criner, Bill Van Praag, Bill Howell and Charlie Gould. They rode at a trot and a lope about eight miles and stopped near the place where the Diamond A fence came to an end and hit a 1200-foot drop off into the Cataract Canyon. The cowboys split up with Bill Howell taking the outside circle on the east side and Ben Fancher going south on the Diamond A fence and the other five men scattered out in between. They were gathering the Babbitt remuda that had been turned out in Little Redlands all summer. On Bill Howell's side of the drive there were many shallow draws and ridges with plenty of limestone outcroppings and a few scrub cedars or pinion pine mixed with chamisa and cliff rose. It had been a good summer and several species of gramma grass were headed out and waving in the breeze. The Cataract Plains is as good a horse or cow country as you'll find, and the Babbitt horses were fat.

When the men ran the horses they had gathered into the pole corrals at Redlands, sixty head were counted into the gate, and they were mixed with thirty more that had been ridden through the summer. Bill Howell wanted to make a quick little drive to gather some cattle south of camp several miles, so he roped a fresh horse for each man out of the bunch they had gathered in Little Redlands. The same seven cowboys saddled up quickly and made haste to get the chore done that Bill had planned with the intention of returning to camp within a couple hours so they could eat a quick lunch and start shoeing all the barefooted horses in preparation for the fall roundup which was commencing even as they got ready to mount up. By coincidence all seven men slipped up on their fresh horses within seconds of each other, and there were seven horses bucking all at the same time. No one was thrown, and they all rode off as if the whole affair was a normal course of events.

The crew spent several days camped at Redlands doing nothing but shoeing their horses. Each man had six or seven horses in his string, or perhaps as many as eight or nine if you were riding some colts. Charlie was in that category, and most of his horses were five or younger, and several would buck when they were fresh, especially a horse named Burro and another called Slick. Slick had been started by a good young cowboy who had just purchased a new slick fork saddle made by the famous saddle maker Ray Holes. The young man with the slick fork saddle never got Slick covered when the bronc decided to come unwound, and because of that the horse acquired the name. Bill Howell

"That was one of the best bronc rides I ever saw."

would tell the story many times how Charlie rode Slick on a very wet rainy day and had put a snaffle bit on the bronc, who was very green. Charlie had greased the leather bridle reins that were attached to the snaffle, and when Slick blew up and went to bucking, the greasy leather reins kept sliding through Charlie's hands. Bill would say that he could see the saddle horn on another man's saddle who was riding on the other side of Slick as the horse bucked with Charlie trying to keep ahold of the sliding reins. Bill would end the story saying, "That was one of the best bronc rides I ever saw."

After getting the remuda shod, the crew gathered all the cows in the Big Cataract Pasture which was over 100 sections in size and had about 1200 cows running in it. They left camp before daylight and made a big flanking drive throwing a roundup together at a dirt stock tank where most of the cattle they gathered had been watering at on a regular basis. On most days someone brought them a change of horses that showed up about the time they got their roundup throwed together. The crew all got a fresh horse with Bill doing the roping of those fresh horses while three or four men held their catch ropes around them making a rope corral. As a man got his fresh horse saddled, he mounted up and went to take the place of another man who was holding the herd while the horse changing process got started. Within ten or fifteen minutes, everyone had their new horses caught and were ready for the rest of the day. Many times there was a bronc ride or two after the new horses were mounted.

On days when Bill Howell anticipated gathering a big bunch of cattle, he had the cook bring them out a lunch, driving a pickup to their location. This would all be prearranged in the morning before the crew left camp with Bill giving the cook instructions on how to find the roundup ground, which many times was in a remote location. As soon as the men had their fresh horses caught and saddled, they would eat, and like changing horses, it was done in shifts: some men eating while others held the roundup together. The eating was done in a hurry so the ones who were holding herd could come and get their turn. This whole process wouldn't take much longer than the changing of horses.

With fresh horses caught and everyone fed, the cattle were held with the men surrounding the herd in somewhat of a circle. One man was told to go out a distance of a hundred yards or so and hold the cut. Another man would ride into the herd and begin cutting out cattle of his choice and thus separating them from the main bunch. The man who was told to hold the cut was responsible for holding the cattle that had been separated from the main bunch. At first, when only one or two animals had been cut out, this task of holding the cut could be easier said than done, but after the first ones were given some company, they settled down. The man doing the cutting was usually the wagon boss; in this case Bill Howell or someone of his choosing. He would position the roundup on a certain place, like soft ground if any was available; and he would have the cut held at a certain spot of his choosing. In other words, the man holding the cut couldn't just lollygag around and let the cut scatter about.

When you cut cattle out of a herd, they naturally will want to go find some company, so holding the cut correctly is important. The cattle are not held tightly, but, instead, they are allotted space so the man cutting can get a good look at them, and also cows and calves that are given room will stay mothered up better. The men on the outside hold the herd as calmly as possible which creates less milling around among the cattle. All of this requires a great deal of learned skill in members of the crew, and the better hands who know when to move and when not to move are held in great esteem.

By the first day of roundup, several more men had joined forces with the seven who had gathered the remuda out of Little Redlands Pasture. Lem Davis, who had been cooking for a year or so, had joined the mounted crew along with Herschel Tipton, Joe Chaves, and a man named Francis Lucas who wanted to be known as Tombstone. Pat Cain and Eph Fancher, who was the Espee camp man, were also working every day.

During this period of the roundup, the cattle that were cut out and separated from the herd were cull cows, which is the term used to describe any undesirable cattle that need to be sold. The majority of these were old cows or bulls that had lived out their useful and productive years and would be sold while they still had some value. It took a very seasoned cowman to ride through a large herd of range cattle and determine which individual cow or bull had reached the end of its career, so to speak. Beings all of this work was done outside, without the aid of corrals, and with limited help made the seasoned hand even more beneficial. And to top all of those various circumstances was the time factor. There were only so many hours in a day and much to be done, so the crew who could accomplish these tasks smoothly and in a timely fashion was much to be praised. The great catalyst that is necessary to do all of this is the wagon boss because his knowledge and leadership make or break a roundup and even the ranch itself. Good wagon bosses or bad wagon bosses are legend, whether they want to be or not, and ranches with bosses who don't know their stuff do not get the good crews.

When the cull cows had been cut out, the crew branded any calves that needed to be branded, which usually wasn't many because most of them had been branded during the spring roundup. On some days there was a branding corral close by where a herd could be penned and the branding done, but on other days where no corral was available, the calves were roped around the neck and drug toward the fire, and somewhere between the herd and fire, another man heeled the roped calf, making it easier to get it down on the ground and branded. Whenever possible Bill Howell sent part of the crew with the cut, trailing it to a holding pasture some distance away. On some days the cut might need to be trailed six or seven miles but on others, perhaps, only a mile or two.

When all of this was accomplished, the men returned to camp where they wrangled the remuda out of a holding pasture and caught fresh horses to ride the next day. The horses were kept up in a corral and fed alfalfa hay and so were ready to ride the next morning.

Gathering and working all of the 1200 mother cows that were running in the Big Cataract Pasture took eight days. At the end of this part of the roundup, all of the unbranded calves had been branded and 200 cull cows and bulls had been put into the Anita Pasture where they stayed until they were shipped about fifty days later.

On the last afternoon the wagon crew worked in the Big Cataract Pasture, everyone rolled up their beds and gathered what little plunder they had with them (wagon bosses frown on men who require too much baggage); and the kitchen was packed up, and the outfit moved camp to a place called Tom Moore in memory of one of Babbitts' earlier wagon bosses. While most of the crew rode in either the chuck wagon or Bill Howell's company pickup, several of the cowboys trailed the remuda from Redlands to Tom Moore, a distance of ten miles. When the horses arrived at the new camp, the cowboys were waiting and the nightly routine of catching horses for the next day's work took place.

The Tom Moore Pasture had 500 cows running in it and was about forty-five square miles in size. The crew took two days to gather those cows, and the procedure was the same, branding any unbranded calves and cutting out all the cull cows and bulls that needed to be sold. On the third day the cut was trailed from a holding trap at the Tom Moore Camp to a pasture at Anita, which was a very long way to go with a herd of cows, close to twenty miles.

The next morning the remuda was gathered, and Joe Chaves, Mike McFarland and Charlie Gould left out with the horses going east toward the C O Bar. The trail they took went across a ranch owned by Cherrie Blair who was the daughter of John Osbourne who had been a boss on the famous Chiricahua Cattle Company on the present day San Carlos Indian Reservation. They drove the remuda, which was close to ninety horses in number, crossing Highway 64 in the vicinity of Valle Junction, and continued east reaching Dent and Sayer Camp around one in the afternoon. Bill Howell and the rest of the crew were waiting for them there.

The Double Knobs Pasture was fifteen miles long east and west and ten miles going north and south, and Dent and Sayer sat about five miles east of the western boundary on the south side. The cowboys spent several days making drives on the western end of the Knobs throwing cattle eastward.

After doing this they rolled up camp and moved eleven miles east to the Tubs, a cow camp close to the east end of the Knobs and the west end of the Mesa Butte Pasture. An old-timer named Jep Stell was the Tubs' camp man, and he, being a lifelong bachelor, had the beautiful rock house all to himself. The wagon crew moved into the house with Jep. The cook had a nice kitchen to cook in, which meant a good wood cookstove and running water in the kitchen sink. There was no electricity, but they had good Coleman lanterns to use. There was a big screened-in porch on two sides of the house with lots of room, and most of the cowboys rolled their beds out on the floor out on this porch. On the north end of the porch, directly out the kitchen door, four big hooks hung down from the rafter joists, and four quarters of beef could be hung on those hooks at night to keep it cool and then taken down, wrapped in big tarps, and left on the cold concrete floor in the daytime. Compared to some of the primitive places the wagon camped, such as Buck Tank, the Tubs was like the Ritz. There was even an indoor bathroom with a shower if, that is, a man thought he might be dirty after three weeks of hard work.

For the next week, the men gathered cattle in the Knobs and worked some big roundups, cutting out short-aged pairs and leaving them back in the Knobs and bringing cull cows and cows with big weaner size calves down into the Tubs. The cull cows were cut out and left in a trap at the Tubs, and the cows with calves that were big enough to wean were turned loose in the

Mesa Butte Pasture. There was lots of herd work every day with cattle being cut and separated and put in several pastures, and in the afternoons everyone rode their best cow ponies. Bill Howell would ride his best cutting horse, Checkers, on many of these afternoons. Checkers was a big streaked-face chestnut that Bill had broke and trained. A cow could not get away from him in an outside roundup, and he could cut cattle for several hours, putting as much effort into his work after cutting a hundred head of cows as he did on the first one. Checkers would cut, turn through himself, and jump sideways at lightning speed; but he always worked with his head and shoulders up, many times having one ear cocked backwards and one forwards and his head tilted slightly sideways peering at his opponent with one eye. No one who ever saw the horse work forgot him.

At the end of eight days, they had put 1100 big pairs, all of the calves big enough to wean, in the Mesa Butte Pasture and had accumulated a couple hundred cull cows and bulls in the Rabbit Corner Trap at the Tubs. Several hundred cows with younger calves were left out in the Knobs. The men gathered the Rabbit Corner Trap and trailed the cull cows east six miles to S P Tank and turned them loose on the east side of the fence in the 89 Pasture where they could drift all the way to Highway 89, twelve miles to the east, if they wanted to.

It was now close to the first of October, and they had been working twenty-eight days with no time off and had no prospects of any free time in the near future. In those days the Babbitt Ranch had no regular payday. Bill Howell had a company draft book with him all the time, and if a man wanted some money, Bill could write him a draft, or if a man happened to be in Flagstaff, he could walk upstairs in the Babbitt building to the ranch office and get the bookkeeper to write him a draft, or if neither of those things happened, a cowboy's wages kept adding up in the ledger. For the most part their money just added up because they kept working.

They rolled up camp the last day of September and moved to Kendrick Park twenty miles south of the Tubs. Kendrick Park, at 8000 feet in elevation, could be a pretty chilly place. The mornings were cold and the fact that the dirt was really soft in the area around camp made for a lot of bronc rides. Charlie had several horses in his string that wanted to buck. The particularly belligerent four-year-old, Burro, was the worst, but there were several others; Chauffeur, Slick and Jazbo being about as bad.

The character known as Tombstone made everyone scratch their heads. Tombstone had come to work a day or two after the roundup had commenced, and by then Bill had issued the best horses to other men. Tombstone got what was left, which amounted to the dregs. Bill had told everyone to keep their mouths shut about the horses he gave Tombstone, figuring if the men talked, it would scare Tombstone off. Among Tombstone's horses were several real buckers including Rabbit, Gayo and Uvalde. Tombstone was not a good hand or a horseman, and he was big, clumsy and slow-witted, but he wallered up on the outlaws and rode them without much trouble.

Camping at Kendrick Park, they worked for five days gathering the Wild Bill Allotment, and they also picked up the help of Raymond Holt, the Wild Bill camp man. Raymond was a small man, equivalent to a little stick of dynamite. He was wired for 440 volts, full of energy, and lots of opinions and forward motion. He didn't have any bad days, just some that were better than others.

As the cattle were gathered they were put in the Kendrick Park holding pasture, and then after five days, when all but a very few had been gathered, the outfit was ready to move camp again. This time they moved to Cedar Ranch, a cow camp four miles south of the Tubs and twelve miles or so north of Kendrick Park and over 1500 feet lower in elevation. Early in the morning, the Kendrick Park trap, over a couple square miles in size, was gathered, which meant both the horses and all the cattle the cowboys had been putting in the pasture for five days, which was over 500 head of cows. The horses and cattle were thrown together near a corral and waterhole not far from camp, and then several men loped over and helped the cook load the kitchen and beds onto the chuck wagon and sent him on his way.

With the cook gone, Bill Howell sent two men north with the

remuda, and everyone else stayed with the cowherd and started it down off the mountain through the pine trees toward S P Pasture. It was a long trail going down by a water hole called Maverick and then C O Bar Tank and then off of the Cedar Ranch rim on the Klostemeyer Rincon Trail and into S P Pasture a little ways above Victor Lake. It was a very crisp fall day, and the fat cows walked along at a good pace doing the twelve miles in six hours. The crew trotted into Cedar Ranch at two in the afternoon.

Cedar Ranch sat under a malpai rim that rises over 500 feet in elevation on the south side of camp, and toward the north the country opens up and levels out somewhat, and from the house and barn a person had a beautiful vista looking north over some of Arizona's most picturesque landscape. Off to the east sixty miles you could see the pastel landscape of the Moenkopi Plateau and Painted Desert. Straight north of camp six miles is Mesa Butte a malpai sentinel that rises a thousand-foot higher than the limestone canyons in the center of Mesa Butte Pasture. On beyond Mesa Butte fifteen miles is Gray Mountain that looms 2000 feet above the Little Colorado River Gorge, and then a hundred miles further and seven degrees to the east is Navajo Mountain sticking up on the distant horizon with its roots being in the state of Utah. There were three houses at Cedar Ranch: a bunkhouse, and a house where Bill Howell's family spent the summer, and a third where Ben Fancher's wife and family were. For Bill and Ben it was a homecoming.

From the sixth of October until the twelfth, the cowboys gathered the 550 pairs that had ran in Slate Lake Allotment all summer. These calves were some of the biggest calves weaned on the C O Bar Ranch, all of them being big enough to brand when they were put into the allotment in early May. For the most part the cows in Slate Lake were young and all of the calves big enough to wean so there was no cutting done while gathering the allotment. The men spent all of the six days gathering the pasture which was about a township in size and had lots of thick pine trees in it. The cattle were put in S P Pasture as they were gathered.

On October 13 they rolled the outfit up again and moved

camp to Harbison, a cow camp that was twenty miles north of Cedar Ranch and on the Kaibab National Forest. Harbison was close to twenty-five miles from Cedar Ranch on the road. Several men trailed the remuda north, and everyone else caught a ride in one of several trucks that were being taken with the outfit.

The cook was an old alcoholic named Earl White who really wasn't much of a cook, just an old drifter who needed a job. His cooking was adequate at best. He had developed a fetish for canned green chilies, and as the roundup progressed, he had taken to adding canned green chilies to every dish he constructed. The first morning the outfit was camped at Harbison, Earl cooked up some hotcakes and had Log Cabin syrup to pour on top of the cakes. Things were going pretty good, at least no one had said anything, and then Bill Howell cut into a large hotcake dripping with Log Cabin, and when he put a big bite into his mouth, he realized there was a full-sized green chili mixed in with the dough and syrup. He decided he had eaten all the green chilies he wanted, and he told the cook his true feelings about that decision. Well, old Earl was deeply offended, and he quit on the spot. Now Bill had to get someone to give Earl a ride all the way to Flagstaff, sixty miles distance, and he also needed to come up with a cook. Bill was thinking to himself out loud and discussing his lack of options when Bill Van Praag offered up the idea that maybe his wife Dorothy could cook for the crew. Dorothy had owned a restaurant and enjoyed cooking, and she could get along alright in the midst of a crew of something less than dignified cowboys, at least that is what Bill Van Praag told Bill Howell.

Having a woman cook on a roundup wagon was not traditional, and the potential problems were both numerous and obvious. Bill Howell thought for a few minutes and decided he would try it, at least until he could find another man to replace Earl. He sent Bill Van Praag to Flagstaff with Earl White and told him to come back to camp with his wife Dorothy, and they would give it a try.

As Bill Howell led the men out of camp on their way to the backside of a pasture, he pondered the paradigm shift that having a woman cooking for the roundup wagon would create. He was sick of green chilies in his hotcakes, and he knew that his crew was just as sick of drunken men cooks as he was. When they reached the backside of the pasture where he needed to start scattering his men, he told his crew, "Let's give this a try, boys. We sure need a cook, and I'm sick of green chilies. Let's see if Dorothy Van Praag can cook and survive amongst a bunch of men. Maybe it will work for a little while."

By suppertime Bill and Dorothy Van Praag were in camp, and there was a pan of the best looking light bread you ever saw in the oven, steak was frying in one pan and potatoes in another, and there were no green chilies. Bill and Dorothy had a baby girl about two years old, and she stared at the crew with big blue eyes; and pretty soon everyone was playing with her. There were no problems. Dorothy knew how to get along with a crew of men, and they treated her like a lady. She cooked for the Babbitt wagon for years.

The next morning the men left camp before sunup, and it was pretty cold, about 20 degrees. Charlie was riding Burro, and as they trotted along through the pine trees, Burro got where he couldn't stand it any longer, and he took to Charlie in a bucking fit. It had been happening pretty regular so nobody paid much attention at first, and then they heard wire stretching and limbs breaking. Tight barbed wire makes a peculiar sound when it is stretched to the breaking point, especially when the horse you're riding has got himself tangled up in it. "Whoa, Charlie! Watch out! Look out!" Men were shouting, and Burro lunged and bucked and squealed and was about to fall over on Charlie and braid him into a witch's knot of mangled barbed wire. Burro finally went down, and Charlie managed to leap out and away from the deadly wire. The horse lay there in a mangled mess and had to be cut loose, but miraculously he was not cut bad.

When they got Burro cut free and stood up, Charlie mounted, and the men rode on into the breaking dawn. Bill looked at Charlie and said, "You know that son of a gun is learning to buck better than you're learning to ride. Maybe you better start riding him every day."

"Suits me."

So the next afternoon, Charlie was riding Burro again. They were gathering yearling heifers and had been working for several days and had all but a few remnants gathered and put in a holding pasture at Lockwood, six miles southeast of the Harbison Camp where the crew was staying. That afternoon Charlie was working with Ben Fancher and Mike McFarland, and they had the use of a dually Ford truck with a stock rack on it. Four horses could be hauled in the truck. Ben left Charlie at a water trough and instructed him to just sit there and wait until some cattle came into water and then hold them at the water until he and Mike returned. They were going to go to several other waters and look for stragglers. Charlie and Burro hid in the trees fifty yards away from the water and waited, but nothing happened. After awhile Charlie got off of Burro and hobbled him and lay down to take a nap. He was riding Burro in a hackamore, and he held on to the end of his hair macate as he lay sleeping.

When Ben and Mike came driving up, they could see what was going on so they shut the engine off of the truck and got out and snuck up on Charlie and Burro. Burro was usually wild and snorty, but he stood like a kid's horse while they slipped a lasso over his head and took the hackamore off and gently laid it on the ground. They unhobbled the bronc and slipped away without waking Charlie up, and they loaded him in the truck and slowly drove off. After going a ways they turned around and went back toward Charlie driving as wildly and fast as they dared. Ben slammed on the breaks and backed up to a bank and jumped out hollering, "Come on! Let's go!"

Charlie picked his head up and pulled on the macate until he had the empty headstall in his lap. He jumped up and looked around and around. Ben and Mike fell on the ground laughing. That night at supper, Ben and Mike tried to act serious, and then they would look at each other and start giggling. Finally Bill Howell said, "What the hell is wrong with you two guys?" When they let the cat out of the bag, the whole crew were holding their bellies and slapping their legs and laughing until they cried.

The pasture at Harbison they were gathering was an allotment on the Kaibab National Forest, and there were 810 head of yearling heifers running there. After working for four days, the crew had all but a half dozen of the yearling heifers gathered. So on the fifth day, they began trailing the 800 yearlings toward the winter pasture east of Spider Web. The first leg of the drive was down Lockwood Canyon and then out onto the Needmore Flat and a corner of the Navajo Indian Reservation. After traveling for about four miles across Indian land, they entered the Babbitt Ranch again, into the Mesa Butte Pasture, and turned to a more easterly course and drove down into Tommy Tank, which had a large water lot around it, and they penned the yearlings there for the night. They had trailed the cattle about twelve miles that day. Bill Van Praag had stayed back and helped his wife, who was now the accepted and well-liked cook, move camp to the Tubs, which was southwest of Tommy Tank six miles. When the crew got the gates securely shut on the 800 heifers, they headed toward the Tubs in a long trot. While all that happened, Joe Chaves trailed the remuda from Harbison to the Tubs, a distance of sixteen miles.

The next morning bright and early, the men rolled their beds and helped get the outfit ready to load up in a pickup again, and then they started out toward Tommy Tank to finish the trail toward the winter range. Bill Van Praag stayed back again to help Dorothy move the kitchen, and Hershel Tipton was given the duty of trailing the remuda to Spider Web, a distance of eighteen miles.

The 800 heifers were let out of the corral at 7:30 a.m. and started down a limestone canyon which was several hundred feet in depth. After a couple miles the canyon abruptly ends and empties out onto a barren plain running northward with limestone mesas and basalt lava flows to the south. As you go south the landscape rises in elevation and good edible vegetation grows thicker. To the north and gradually decreasing in elevation is the Navajo Reservation, which because of gross mismanagement and overgrazing is bare basalt and sand mixed with limestone outcroppings and very little growing except a few scrubby shadscale plants and an occasional stunted stick cholla. Scattered about are a few bunches of wild Navajo ponies of every color and description and mostly in poor body condition. A horseman riding across this place will also spy an occasional band of Navajo sheep or hair goats accompanied by a lone herder, most of which will be a child or woman. The Navajo ponies and sheep graze for the most part on sand, and by some quirk of nature that scientists cannot explain, they manage to extract nourishment from it.

At a gate three miles below Tommy Tank the Babbitt cowboys put the 800 Hereford heifers out onto the reservation and continue east toward Spider Web. The scene at this point could be compared to one of John Ford's Western movies filmed in Monument Valley, which is a little over a hundred miles to the northeast. With the towering cliffs of Gray Mountain looming twenty miles to the northwest, a man could easily envision himself being in a column of mounted cavalrymen following John Wayne across the sand between columns of beautiful rock sentinels. Instead the Babbitt crew, including Charlie Gould, were following Bill Howell as he pointed the trail herd east, trying very hard to avoid the sand-eating sheep as they rode along.

After an eight mile stretch of trailing across the reservation, they came to a gate going into a Babbitt pasture known as Prosperity. As they stared northward down the fence line between Prosperity and the reservation, a distinct line could be seen with virtually no grass on the reservation side of the fence and plentiful grass on the Babbitt side. The Babbitt cowboys put the 800 heifers through the wire gate and then stopped them by holding them up against the fence on the Babbitt side. Hershel Tipton had trailed them up bringing the remuda behind them, and when the horses were through the gate, half of the crew unsaddled and threw their ropes up between each other, and Bill Howell started roping each man a fresh horse. As soon as a man got his fresh horse saddled, he loped to the herd and traded places with another man, and he would get himself a fresh horse also.

Bill and Dorothy Van Praag showed up in a pickup with a lunch and Bill Van Praag's saddle, and a horse was caught for him also. When everyone had eaten a piece of steak and a piece of bread washed down with black coffee, Dorothy left with the pickup that had a chuck box mounted on back, and Herschel continued on east with the remuda toward Spider Web, a distance of four miles. The crew that was left with the herd—Bill Howell, Ben Fancher,

Bill Van Praag, Mike McFarland, Harvey Howell, Raymond Holt, Joe Chaves, Eph Fancher, Lem Davis, Tombstone, and Charlie Gould—now commenced to sort the 800 heifers. About 400 of the heifers were going to be shipped and the remainder kept for replacements, so the crew held the herd up against the reservation fence, and Bill Howell began the process of cutting out the heifers that were to be sold. Before it was finished, Ben Fancher and his father, Eph, also took a turn at cutting, and the whole process took close to three hours. Tombstone held the cut while all of this took place, and when the cutting was finished, the cut was driven to a waterhole in the Prosperity Pasture, and what was left was trailed on to Spider Web. It was now the nineteenth of October, and it was sundown when the men were finished catching and feeding horses for the next day.

The next morning the replacement heifers they had driven from Harbison were trailed a mile east of Spider Web and turned loose in a pasture known as the Northside whose eastern boundary was the unfenced Little Colorado River twelve miles to the east and a thousand feet lower in elevation. The men had a few hours to put new shoes on some horses or go to town, thirty-five miles away, and blow off some steam. They now had worked for six weeks without a day off and were looking at another six weeks of the same.

On the October 21, the crew began to gather the cull cows that had been turned loose in the 89 Pasture a week or so before and bring them down to a trap near Spider Web. And then on the twenty-fourth and twenty-fifth, they bunched up the 1200 cows that had big weaner calves on their side, and on the twenty-sixth this big herd of cows and calves were driven into a set of corrals at a camp called Aso that was fifteen miles west/southwest of Spider Web. That morning, October 26, the calves were separated from their mothers. With that being accomplished by 11:00 a.m., Dorothy brought the crew a simple lunch, and at noon the herd of cows, a little over 1200 in number, were pointed east toward their winter range.

The 1200 big calves that had been separated from their mothers were bawling and walking the fence like angry prisoners of war, and the herd of cows were bawling on the other side, acting like mothers whose children had been kidnapped. There was lots of noise, and the Babbitt crew had to ride hard and whip and spur, putting the cows into a forced march away from their offspring. This was one situation where a cow running off was a welcome sight as long as she was headed east, away from her calf. It was a long hard fight for fourteen miles, making the cows walk until they reached a very large corral about the size of the Prescott, Arizona, rodeo arena where the cows were locked up for the night. For the next three days, the cowboys would let the cows out of the corral and let them graze for about an hour, and then they would lock them up again. After several days the cows' udders were swelled and chapped and sore, and they had all bawled and bellered until they sounded hoarse. On October 30 they were trailed east another eight miles and turned loose at a cow camp called Savage Well. Out the back door of Savage Well were cliffs 500 feet high that dropped down into the Little Colorado River Valley, the river being visible four or five miles farther east. And out of the sandstone mesas sloping upward and eastward from the river was the Painted Desert, colored in shades of pastels and ocher made so famous by a million classic photographs that were put on postcards.

On October 31 Bill Howell sent Joe Chaves, Herschel Tipton and Tombstone over to the cataract ranch to help Pat Cain and the W Triangle crew start gathering yearlings of which there were about 3720 that needed to be shipped. Those three cowboys and their horses were hauled in a truck to a cow camp known as Tin House where the crew would be camped during the shipping of those yearlings. While Pat Cain and that crew started the yearling gather, Bill Howell and the men camped at Spider Web shipped the C O Bar cull cows of which there were 250 cows and 25 bulls. This was done on November 2, and then on November 3, the yearling heifers that had been left in the Prosperity Pasture a few days earlier were loaded on trucks. With this accomplished, Bill and all the men left at Spider Web moved over to Tin House to throw in with Pat Cain's crew and ship the yearlings at Tin House. All of these yearlings were shipped on three dates, November

5, 7 and 8, a total of 2160 steers and 1560 heifers. The steers which weighed an average of 715 pounds going on the fifth and seventh, and on the eighth the heifers that weighed 700 even.

During this first week of November, there came a big storm with several inches of snow and then rain, and the big Cataract Creek that heads out on the north slopes of Bill Williams Mountain, forty-five miles to the south, ran big for several days. And then it turned cold enough to freeze ice on the water holes about an inch thick.

On the afternoon of November 8, the wagon moved to Tom Moore for the second time that fall so the cows could be gathered and the calves weaned. The first morning they worked in Tom Moore, Bill Howell led the crew upstream in the bottom of Cataract Creek, and there were still numerous pools of water left over from when the creek had run a week or so before. The trail in the bottom meandered back and forth across the creek bed, and the men followed Bill single file as they traveled along riding in a trot when on dry ground. At one place where the trail crossed the bottom, the horses had to walk through water a foot or so deep, but on each side of the crossing, the water was much deeper, about four feet or so. The trail had cut through the bank, but on either side it was straight off several feet and down into a pool of icy water.

Ben Fancher was riding a big jug-headed outlaw known as Hammer, and Charlie was riding the infamous Burro. Lem Davis, who claimed to have been a rough string rider in his younger days, had his new Bob McCray flower-carved form-fitter saddle strapped on a Clabber horse known as Cacahuate. Cacahuate was short and stout with a big belly and a pole in his heavy-muscled neck, with a long curly mane and tail that drug the ground. His fetlocks had feathers like a Clydesdale, and he was solid brown in color. Cacahuate had been known to buck, and when he did he had alot of kick in him as if he had been flanked. Just as Lem was easing Cacahuate down the muddy slope into the shallow crossing, Ben and Charlie came charging from behind and spurred their horses off of the shallow cliffs on either side of Lem, and their horses splashed into the icy pools below. The men's shouts and the horses splashing into the deep water were too much for

Cacahuate, and he jumped through himself and kicked over his head, and Lem turned a somersault ten feet in the air and came down and out of sight into the deepest part of the water. The first thing that floated to the surface was Lem's cowboy hat, and then he surfaced, his bald head appearing first, and blew water and air out of his mouth like a breaching whale. Lem stood about five feet three and was just as wide, and he came puffing out of the water like a walrus trying to secure a perch on dry land. Someone caught Cacahuate and led him up to Lem who stepped on him and gave Bill Howell a look as if to say, "Working for you isn't easy!" In respect of Lem, it should be mentioned that he did not ask to be excused so he could change clothes, but gritted his teeth and worked on in wet and icy attire. Bill spurred his horse upstream and resumed his quest to the backside of the morning's circle. It was 20 degrees above zero.

Gathering the Tom Moore cows took two days, and they were deposited in a trap at Little Rogers Tank on the west side of the Tom Moore Pasture and then trailed to Tin House where the cows and calves were separated and then the cows were driven back to Little Rogers. The gates on the backside of the Little Rogers Trap were opened and the cows allowed to drift back into Tom Moore, but they stayed on the west side of the trap for several days, bawling and looking off toward Tin House and their babies. Two good fences and five miles separated them.

The wagon then moved to Redlands for the second time that fall, and the cows in the Big Cataract Pasture were gathered, and the calves weaned in the corral at Redlands, and the cows trailed to Box K eight miles to the north.

On November 14 the crew rose early and hauled their horses ten miles to Anita and gathered the 200 cull cows and fifteen old bulls that were being sent to the slaughter house. The old Atchison, Topeka & Santa Fe Railroad line was still running between Williams and the Grand Canyon Village and there was a set of railroad shipping pens a mile south of the Anita Camp, and a train with cattle cars was scheduled to come and load the cows at 10:00 a.m. At 11:00 it hadn't appeared, so Bill Howell got on his newly acquired radio phone that had just been installed in his company pickup, and he inquired about the arrival of the train. He was told that the train had been held up for some reason, and it wouldn't arrive until late afternoon, maybe 4:00 p.m. Bill's family was living at Cedar Ranch some sixty miles to the southeast, and he hadn't been home for a couple weeks, and neither had Ben Fancher whose family was also there; so he instructed Pat Cain to take over the shipping responsibilities so he and Ben could go home to see their lonely families. The dust hadn't settled from Bill's pickup driving east toward Highway 64 ten miles away when Pat Cain announced that he was going to the Tusayan Saloon to have a drink. He also allowed that there was a telephone at the saloon, and the whereabouts of the train could be investigated. He let it be known that everyone who was thirsty was welcome to come.

There were two dirt roads leaving Anita and ending at Tusayan. Bill Howell and Ben Fancher left going straight east on the one, but Pat Cain chose to go straight north on the other, but the mileage is about the same. Pat Cain and the remaining crew, including 18-year-old Charlie Gould, pulled into the Tusayan Saloon seventy feet behind Bill Howell and Ben Fancher who had turned north toward Tusayan when they hit the highway instead of going south toward Cedar Ranch. The Babbitt Cowboys invaded the saloon like cowboys will do, but Pete, the cranky old bartender, wouldn't serve anything to Charlie except soda pop. They drank their refreshment of choice, and after several hours Pat Cain wandered to the phone booth to check on the Santa Fe. Bill and Ben left to go to Cedar Ranch. The train was having more difficulties. They stayed and it got dark, and every hour or thereabouts Pat would go to the phone booth. Charlie got sick of Coke and played pool and beat up on everyone because he was sober and they weren't. Finally, at nine o'clock, Pat's thirst was quenched, and they headed back toward Anita taking several bottles of Seagram's VO with them.

The train arrived about 11:00 p.m., and the engineer backed the cattle cars onto the siding that ran up close to the loading chute, and about the time the brakeman spotted the first cattle car, another railroad man who was running the switch that turned the train into the siding started waving his lantern to stop the train.

He ran to the engine and had an excited conversation with the engineer as the cowboys sat on their horses drinking Seagram's VO. The conductor came and announced to Pat Cain that the switch was not functioning correctly because of the fact it hadn't been used in a year, and they were worried about derailing the train. The conductor was using railroad vernacular not understood by drunk cowboys. Pat Cain assured the conductor the cowboys had full faith in the Santa Fe employees' capabilities, and to not worry about the #@$%^&* switch and get them cattle cars up to the chute. The conductor left and had a consultation with the engineer and brakeman, and then he came back and told Pat Cain that they would load the cattle but would not be held liable if there was a malfunction. "Get them damn cars spotted so we can load these old cows! Hell, they're going to die if you don't get 'em to California!" Pat told him. The conductor instructed the engineer to proceed.

The cars were spotted one by one, a total of six, and the old cows and bulls were loaded. Sometime about the second car, Pat Cain disappeared, although no one noticed because they all knew what to do without him, and then he appeared standing on top of the third car as the other cowboys were loading it. He had found a harmonica in his coat pocket and stood on top of the cattle car playing "The Wreck of Old 97" in the key of G. The brakeman hollered at him to get down, but Pat hollered back telling the man to spot another car. He took a drink of VO and "The Wreck of Old 97"resumed.

When the last car was loaded and the gate shut, the conductor appeared with the bill of lading and asked for someone to sign it. He also had a release form stating that the Santa Fe would not be responsible for the cattle if the switch malfunctioned when they pulled onto the main track. Everyone pointed at Pat Cain who was now not only playing the harmonica but also dancing on top of the cattle car. The conductor was told that Pat was the boss. "You need to get down off of there! We need you to sign these papers!" The conductor shouted.

"Get that boy there to sign 'em! He's the only one sober." Pat pointed at Charlie.

The conductor handed Charlie the papers but Charlie turned his back on him. "I'm not going to sign those papers."

The conductor climbed up the ladder attached to the back of the car and approached Pat who picked up his bottle and staggered to the opposite end of the car, running away from the conductor and playing his harmonica. Those were the last Babbitt cows that were ever loaded onto a railroad car.

On November 15 the wagon crew moved back to the Tubs where they finished working the C O Bar cows. They moved all of the cows with calves that were too young to wean into the Mesa Butte Pasture where they would spend the winter. All of the C O Bar bulls were trailed to Lockwood ten miles north of the Tubs where they would spend the winter. And another 500 calves were weaned and their mothers trailed east to the winter range east of Highway 89. The Babbitt cowboys had worked every day from Labor Day until Thanksgiving when the roundup officially ended.

The Great Babbitt Horses

When the branding was all done the end of June of 1970, Bill Howell sent Charlie and Dewey Brown back to the Well Camp to stay with Skeet and Diane all summer. The three of them, Skeet, Charlie and Dewey all had four broncs to break and all of July and August to do it. The colts were three-year-olds sired by the stud everyone called Breeze who was out of Breeze Bars, an own son of the great Three Bars. No one at the ranch knew that much about Breeze's sire, Breeze Bars, at least it was never talked about much; but every cowboy who worked for Babbitts in the 1960s and 1970s has a few stories to tell about the Breeze horses, and the stories are all about the horses' ability and propensity to buck. Maybe it wasn't the stud's fault, and the blame should be put on the Clabber mares he was crossed with. The Clabber horses would buck also, but they were favored by the cowboys over the Breezes because at least they would watch a cow, a quality the Breezes did not possess.

When Bill Howell took over the reins as the Babbitt Ranch manager, he inherited a remuda that was full of real buckers. Even for that day in time when there were other ranches in the Western United States that had remudas full of buckers, the Babbitt Ranches were well known. Frank Banks was a top notch cowboy by anybody's standards, but he was not concerned with having a reputation as a man who had a lot of gentle cowponies at his disposal. The story has been told many times how Ben Fancher ran into Frank on the streets of Flagstaff one day after not seeing him for several years. They went into the 66 Club on Santa Fe Avenue to drink a beer and visit. "How's the horses doing out there, Frank?" Ben asked.

"Oh good, Ben. Good! We killed three Indians at the Powwow this year," Frank answered happily. The best part of the story is, Frank was telling the truth. Babbitts supplied the bucking horses for the all Indian rodeo that was held annually on the Fourth of July weekend. Most of the horses were Babbitt Ranch brood mares plus a few geldings out of the remuda, and there were three Indian bronc riders who had died as a result of getting on Babbitt broncs at that year's rodeo. The year was 1964. Frank was just as proud of that as if he had won the NCHA Futurity while riding a Babbitt horse. Frank's view of horses had nothing to do with a lack of horsemanship or cowboy skill, but instead, it was a result of Frank being a product of a different time and place. The cowboy culture that he was a part of knew very little of cow horse pedigree or cutting contests. Frank probably didn't even know what the NCHA Futurity was, but he did know how to ride the fresh off of a snorty horse herding cattle all over the Coconino Plateau and Little Colorado River Valley.

Comparatively speaking, Bill Howell was from the new school, at least in 1969. In 2005 Babbitt Ranches won the coveted AQHA Ranch Remuda of the Year award which can be accredited to Bill and later Vic Howell's vision and guidance about the Babbitt horse program. The big turnaround for the Babbitt horses was when Bill purchased the first good Driftwood stud for the ranch on January of 1975. But in 1970 that was still way off in the future.

One day that summer of 1970, Charlie Gould and Dewey Brown left the Well Camp on Burro and Pole Cat who were both very green. They traveled up Pine Canyon above Holesapple Well toward an old camp known as Metzger. They were looking for some cattle to harass in some fashion, which was an activity they figured would benefit their green broncs. After going a ways they turned back south toward the limestone rim that rises above Holesapple and continues on toward Buck Tank. Presently they rode up on two big unbranded calves that had been missed during the spring roundup, so they discussed that fact, and since

Dewey was in possession of a good running iron, they decided they would rope the two slick calves and put the Babbitt brand on them. They cinched up good and tight and pursued the calves that weighted about 350 pounds, and right away the calves turned downhill going off the limestone rim. The two cowboys were in top form because about all they had been doing with their time was roping on their colts, and they got the calves caught about halfway down the slope, and they tied them down about fifty yards apart. They stepped off the distance and built a fire exactly halfway in between the two calves, and when Dewey's running iron was hot, they applied the Babbitt brand to the calf Charlie had tied down.

They walked back to the fire and began to reheat the running iron which was a two piece affair with a piece of three-quarter inch pipe for a handle and a round rod that was threaded on one end and could be threaded into a nut that was in one end of the pipe. If you stuck the threaded end down through the pipe handle and screwed it tight, it was short and easy to carry tied on your saddle. When you needed to use it, you simply unscrewed the rod that was in the handle and then screwed it back in from the outside, which extended the whole affair and made it long enough to brand with. On the opposite end of the threads, the rod had been heated and beat into a large U shape, and that was the end that was always heated and used to mark the critter. The U on this particular iron that Dewey possessed was quite large, especially for a portable iron, but it was what they had and it worked great.

When the running iron was hot the second time, Dewey mounted Pole Cat, and Charlie handed him the running iron. Dewey was going to lope the twenty-five yards to the calf thinking it would be faster than walking, and therefore the iron would still be hot when he got to the calf. When Charlie handed Dewey the iron, Pole Cat snorted and threw a fit; and in the midst of the ruckus Dewey dropped the hot iron, and it landed perfectly, the oversized U being the correct size to settle nicely on both sides of the horse's neck and stay there. Smoke rose from somewhere in front of Dewey's saddle, and the smell of burning flesh filled the atmosphere. Charlie watched in amazement as Pole Cat bucked and pawed and squealed down the limestone mountainside disappearing at times in a cloud of smoke. The bay horse was no slouch as a bucker, and Dewey had his hands full trying to stay on and could not lift the red-hot iron off of the melting flesh. Dewey didn't come back for a long time, and Charlie had to turn the unbranded calf loose.

Joe Chaves was typical of cowboys who drifted around working on big ranches. Typical as far as the places he had worked and different crews he had worked with and experiences he had accumulated. He was untypical in temperament because of a bent toward melancholy, and at times he would descend into a dark hole and reside there for days. At other times he would be happy and talkative, appearing to be riding on Cloud Nine. He was, in spite of his irregularities of spirit, capable of making a hand, especially if he was in the mood to do so. He was not, however, a bronc stomper and never had been. He was working at Babbitts in the fall of 1971 when Charlie was there. Joe had a Clabber horse named Moonshine in his string that was humpy when he was fresh: fresh meaning if he had not been ridden in two days. Joe could get on old Moonshine and get away from camp without the horse bucking if he was given the time to baby him along very slowly for a couple hundred yards. The old horse knew that Joe was incapable of making the whistle if he took to him in a bucking fit and so he played the situation for all it was worth.

One morning the men were saddling up when it was just beginning to get light, and it was very cold. They had penned several hundred cows in a large corral just a short distance away from where they were saddling their horses. Joe was the first man to get saddled and ready to ride. About the time he pulled his cinches tight, Eph Fancher looked up and saw that somehow a gate had got opened on one end of the corral that held the herd of cattle "That damn gate got knocked open, and the cows are about to get out!" Eph yelled.

Bill Howell looked up as he was wiping dirt off of his horse's back. The cows had spotted the open gate and were headed toward it. He looked around and saw that no one was saddled and ready to ride except Joe. "Joe, jump on and keep them cows from gettin' out!" Bill shouted.

Joe saw the wreck about to commence. He was the same distance to the open gate as the lead cow headed toward it. A man on a fast horse could easily save the day. He mounted Moonshine and turned him toward the gate. At first old Moonshine refused to untrack but finally began taking short little tippy-toe steps. The cows looked from Moonshine back to the open gate, and they increased their speed. Moonshine needed to run, but he walked slowly as Joe carefully spurred him with the calves of his legs making sure no spur iron touched his belly.

"I'll bet five dollars on the cows!" Eph hollered.

"Jiminy Crickets, surely he'll get to the gate before them," Mike McFarland said quietly.

Joe now had Moonshine pickin' em up and sittin' em down in a regular walk. He needed to be runnin'. "Hell, I'll bet ten dollars on the cows," Ben Fancher said.

"Joe will make it," Pat Cain said.

What Bill Howell said can't be repeated, but the end of the story is only a dozen cows got out of the gate before Joe and Moonshine got there and plugged the hole.

Later on that fall the wagon was camped at Redlands for the late works when all the calves were weaned. It had stormed and a lot of water had run filling the dirt tanks all over the ranch. It was the same storm that caused Cataract Creek to run and create the pool of water that Lem Davis was thrown into when Cacahuate came unwound riding up the creek from Tom Moore.

The big dirt tank north of the horse corral at Redlands had filled up and run around the spillway, and it was backed up and outside of the big water lot toward the west and into the Little Redlands Pasture. The fact that the high water was plumb out of the corral going west created an island on the north side of the barb wire water lot that covered about ten acres in size. One evening the crew penned a number of cattle in that water lot intending to leave them there overnight and then do something with them the next day. The morning of the next day broke early and cold, and there was an inch or more of ice on the surface of all the dirt stock ponds.

All of the cattle that had been left in the big water lot north of the corrals had walked across the water and were standing on high ground against the north fence and staring back south at the cowboys as they saddled their horses as the first ray of sunlight peaked over the eastern horizon. Someone was going to have to ride across the icy water and bring the cows back to the corrals, and for some reason Joe Chaves volunteered and rode out in front of the rest of the crew to do the job. He was riding old Moonshine, and as usual the horse was humped up, and Joe was coaxing him along, nudging him gently with the calves of his legs but being careful to not spur him. Moonshine was movin' pretty slow as he broke through the ice at water's edge and started across the body of water that was fifty yards wide and three feet deep at Joe's selected heading.

All of the cowboys were watching and, not wanting to ride through the ice themselves, were content to wait while Joe retrieved the cattle who were also watching, being crowded up against the fence 150 yards distance. About thirty feet into the water, Moonshine stopped and humped up and acted like he might buck. Joe had his hand on the saddle horn and pulled back on the reins to keep the horse's head up. He clucked to him, pleading in a low tone of voice for a little forward motion. Finally Moonshine responded to the gentle nudging of Joe's legs squeezing him in his big belly. They moved forward another thirty feet breaking ice as they went. The sun was now fully up over the horizon and reflecting off of an infinite number of frost sparkles covering the landscape in every direction. Everything looked like a shiny Christmas card as the cowboys watched Joe's slow crossing of the icy waters of tribulation. At sixty feet Moonshine stopped and refused to move. The ice was up to the horse's belly and the soles of Joe's cowboy boots. His hand squeezed the saddle horn tightly. Everyone thought the horse would buck Joe off. Instead he acted like he wanted to lay down. Joe pulled on the reins and pleaded, "Moonshine!"

Bill Howell was getting pissed, he had a very large day planned. "Spur that @#$%^&*(). Spur him! Spur him!" Bill hollered.

"I'll betcha' five bucks he lays down with him," Eph Fancher said.

"Spur him!" Everyone hollered in unison. Moonshine continued his spiral downward until his whole body disappeared under the ice. Joe, by that time, had stepped off and was marching toward shore in ice water that was up to his rotund belly, and he was exuding great gusts of wind with each stride. Awoosh! Awoosh! Awoosh! Awoosh! He strode out of the water sucking and blowing great gasps of oxygen as if he was a huge bellows casting needed air into a red hot bed of burning coal. He gritted his teeth as he walked past the crew, who had quit trying to control their laughter, and marched toward the bunkhouse to get a set of dry clothes. Old Moonshine stood up and came to shore after he had cooled off.

Pat Cain loved horses and had broke lots of them in his younger years in Wyoming and then on other big ranches in Arizona after he moved south in 1948. He was a happy-go-lucky individual who traveled at his own speed, and he seemed to let a horse do the same thing. He never trained on a horse but instead just rode them and let them do as they wished. His old rough out, swell fork saddle had never seen or felt the caress of a wet rag lathered up with saddle soap or neatsfoot oil, and his latigo bridle reins were cracked and on the verge of breaking in two because they were so brittle. He owned one bridle with an old Kelly Brothers grazing bit with 1 ¼ inch silver conchos on the side where the mouthpiece and cheeks were welded together, and the curb strap hung so loose that it was almost impossible for it to touch the underside of a horse's chin.

One day during the fall roundup of 1971, the Babbitt crew was sorting a large herd of yearling heifers at Tin House. There were over a thousand head of cattle, and Bill Howell was riding his famous cutting horse Checkers, and Pat was riding a bay five-year-old bronc known as Coon. Coon was a Clabber bred horse and was very quick and agile and had been started by a friend of Bill Howell's from Montana whose name was Gene Ewalt. Gene Ewalt had come down and worked at Babbitts for a while and then moved back to the north country. He later ended up owning a cow ranch near Douglas Lake in British Columbia.

Bill and Pat Cain were in the large herd of heifers doing the cutting. Several times Coon stopped and stretched out like a horse that wanted to urinate, and Pat sat calmly on his back, lighting his corncob pipe, giving the bay bronc plenty of time to do his business, but the horse didn't get anything accomplished. Then all of a sudden while Pat was trying to maneuver a yearling out of the herd, Coon blew up and bucked Pat off. The bucking was spectacular and surprised everyone because the horse had never bucked in his life. "Boy, I didn't see that comin'," Pat said as he picked himself up off of the ground.

"Well, I don't know why you didn't; he stretched out and measured you two or three times," Eph Fancher said.

Pat's favorite horse was a big sorrel Clabber he called Oxbow. Oxbow was about fifteen hands one inch high and weighed close to 1300 pounds and sported a big belly. He was gentle, and Pat liked to ride him when he sorted cattle. The big pot-bellied horse would watch a cow a little, but Pat couldn't turn him around in forty acres. When he pulled on the bridle reins connected to the Kelly grazing bit, it seemed to turn over in the horse's mouth similar to cherries rolling around in a slot machine. A toothpick stuck in his mouth would have had just as much effect on Oxbow as a bridle bit. If Oxbow broke into anything faster than a slow trot when cutting a cow, Pat would swing a doubled up pigging string over the horse's ears when he wanted to get the horse to stop.

Ben Fancher had started a big Breeze he named Quatro de Julio, or Julio for short. After about twenty rides, Pat asked to have the horse in his string. Over the next several years, he only rode him two or three times, and Julio got snortier and snortier and grew to over fifteen hands and over 1200 pounds. By the time the horse was five years old, he was extremely intimidating on the ground. He would roll his nose and snort and make a person think he was going to paw your head off or kick you and break your leg. At five years old he might have been ridden a total of thirty times. He was very scary.

The crew was sorting some cattle in the corrals at Redlands, and Pat was riding old Hooley, which was what he called him. The bronc's mane and tail had not been combed out in several years, and he had long tangled witch's knots in both, and mixed into the tangled, knotted hair were pieces of grass, dried out tumbleweeds and bits of other trash picked up out on the range. His tangled, matted tail drug the ground, and besides all the tumbleweeds stuck in the hair, a long stick had been snagged by the tail and was dragging behind the horse like a travois.

Pat was riding Julio in a hackamore and seemed to have no fear of the horse, although no one else wanted to get near him. He had not curried him off when he saddled him, and he had a considerable amount of dried mud all over his body as a result of rolling in the mud on the edge of a dirt stock tank. Pat was on Julio and sitting in a gate working and allowing some cattle to be cut through the gate while holding others back. The bronc was snorting and would occasionally look back at the dragging stick connected to his tail and act as if he wanted to kick it. Just as a cow was being cut through the gate and both Pat and Julio needed to be paying attention, a black cat ran behind Julio within inches of the dragging stick, and Julio turned his eyeballs backwards looking, and then kicked the cat with his left hind hoof and sent the cat sailing plumb over the fence on the lower end of the corral where he landed in the Promise Land.

He was very scary.

Jodie

Bill Howell owned a black mare that he thought a lot of who went back to a stud named Music Mount, and he raised several good colts out of her, the first of which he named Tiny Bull. Bill bred the black mare, which was the only name she ever had, to an own son of Spotted Bull in Montana and then hauled her south to Arizona and the Babbitt Ranch. Tiny Bull was a blood bay with no white markings and became one of the great team roping horses of his time, and Bill won a lot of money and silver buckles riding him. In the mid-70s Bill turned down $5000 that a famous roper offered him for the horse, and in that day and age, that was a lot of money.

After the black mare gave birth to Tiny Bull, Bill bred her to a Babbitt stud named Little Pard who only sired a few horses on the ranch. The result of that union was a seal brown horse colt he named Jodie. The spring Jodie was three years old, Bill had a cowboy who was working for him at the time put a half dozen rides on Jodie, and the cowboy and colt got on nicely; but then the cowboy quit and went off to seek his fortune elsewhere, and Jodie went unridden for a month or two. After Charlie had worked for the outfit several days, Bill recognized that Charlie was very capable with a horse, and he asked Charlie if he would ride the brown colt, and Charlie said yes.

On one of the first rides Charlie put on Jodie, they were trailing 150 pairs up the mountain above Cedar Ranch with Slate Lake as their destination. The cowboys always enjoyed trailing cattle to Slate Lake because they had to make the cattle walk across Highway 180 a mile south of Slate Lake, and there were usually some cattle that wouldn't want to cross and would have to be roped and pulled across. Any excuse to rope something was welcome. As expected several cows wouldn't cross the blacktop and painted white lines, and they tried to run off. Charlie ran up on a big horned Hereford cow and roped her clean around the horns and stopped her. That day was the seventh or eighth time Jodie had ever been ridden.

Bill Howell rode up to Charlie and offered to help. "Here give me your rope and I'll drag her across the highway for you," Bill said.

"By golly, I roped her so I'll drag her across myself," Charlie replied, and he led the cow across the pavement with very little trouble.

Charlie rode Jodie with the Luis Ortega hackamore and the Blind Bob macate, and the colt kept his head up and ears forward and moved with a purpose. He had a fast and comfortable walk and was very enjoyable to ride. He was one of those horses that wanted to get along, and instead of being bowed up and obstinate when faced with a new challenge, he would act as if

Any excuse to rope something was welcome.

he was curious and wanted to see if he could figure things out. Charlie loved him and rode him all spring and into the summer, and then in the fall of 1970, Bill turned him out in the Little Redlands Pasture with the intention of letting the colt grow up and get stronger.

In the spring of 1971 around the first of May when the extra horses that had been turned out barefooted all winter were gathered for use during the branding wagon, Jodie was missing. No sign of him was found, no bones or carcass or anything. Then in September when the extra horses were gathered out of the Little Redlands Pasture, the brown colt came up missing again, and he was presumed dead; and although it was a loss to Bill, not much more was thought about it. On a big ranch covering hundreds of square miles of broken landscape, cattle and horses die from lightning, snakebite or sickness, and the fact that they are never found isn't out of the ordinary.

The Little Redlands' pasture fence on its west side was the boundary fence between the Babbitt Ranch and the Diamond A. Before you got to the southern end of Little Redlands, the Diamond A fence cornered and went straight west eight miles, and south of that fence was another Babbitt pasture known as Blanco. The pasture on the Diamond A side of the fence in that corner was called Broken Axle, and there was a dirt tank bearing that same name off to the west several miles. The Broken Axle Pasture was 70,000 acres in size.

Going northwest from Redlands was a dirt road that passed through the Diamond A fence six miles northwest of camp and eventually turned in a more northerly course toward what was known as Hualapai Hilltop which was the jump off point for the trail descending down into the canyon and the Supai Village and the beautiful Havasupai waterfalls near the bottom of the Grand Canyon. Occasionally a lost tourist would drive through Redlands and go out on this road out of ignorance because the road was very primitive for the thirty-mile stretch from Redlands to Hualapai Hilltop. But nevertheless the pilgrims would come, and often they would leave the boundary gate between Babbitts and the Diamond A open. This was a real problem for Babbitt livestock because they would get out of the gate while it was open, and then not knowing where water was, they would try and come back; and sometimes they would get hung up and dried out walking the fence and trying to make it back to the east to find water. Whoever was living at Redlands had to keep their eye on the situation because more than once livestock had died of thirst walking the fence. That fence was checked several times when Jodie failed to be found, but no sign of him turned up.

The Diamond A Ranch bordered the Supai Indian Reservation on its northern boundary and the Hualapai Reservation to the west, and for many years the Diamond A had a huge problem with wild Indian horses crossing from the reservation onto the Diamond A and running on the northern half of the Diamond A. This half of the ranch north of Rose Well covered about 500 square miles and was part of the country known as the Cataract Plains. The plains are a limestone country being quite open but not flat but, instead, contain may shallow draws and ridges with limestone outcroppings and lots of gramma grass growing in the rich but shallow soil. There is also chamisa and cliffrose in some places and an occasional juniper or pinion tree, but for the most part, it is an open rolling country. It is excellent cow and horse country.

The Indian horses were a constant headache, and finally about 1970 Jim Lowrance, the Diamond A manager, decided he would deal with the Indian horse problem once and for all time. He got the authorities on his side and announced that the Diamond A cowboys were going to corral the Indian horses, and the Indians would have to sell them and dispose of them permanently. It was a good idea and sounded feasible on paper but was not easy to accomplish. The Indians would gather some of the horses and run them back onto the reservation only to turn them back onto the Diamond A when Jim Lowrance and his crew weren't looking. It was a cat and mouse game of large proportions that went on for a number of years.

The Diamond A camped their wagon crew, with sometimes as many as twenty cowboys, out at various spots on the plains in the summer of 1970 and spring and summer of 1971 and 1972, chasing and gathering wild Indian horses; and hundreds of the horses were shipped, but they kept reappearing. The Indians had lots of them.

Southwest of Redlands twenty miles and ten miles west of the Babbitt cow camp known as Tin House was a cow camp on the Diamond A Ranch known as Black Tank. Black Tank was a beautiful spot nestled in a canyon under a malpai rim on the south that was covered with juniper and pinion pine and other brushy vegetation and good grass. To the south and west of the camp, the country rose several hundred feet and became part of what the Diamond A referred to as the top country. Going north a short distance from Black Tank, the country opened up onto the hundreds of miles of Cataract Plains.

Black Tank was an isolated place, and whoever was given the job of staying there and taking care of that part of the huge Diamond A Ranch was never bothered much by the boss. If a man didn't need people around all the time, it was a good place to be. In the winter months of 1971 and 1972, Jim Lowrance put two bachelor cowboys at Black Tank. Their names were Dale and Ray. They had been part of the Supai and Hualapai Indian horse roundup earlier in the summer of 1971 and had worked for Mike Landis, the Diamond A wagon boss, that fall. Dale and Ray were present on the wild horse roundup the day Dave Ericsson roped an unbroke seven-year-old bay stud, and with several cowboys help, he tied him down and rolled his saddle under him and rode him up back into camp. Dave named the stud Prisoner, and he continued to ride him, and the horse made a good ranch horse.

On that horse roundup, the Diamond A cowboys gathered about 500 wild horses and eventually got them all corralled in the shipping pens at Camp 16 on the north end of the ranch some sixty miles north of Seligman. The whole process took several weeks of hard riding, culminating in many semi loads of horses being trucked to a distant slaughter house where they were transformed into dog food. For the most part the horses were small, hatchet-hipped, jug-headed, broom-tailed mustangs, but there were a few exceptions like Prisoner who became a respected part of the

Diamond A remuda. The successful gathering and shipping of 500 head reduced the wild horse problem considerably, but did not totally eliminate it.

At the end of the roundup in the fall of 1971, Dale and Ray moved into Black Tank for the winter. Their duties for the winter included making the rounds on a number of dirt tanks and water troughs, cutting ice so the livestock could drink as well as keeping cottonseed cake put out in feed troughs for some herd bulls that were going to be wintering near Black Tank. For two men working together, it was not a difficult job.

At some point the two men dreamed up a scheme to make some extra money. They had seen a few Indian horses running wild in the Broken Axle Pasture. Going straight north from Black Tank, it was a twelve mile ride to the south side of Broken Axle and another twelve miles to the north end of the pasture at Platinum Point. From the southeast corner of Broken Axle Pasture and a water hole known as Hazen Hole, it's nine miles straight east to the Babbitt fence and Little Redlands Pasture.

Several other Diamond A cowboys besides Dale and Ray had seen a small bunch of wild Supai horses running in Broken Axle, and among them was an abnormally good looking brown gelding. Very good looking if compared to the horses he was running with. The brown gelding was Jodie. Apparently sometime after the end of the summer in 1970 when Charlie Gould pulled the shoes off of him and he was turned out to rest in the Little Redlands Pasture, Jodie walked through an open gate or got through the fence from Little Redlands and into Broken Axle. And then he threw in with a bunch of wild Supai horses and ran with them for a number of months. Somehow the bunch had escaped the snare of the big wild horse roundup.

Dale and Ray's plan was to gather a few of the wild horses on the sly and trail them south into Black Tank and pick out the best looking ones and then sneak them off of the ranch and sell them and pocket the money. If you went east on a dirt road from Black Tank you entered the Babbitt Ranch, the fence being five miles distance from Black Tank Camp, and then it's another five miles on into Tin House and then about eighty-five miles on to

Flagstaff and points beyond. They figured that if they played their cards right they could slip the stolen horses off the Diamond A Ranch undetected. The plan in their mind was fool proof. If they got the first load out, perhaps they could high grade a second or even third load. They imagined they were sitting on a virtual gold mine.

The two Black Tank men left camp one cold January morning and rode straight north in a long trot, and after going twelve miles they came to a wire gate about two miles east of Hazen Hole that would let them into the Broken Axle Pasture. It was cold with an overcast dirty sky keeping the temperature barely above freezing. There were large patches of snow on the ground that covered about one half of the landscape with the remainder being bare ground with gramma grass exposed for livestock to graze on. The two men took the time to build a fire made from the limbs of chamisa and old cow chips. As they stood warming their feet against the small flames, they cursed the cold and wind and the smell of the fire. "Maybe," Ray said, "we could make enough money on our horse venture to vacation in a warmer climate like Tucson or Nogales. There were lots of dark-skinned girls in Nogales, at least I heard that from several cowboys who have been there."

They decided to split up and travel northeast on both sides of the waterline that originated at Rose Well fifteen miles to the southwest. Ray would go a mile or so north of the pipeline, and Dale would stay on the south side. They agreed to high point every mile or two and see if one man or the other had spotted the band of horses.

About six miles and an hour and a half later, Ray spotted five head of loose horses a quarter mile north of a storage and water trough on the pipeline that was known as Number 13. He went way wide to the north until he was north and a little east of the horses and then he approached them, and when he was a half mile away, the five horses started traveling south in a trot. Dale had been watching and was positioned a mile south of Number 13. He had dismounted and was standing next to his horse hoping the wild bunch would recognize the horse but not the man. He played his hand perfectly, and the five horses loped his way, and when they were 400 yards away, he slipped up on his horse keeping his head bent low over the fork of the saddle; and he kicked the horse underneath him into a lope and started toward the southwest. The five loose horses took his bait and followed.

The horses he and Ray were riding were grain fed and hard, and Dale stayed out in front of the wild ones several hundred yards distance and never acted like he cared if they followed, while Ray stayed behind and made enough noise to make the wild ones think they were being pursued. By the time they reached the wire gate they had ridden through several hours earlier, the five loose horses were traveling fifty feet behind Dale who never looked back. He had convinced them that he was their leader, even a friend. Jodie was among the five, and the fact that he was broke to ride and had been driven in this same fashion is probably what made it go so smoothly. They had left the wire gate open, and Dale never slowed down while he rode through and turned directly south toward Black Tank twelve miles away. They reached the horse corral at the Black Tank Camp at two thirty in the afternoon with Dale leading the five loose horses and Ray driving. The wild bunch trotted right through the open gate with Jodie leading the way.

"Where in the hell do you suppose that brown horse came from? I ain't never seen no Supai Indian ridin' a horse that is that good lookin'!" Ray said as he unsaddled his tired and sweaty horse.

"I been wonderin' that myself! I haven't seen a brand on him, have you?" Dale replied.

"No, there ain't a mark on him!"

"He can't be a Babbitt horse. They always brand 'em."

The fact is, Bill Howell, in a rare case of not tending to business, had never put his brand on the colt. It was one of those things that a man intends to do but because of circumstances, like being very busy, never gets done. It was a mistake that he would always regret.

The other four horses that Ray and Dale had gathered were run-of-the-mill Supai Indian horses, or the equivalent of a typical mustang you would find on the Owyhee Desert of Northern

Nevada or the Red Desert of Southern Wyoming. The two cowboys had never intended on riding the horses but were going to haul them out through the Babbitt Ranch and sell them for dog chow prices to a horse trader in Flagstaff. But seeing Jodie in the bunch changed things. He was gook looking and obviously well bred and acted gentle. They roped the brown horse who was now a coming five-year-old, and Ray saddled and rode him, and he rode around like a well-broke horse. They were happy because the horse would obviously be worth a lot more than the other four.

Then on the afternoon of the day after they had gathered the five horses, Ray and Dale fell upon bad luck. A pickup pulled into camp carrying a young cowboy who worked for the outfit and was staying at Rose Well about twenty miles to the west. They hadn't planned on having company before they could get the stolen goods snuck out and into town the back way. But when they saw who it was they relaxed somewhat, the cowboy was a friend, and no one on the ranch really cared about Indian horses anyway. So what if a Diamond A cowboy made a little extra cash; it was doubtful anyone would care. But as luck would have it, their visitor spied the wild horses in the corral and out of curiosity went to investigate. The young visitor was totally innocent. He didn't care what Ray and Dale were doing and wasn't the type to stick his nose in other people's business, but when he saw Jodie his countenance changed, and Ray and Dale could see the change.

Nobody knows for sure what happened next. It is unclear what if anything was said between the three men. Perhaps there was nothing said, but just the look on the young man's face was all it took. We will never know for sure. But as bad luck would have it, the young man who drove up unexpectantly in the pickup and laid his eyes on Jodie was also a friend of Bill Howell's, and several years earlier he had worked on the Babbitt Ranch. He was also the first man who ever rode the brown colt a month or so before Charlie Gould went to work for the outfit.

After a short stay at Black Tank tending to whatever business that had brought him to the camp, the young cowboy drove back to Rose Well, and then later on that evening he drove on south to Seligman, fifty miles distance, and to a telephone. He phoned Bill Howell, and after saying hello he spoke one short sentence, "Bill, if you ever want to see your Jodie horse again, you better go to Black Tank." With that said he hung up the phone and drove back to Rose Well.

The phone call, as short and to the point as it was, created somewhat of a dilemma for Bill. Although the young man's message was lacking in details, he could put two and two together and come up with a pretty accurate scenario. He knew all about the wild horse roundup, and he knew how isolated Black Tank was, and he knew who was spending the winter there, and his imagination could fill in the blank spots. He thought about the situation and weighed his options. He was very busy and had a lot on his mind concerning running the Babbitt Ranch and hardly had the time to go snooping around on the neighbor's place. There was also the fact that Jim Lowrance, who managed the Diamond A Ranch, was a good friend of his. Jim Lowrance had worked for Bill before getting his big job running the biggest ranch in Arizona, and Bill didn't want to get pushy by barging in and causing trouble with some of Jim's crew. Bill was a believer in following proper cowboy etiquette. He thought the retaliation against him showing up where he didn't belong might do the Babbitt Ranch more harm than it was worth. In the end, right or wrong, he chose to take no action.

As the evening of the day the young cowboy from Rose Well showed up and saw Jodie and the four Indian horses in the Black Tank horse corral wore on, Ray and Dale became increasingly paranoid. They drank whiskey as they sat by the woodstove that evening and envisioned deputy sheriffs and brand inspectors driving up with handcuffs in one hand and a loaded gun in the other. As the night wore on, their position seemed less glamourous and began to leave a sour taste in their mouths that Jim Beam couldn't wash down; and by sun up the next morning, they had made their decision.

East of the Black Tank Camp several miles is a finger of a long mesa running north and south extending several miles northward jutting out like a sentinel looking out over the thousand square miles of rolling gramma grass plain. The last three miles of this mesa is less than a mile wide going east and west and rises 500 feet above the plains to the north. There are a good many juniper and pinion trees on the top, and a black malpai rim rock around its edges that make it a landmark that can be seen for thirty miles. The north/south boundary fence between Babbitts and the Diamond A comes off of the plains going south and goes right up the northern end of the mesa splitting it evenly between the two ranches. They call this landmark Long Point, and on the west, or Diamond A side, of Long Point there are several short little arroyos falling downward to the plains below.

At daybreak the morning after being found out by the young man, Ray and Dale left the Black Tank horse corral driving four broom-tailed Supai horses and a good looking five-year-old brown gelding and headed east toward Long Point, and when they reached its slopes, they pushed the five horses halfway up the bottom of a rocky arroyo and into a spot that was steep and rocky which made the five loose horses content to stop. There in the shadow that was given to them by the fact that the sun had not topped out over the mesa above, Ray stepped off of his horse and took a .30 .30 Winchester out of a saddle scabbard. He had a new box of ammunition in his coat pocket, but it was unneeded because the five horses were held in close by the boulders and steepness of the terrain. When the tubular magazine underneath the Winchester's barrel was empty, all five of the horses including Jodie lay there dead.

Eighteen years later Bill Howell received a three page letter from Ray admitting what had taken place and explaining it in some detail. No apology was offered or forgiveness asked, just a simple explanation. Jodie's bones are laying there today bleached in the sun.

Slim Gilliam

When Charlie went to work at the Diamond A Ranch, Slim Gilliam was sixty-four years old and one of the oldest men on the crew of twenty or so cowboys. He was a tall, slender man with chiseled features handsomely laced together with muscle and sinew, and an erect posture and bearing of a natural born leader. He always conducted himself with a purpose, a member of a crew who did his part to make the work successful. He was exceedingly intelligent.

He had the habits of an outdoorsman such as carrying his own personal double-bitted axe rolled up in his bed. He would keep his axe honed razor sharp with a whetstone he also carried and could cut firewood for the roundup cook faster and more precise in size that a man wielding a sharp chainsaw. He could read sign and outthink a herd of wild horses or cows better than any man on the crew.

On one of the first days that Charlie worked for Mike Landis, the crew had gathered a holding pasture at Farm Dam, ten miles north of Black Tank Camp and ten miles east of Rose Well. A small herd of cows with short-age calves from the previous year had been gathered into the holding pasture, and the ranch manager, Jim Lowrance, had sent word to the wagon boss, Mike Landis, that he was sending a truck out to Farm Dam to haul the calves back to Pica Camp some forty miles to the south. There was a small and crude corral and loading chute at Farm Dam where the calves could be loaded but very little else in the form of corral facilities existed.

Mike Landis had most of the crew holding the herd of cows and calves as several men rode into the herd and hoolihanded the calves around the neck and drug them through a gate into a small corral adjacent to the wooden loading chute. Charlie Gould, Larry Leist, and Ray Lambert were afoot in the corral and had been instructed by Mike Landis to take the ropes off of the calves. Mike had also told Slim Gilliam to rope the calves by the heels as they were drug through the gate. Slim Gilliam positioned himself on the right side of the gate, sitting on a buckskin horse and ready to take a shot at the heels of the jumping and bawling calves as they were drug past him by the cowboys who had roped them around the neck. Slim roped fifty-two calves by both hind feet without missing a loop and barely moved the buckskin horse the whole

Slim roped fifty-two calves by both hind feet without missing a loop...

time. He dallied his rope, without slipping a leg, on a short, little tie-hard horn with a small cap which was wrapped with nothing more than the original leather that was stretched over the rawhide-covered saddle tree. Charlie Gould and Larry Leist would tell of that day for decades to come. They both told the story separately on numerous occasions, but it was told the same way, and they said it was the most impressive job roping they ever witnessed.

Slim Gilliam was born in Washington State in 1908. His father had work horses and would contract to harvest wheat and other jobs that could be done with teams. When times got modern, they used steam engines to do the work that had been done by horses. Slim dreamed of being a cowboy, and in 1921 he lit out by himself to Arizona to pursue his dream, ending up in Phoenix looking for a job but having no connections. No one on the big ranches wanted to give a green kid with no skills a cowboy job, those being available to only the experienced hands. But how did one become experienced? He eventually acquired work on several outfits around Roosevelt Lake where he worked as a flunky, chopping wood for the cook and other menial tasks, being paid pennies a day and sometimes less. At times he worked for nothing more than the right to roll his blankets out among the cowboys and some food to eat.

Eventually he found his way to Northwest Arizona where his prospects looked better. He worked for ranches in the Hualapai Valley and the Big Sandy River where he learned the art of gathering and leading wild cattle and capturing wild horses, and by 1930 he was considered a top hand. Before the Taylor Grazing Act was passed by congress in 1934, the remote cattle country of Arizona was still a wild place with huge expanses of open grassland that were still unfenced, and getting into the cow business could be done by acquiring the claim to a water right at some spring or water hole and then roping a few unbranded cows and applying your brand to their hide. Several men were shot and killed in Seligman, one while sitting in a barber's chair, over an argument about water rights and the rightful ownership and horses. These things were current news when Slim first appeared there in the early '30s.

He met a young girl in Seligman named Dorothy Shuckings who had grown up on a homestead east of town near Floyd Mountain, a prominent landmark that is now part of the 7s Ranch, and just east of the Diamond A boundary fence. Slim and Dorothy married in 1934, and they moved south of Seligman thirty-five miles, set up camp, and proceeded to make a living by running, capturing and breaking wild horses to ride and then selling them as broke saddle horses. They worked together capturing the wild horses with Slim placing Dorothy in strategic places where she could turn horses toward a trap or help Slim lead a wild one into their camp. She was an exceptional cowgirl as well as cook and camp tender. She cooked in dutch ovens on an open fire, and for the first two years of their marriage, Dorothy was content living with Slim in a canvas tent at various spots on the north end of the famous Baca Land Grant.

For awhile during those first years of marriage, Sam Fancher, who was a good friend of Slim's, stayed with Slim and Dorothy and helped them gather wild horses. One day they were working out on the far northern points of Cow Creek Mesa, and Slim had tied a wild horse up to a tree with plans to lead him back into camp. Dorothy and Sam were with him and it was summertime. About the time they were getting the bronc loose from the tree, a big thunderstorm erupted, and it started raining violently over a large piece of country. Slim told Dorothy and Sam to take off and go to camp telling them he would deal with the colt by himself. The camp was south of where the colt had been tied and across several canyons, and Dorothy and Sam rode up to the edge of one that was running water over its banks, and they could hear boulders rolling under the rapids. Sam was in the lead, and at water's edge he hesitated, but Dorothy spurred her horse off into the deep water and was immediately swept downstream for a ways but managed to ride out to the other side and high ground a hundred yards downstream. Sam went against his better judgement and spurred his horse off into the rolling water. "I'd a' never went off in there if she hadn't went first!" He told Slim later on.

Slim and Dorothy made their living capturing and breaking wild horses to ride for the first two years of their marriage, living in a tent on the Grant the whole time, and then late in 1936, just before Clifford, their first child, was born, they found a real house to live in.

For a good while Slim worked for Clarence Denny on his ranch near Seligman, and Clarence paid Slim $175 a month, and Dorothy $75 a month to cook for his cowboy crew. Several of Clarence's neighbors complained to him about paying Slim such high wages because most cowboys were making half that much or even less. "I believe in paying a man what he's worth, and Slim Gilliam is worth that much to me," was Clarence Denny's reply. Slim also worked for the 3 Vs in those days.

In 1943 Slim and Dorothy bought a ranch on the Humboldt River near Imlay, Nevada. The ranch had 5000 deeded acres and the second oldest water rights on the Humboldt River, and Slim and Dorothy bought it for $20,000. They held onto the ranch for several years and tried to increase the size of their operation by purchasing more country on the Black Rock Desert but were never able to put a deal together. After three years they sold the ranch for a profit and moved back to Seligman.

When Kern County Land and Livestock Company bought the 3 V Ranch in 1949 and brought Leland Larson in from Southern New Mexico to manage it, Leland hired Slim to be the wagon boss for him, a position he held for several years. About this time a professional photographer took a picture of Slim dragging calves to the branding fire at Rose Well, and the picture became famous and appeared on Stetson hat boxes for many years. Slim could and would rope and drag calves to the fire with either his left hand or his right.

In the 1950s and '60s, Leland built hundreds of miles of fence on the Diamond A Ranch, and he awarded Slim and his two sons many of the fence contracts. They could make very good money building fence, and they would also trap coyotes and bobcats in the winter because fur prices were very good in those days.

Slim and Dorothy built a house in Seligman and lived there when they weren't out camping in some remote place building fence or trapping or cowboying for someone. They were both avid hunters of Indian artifacts and had many collections of beautiful arrowheads, spearheads and stone axes. They were well known for their collections.

On one fine day during the spring roundup of 1972, Cole Moorhouse and the rest of the Diamond A crew were gathering cattle in the Lower Sandstone Pasture east of Rose Well. Cole was a Texan and talked real slow with a Texas drawl. He thought a lot of Slim and looked up to him. As Cole rode along he looked down and saw a large black stone that looked like a spearhead that had been fashioned by some wild Indian several hundred years earlier. He jumped off his horse and picked the spearhead up. He was very excited because he had never found anything like an arrowhead or an artifact of any kind. It was a beautiful specimen, except about a third of it was missing, including the sharp point, but Cole thought he had made a good find anyway. He spied Slim riding along a quarter mile away following some cows, so he loped over to show Slim his spearhead. "Slim! Look what I found a minute ago," and he handed Slim the black piece of stone.

Slim held the rock in his hand as he rode along and turned it over several times, inspecting it. "Yeah, it's a spearhead alright. Too bad the tip's broke off of it." And with that said he threw the broken specimen as far as he could, and it disappeared in some tall grass a hundred feet away. To Slim it wasn't worth keeping. Cole stood there looking off into the distance for quite a spell. Years later Cole told a friend, "It was the only arrowhead I ever found." Cole would laugh about it when he told the story. Slim didn't mean to be ornery or disrespectful, he was just used to finding perfect specimens.

The Diamond A

W hen the fall roundup of 1971 came to a close at Babbitts, Charlie migrated west to California where his brother Skeet and sister-in-law Diane had located. Charlie spent the winter in the Coalinga area day working, breaking colts, and helping Skeet. For recreation he did a little team roping. And then on his nineteenth birthday, May 9, 1972, he showed up at Seligman and went to work for the Diamond A Ranch, also known as the Boquillas.

Leland Larson had managed the Diamond A for twenty years beginning in 1949, and then through the '50s and '60s. He was a big man and a very good cowboy with above average intelligence and an aptitude to take his mental thought processes and turn them into visible physical accomplishments. He was the man who took the huge ranch that was raw land and fenced it up into many pastures that were well watered by hundreds of miles of pipelines with millions of gallons of storage capacity. Leland was a dynamo and was well liked. For most of his tenure at Seligman, he ran a good outfit owing a great deal to his top men who served as wagon bosses under him: the most well known of these being Slim Gilliam and then for many years Tom Dolan, both of them being well respected by their peers. There were lots of famous cowboys on the outfit in that time period including Burley and Elmer McDonald, Ally Sifers, Carl Welsh, Pat Cain, John Andrews, Marion Deurenburger, Alvin Wagner, Raymond Scott, Jerry

Leland Larson had managed the Diamond A for twenty years.

Osborn, Dob Earnest, Jep Stell, Raymond Scott, and Chief Bernard. There were others and it was a cowboy outfit.

Tom Dolan got old and retired, and the late '60s saw a change in the old guard, and to many who lived in that era, it seemed that perhaps Leland was reluctant to promote a top cowboy into the wagon boss position. Several who were promoted to that position would make you wonder if that wasn't true. One man whom Leland promoted was so unsure of himself that his fear of Leland became a legend. One morning way before daylight, the wagon crew was drinking coffee in the cook tent and waiting for the cook to holler chuck when one of the men saw the headlights of a pickup approaching from several miles away. The cowboy hollered, "Pickup's a comin'," and with that the wagon boss threw his coffee cup in the air and walked in circles for a moment becoming paralyzed by the fear that Leland was going to find the men in camp. He finally mustered the presence of mind to spring into action and ran to the corral and went to catching horses for his crew as the vehicle drew closer. When he caught his horse, he hurriedly saddled him and stepped aboard and took off in a run. He loped for a half hour and finally pulled up and looked around and saw that only one of his dozen cowboys was with him. He had a high-pitched voice and squealed, "Where in the hell is everybody?" The other man replied matter-of-factly, "You lit outa there in a dead run before anyone else got saddled up." Another one of Leland's wagon bosses was so out of touch with traditional cowboy ways that he chose to lead drives mounted on a Honda motorcycle. People began to talk.

Mike Landis was running a ranch in the Cerbat Mountains north of Kingman, and he had become close friends with Leonard and Johnny Neal who were well-known and successful ranchers in Mojave County. Johnny Neal was married to one of Leland's daughters. The Neals recommended Mike Landis to fill the wagon boss position, telling Leland that Mike was all cowboy and perfect for the job.

When Jim Lowrance succeeded Leland as manager, he chose to run two wagons with Mike running the crew that worked the south end of the operation and Burley McDonald running the crew that worked the northern end of the huge ranch. Burley was well liked among the cowboys having a reputation for being a very smooth hand, and he also possessed an above average knowledge of cattle. He was famous for his photographic memory of cattle, a quality that Bill Howell at the Babbitt Ranch also possessed. More than one cowboy would tell stories of Burley riding through a herd of hundreds of Hereford cows and leaning out of the saddle and petting a certain cow, who to most cowboys looked no different than any other. When questioned later why he fawned over that particular cow, he would call her by name and say that years before he had fed her with a bottle because she was an orphan, and he could still remember her. Burley was not only a cowboy but a cowman. There is a difference.

The Diamond A had been operating for several years with two roundup wagons when in September of 1971 Burley got bucked off and hurt. He and his crew were camped at Keseha and were making a circle into Jones Tank in the Trinity Pasture, and below Jones a ways some cows took off running and trying to escape through the trees, so Burley spurred his horse down a steep hillside in an attempt to get in front of the cattle. He was riding a big brown horse called Freeze, and in hot pursuit he rode the horse between two cedar trees where there was barely room for him and Freeze to squeeze through, and in the process, the trunks of the trees drug Burley's feet backwards, and he spurred the horse in the flanks, and Freeze came unglued and bucked Burley off and hurt him pretty bad. And then while Burley was in the hospital recovering from that wreck, the doctors discovered that he had cancer. As a result of that run of bad luck, Burley was out of commission for a few months, and Jim Lowrance, the Diamond A manager, put Mike Landis in charge of both wagon crews, instructing him to gather and work the whole ranch.

When Charlie showed up on the outfit, the crew consisted of Dale Lee, who was Mike's jigger boss, plus Elmer McDonald, A. D. Mays, Wayman Vessels, Tom Reeder, Lloyd Hodges, Ray Lambert, Glen Paya, Larry Leist, Cole Moorhouse, Earl Prosser, Bert Davis, Tommy Truba, Alvin Wagner, Slim Gilliam, Truman Rustin, Rex Williamson, Kelly Street; and Johnny Nichols was wrangling horses. Raymond Scott was the Denny Ranch camp man, and Jim Lowrance hired a local boy named Dave Robinson to help him brand the calves in that country, and Alvin Wagner would brand calves on the 7s Ranch where he lived with some extra help, but Mike and his wagon crew were supposed to get around most of the outfit which was 1500 square miles of country when you counted the Denny Ranch and the 7s Ranch together with the Diamond A proper. The Denny and 7s were leased ranches that joined the Diamond A: the Denny on the southwest side and the 7s on the east side.

In those days the Diamond A was running over 17,000 mother cows, all of them Hereford. When the Hereford cowherd was liquidated in 1973, the official count taken by Arizona State Brand Inspectors was over 17,000 mother cows. It was common knowledge that Diamond A managers had the habit of telling the head office of Tenneco Oil Corporation and Kern County Land and Livestock that the ranch had several thousand fewer cows on the ranch than what was actually there. The lower numbers made the calf crop percentage look better and consequently made management practices look better than what was reality.

Jim Lowrance had been the manager for several years when Charlie went to work there in 1972. Prior to being the big boss there, he had worked a short while at the Babbitt Ranch for Bill Howell, and the two men were friends. For a while he had filled in as wagon cook when he worked for Babbitts: a fact that he didn't want to talk about. Lowrance bought a big Cadillac car for his wife who was beautiful like Elizabeth Taylor, and he always wore a starched white shirt and high-heeled Paul Bond boots that were shined to perfection. To say he was enjoying the life of being the manager of one of America's biggest ranches would be an understatement. One day the crew was sitting around the cook tent waiting for the cook to holler chuck. There was a young cowboy who was completely enamored by Dale Lee who was an old hand who sported a handlebar moustache with forty years of hard riding and a questionable history in his trail. Dale was the quintessential big outfit cowboy, and the kid was a gunsel. The kid was asking Dale about his experiences, and Dale was laying it on pretty thick while Jim Lowrance stood nearby drinking coffee and showing off his newest pair of Paul Bond boots and 10 X hat. "What about that Babbitt outfit, Dale? You worked there didn't you?" he asked.

"Yeah, sure did and it's a hell of an outfit, too!"

"Man, Dale, tell me about it . . . is it a big outfit like this one?"

"BIG OUTFIT! Hell, kid, the guy that manages this outfit used to be the cook over there!"

Jim Lowrance threw his coffee cup into the roundup pan and stomped out of the cook tent and got in his new Chevy pickup and drove off in a cloud of dust while Dale Lee rolled a Bull Durham cigarette and blew a smoke ring into the air and continued telling the kid stories.

In those days the Diamond A Ranch was a big deal, there was nothing else like it in Arizona. While the Babbitt Ranch was almost as big in total land mass, the Diamond A had over three times as many cows grazing in its pastures, and three times as many men on the payroll. The Babbitt Ranch was very well managed and consistently got a good calf crop and was run like a well-oiled machine, but there were no frivolities. If the Babbitt Ranch ledger said there were five thousand cows on the ranch, the cows were there, and the men could gather them. The two big ranches were always thrown up against each other when people who liked to talk about such things went to trying to outdo each other with their knowledge. In contrast to Babbitts, the Diamond A Ranch was a big splash similar to comparing Marilyn Monroe with a plain farm girl who didn't know how to put on makeup. The Diamond A manager's wife drove a new Cadillac compared to the Babbitt manager's wife who drove a very used Chevrolet. The Diamond A manager really had no idea how many cows were on the outfit but claimed to be getting a 90% calf crop. The Babbitt manager knew what his calf crop was and could prove it. Everything about the Boquillas was done in a big way, and in the wake of its activities, there was always a very large cloud of dust.

When Charlie went to the Diamond A in '72, the crew being led by Mike Landis was running Indian horses out on the plains, and all the talk was about the finer art of pursuing and capturing wild horses. Slim Gilliam and Dale Lee had both run lots of wild horses, and on more than one occasion, one of them would disappear from the crew without saying anything and show up at some distant spot just in time to plug a hole or turn the leaders in the correct direction and therefore save the day and resurrect success out of a situation that looked hopeless. The two men, especially Slim, had forgotten more about running horses than most of the crew combined would ever know, including the boss.

Conversation about Bill Howell's dead horse Jodie surfaced, and Charlie learned of the horse's fate for the first time. He confronted Ray and Dale, who didn't deny anything and offered no explanation. In their opinion, it was just one of those unlucky circumstances that arise now and then.

Mike Landis was in his heyday being wagon boss over the whole crew with more cows to gather than he could count. He had worked in Texas for both the upper and lower Matador as well as the JA in Palo Duro Canyon, and his experiences there served as the template for his style as the supreme leader of the Boquillas.

The main ingredient in Mike's cowboying was speed. He got up in the middle of the night and ate breakfast fast, several hours before sunup. When he stepped out of the cook tent into the pitch black of night and headed to the corral to rope horses, he wanted his men following on his boot heels and wanted them to have an eager grin on their faces. When the horses were caught, he saddled his fast, always making any necessary adjustments to his cinches or headstall the night before so nothing could or would slow him down. When his horse was saddled, he stepped aboard and whipped him down a hind leg and expected everyone to be following. If you couldn't get your horse saddled in time, he would leave you behind and fire you at noon or whenever he made it back to camp. It was a young man's outfit and, for the most part, the younger men liked his style. He had absolutely no empathy for anyone who would slow him down. His habit was to be riding hard and ten miles from camp when the sun peaked over the horizon, and on most days he found time to take a nap in his teepee tent in the afternoon. He always had a Louis L'Amour novel, or something like it, by his bed.

When Mike's crew finished with their wild horse roundup on the plains north of Rose Well, they started branding calves. Mike had announced to everyone that they were going to do all the branding that spring holding the cattle rodeer style, outside without the use of a corral, even though there were branding corrals scattered about all over the ranch. That's the way it had been done on the Matadors and JA, and that's the way they were going to do it there. He told Jim Lowrance of his plan, and Lowrance concurred, saying it was the cowboy way.

On one of the very first days of branding, they made a big fast flanking drive into a large dirt tank known as Platinum, west of Number Five Camp where the wagon was set up. Platinum was one of the major waterholes anywhere on the north end of the ranch, and they threw a big bunch of cows together. An old man named Johnny Nichols was serving as horse wrangler for the outfit, and Mike had instructed him to show up at Platinum with a change of horses about 9:00 a.m., when Mike figured they would have their rodeer throwed together. Johnny Nichols never showed, perhaps because he had found some moonshine in someone's teepee; but for whatever reason, fresh horses never appeared, so Mike and the crew went to branding calves on tired horses. Mike had about half of the twenty-man crew hold herd while several men were roping calves around the neck and dragging them to the fire. Several sets of flankers worked at getting the calves down and the rope removed from their neck while others did the branding, castrating and vaccinating. Mike had the men rotate jobs occasionally so no one had to do all the dirty work like flaking, or no tired horse had to do all the dragging. It would be one of the biggest brandings of the spring roundup, over 300 head, and all done on tired horses.

When the last calf had been branded, Mike Landis gave the order to turn the large herd of cattle loose, and when he and all the men who had been working on the ground, flanking, branding and vaccinating, got mounted on their horses, he took off toward camp in a high lope. For a mile or so everyone followed the wagon boss close by, but then Charlie pulled up and let his tired horse walk. He was riding a yellow colt named Gato that had been started by Dave Ericsson a few months earlier, and he roped lots of calves and drug them to the fire. Larry Leist and Ray Lambert were also riding young horses that they felt had been ridden hard enough to deserve to not be pushed hard all the way to camp, which was about four miles away. Mike and the rest of the crew disappeared over a ridge and out of sight. Charlie, Larry and Ray knew that they were not going to do anything the rest of the afternoon except take a nap and catch horses for the next day, and that would be done late in the afternoon.

When the three cowboys rode into camp close to an hour later, Mike Landis came walking to the corral to meet them as they were unsaddling their horses. He was mad. "I expect a man to keep up around here," he said angrily as he looked at the three cowboys.

"Well, Mike, where I come from a man is expected to take care of his horses," Larry answered him.

"Well, you're not where you come from! From now on you keep up or else," Mike said, and he turned and walked to his teepee and laid down on his bedroll. He as well as the rest of the crew except the three late cowboys had already eaten.

From that day on, Larry, Charlie and Ray kept their horses' noses within five foot of Mike's stirrups as he led his crew about the huge ranch in a high trot and lope. Earl Prosser, who had been Mike's boss twenty years before on a ranch in Nevada, wasn't afraid of Mike or his position. After that day Earl would ride along when Mike was leading the crew back to camp in a cloud of dust and pet his horse's neck and say, "I know that you're tired old hoss, but we gotta keep hurryin' so Mike can get back to camp and read his Louis L'Amour book so he'll know how to lead the drive tomorrow." Mike Landis would act like he hadn't heard Earl's comment and would keep trottin', and when he got back to camp he always took a nap and fell asleep with a Louis L'Amour book in his hand.

With his large crew of twenty men, Mike Landis swept over the big Boquillas making big flanking drives and throwing big roundups together, and every day they branded outside, rodeer style, even if there was a perfectly good corral nearby. The calves were roped around the neck and brought to the fire bouncing and bellering out on the end of a nylon rope. As was the custom on most ranches, the ear off of an earmarked heifer and the bag off of a castrated bull was kept in a pile and counted after the last calf was turned loose each day. But at the Boquillas every tenth ear or bag was thrown away and not put in the count, and because of that the correct number was easier to gather in the fall. There was always enough cattle, more cattle of every class than anyone knew the outfit possessed including the manager or owners. That was the way they wanted it.

Mike Landis's main objective as wagon boss was to get the cow work done in as Western a fashion and style as possible. He was a good storyteller and on a regular basis told about how Western the Matadors and JA had been when he worked for them in the late '40s. He talked of the great quantity of good horses those two famous Texas ranches had and how each man would have ten or twelve horses in his string, perhaps even more if he was a bronc man. He tried to imitate the Matadors and JA and incorporate his memories of those ranches into his style of running the Diamond A wagon. First and foremost in that style was speed, and his quest for speed surfaced in odd ways. While being wagon boss at the Diamond A, he decided it was unnecessary to clinch the nails when shoeing his horses. It was, he said, wasted effort. The shoes would stay on fine if you just cut the nails off but did not bend them over—it was faster.

It was also a rule that a man should not expect to ever go home until after the roundup was over. Several of the men on Mike's wagon were married with a family living in a cow camp on the ranch. Tom Reeder's wife was home alone at the Keseha Camp fifteen miles south of Rose Well. When the wagon moved within ten miles of Keseha, Tom asked Mike if he could go home in a company pickup and spend the night and return in time for breakfast the next morning. Mike refused to let Tom have the use of the truck so Tom quit.

About this time Mike had the wagon camped at Red Lake between Rose Well and Keseha on what they called the top country. They were making drives in the cedar breaks and continued to brand everything outside without the use of a corral. They made a fast drive between Murphy and Johnson and the Trinity fence and gathered a dozen head of cattle and held them up. After looking at the herd for a minute, Mike Landis saw that there was only one unbranded calf, so he announced that they would brand the calf real quick and then turn the cattle loose and go look for some more. The hood had showed up in a pickup with all the branding stuff, such as a small propane tank with a torch used to heat the irons and the Blackleg vaccine. Mike bailed off his horse and lit up the torch with a match and proceeded to get the branding iron hot. While he was doing this, the rest of the crew sat on their horses holding the small bunch of cattle. There were eleven men on horseback, and Mike Landis on the ground with his horse being hobbled was number twelve. There were twelve head of cattle in the herd including the unbranded calf which was the only critter that really mattered at that time. Every man had his rope down and had a loop built, holding it in his hand. Ray Lambert was sitting on his horse directly in front of a big

Hereford bull that stood facing him ten feet away and chewing his cud and acting gentle. Truman Rustin sat on his horse a few feet to Ray's right, and Truman looked at Ray and grinned. "Catch him," he said, gesturing at the bull with his chin like a Navajo Indian would do.

Ray shrugged his shoulders as if to say "whatever," and he hoolihanded the bull, catching him around the neck. And then like spontaneous combustion, every man threw at a critter and caught it. Twelve head of cattle and eleven mounted men, all of them with a critter bawling and bouncing out on the end of their rope. The only critter that didn't get caught was the unbranded calf who threw a figure-nine in its tail and took off for the cedars. Someone hollered at Mike, "The calf's getting away, the calf's getting away!" Mike jumped on his horse and spurred him into action, but in the process one of the horse's hind legs got tangled in the rubber hose connected to the propane torch which launched it into a flaming spiral, and Mike's horse's tail was completely burned off. The calf was never caught. According to legend, the crew didn't say much the rest of the day.

The next day things went south. For some reason no one remembers now, the relationship between the cook and crew had deteriorated badly, and it came to a climax when a couple of the younger men turned the outhouse over on him—door down. That night nine men quit including Charlie Gould. They were pretty much done branding anyway, and most of them came back the next fall and went back to work for the outfit again.

Top: Bowman Ranch at Hillside.
Above: Skeet Gould, 1948.

Left: John, Sam and Cole Gould.

Below: Cole and Sam Gould at Halfway House.

FVERETT BOWMAN, PRESIDENT
COWBOYS' TURTLE ASSOCIATION
HILLSIDE, ARIZONA

Mr. John Gould,
22 East Ave.,
Riverside, Ill.

HOTEL BELVEDERE
319 WEST 48th STREET · NEW YORK CITY

Mr & Mrs John Gould
Hillside,
Ariz.

Top: Letter from the Bowmans, postmarked 1939.

Above: Letter to John Gould from the Bowmans, mailed from New York.

Left: Charlie and his mother, Margaret Gould, Rancho Moana, 1991.

COWBOYS' TURTLE ASSOCIATION

OFFICERS

EVERETT BOWMAN
PRESIDENT
HILLSIDE, ARIZONA

HERMAN LINDER
FIRST VICE-PRESIDENT
CARDSTON, ALTA., CANADA

RUSTY McGINTY
SECOND VICE-PRESIDENT
PLAINS, TEXAS

HUGH BENNETT
SECRETARY-TREASURER
FORT THOMAS, ARIZONA

DIRECTORS

EVERETT BOWMAN
HILLSIDE, ARIZONA

PAUL CARNEY
GALETON, COLORADO

EDDIE CURTIS
EL RENO, OKLAHOMA

HUEY LONG
CRESSON, TEXAS

RUSTY McGINTY
PLAINS, TEXAS

JAMES MINOTTO
PHOENIX, ARIZONA

EVERETT SHAW
STONEWALL, OKLAHOMA

Hillside, Arizona,
June 19, 1939.

Dear John and Margaret:

I received your letter a day or two ago and will say we were surprised to hear from you. What was so funny though we got your license plates before we got your letter and I told the boys that you would be blowing in now any day. Every time a car would come up the road we just knew it was you. Bryce and Albert was dissappointed to hear that you were not coming until September. I don't think you get any more homesick to see us as we do you.

We have got a little house built down from our house that the man and his family stayed in and since Bryce came back and we laid off the man I have fixed it for a bunk house for the boys. Bryce had it all figured out that you and your wife could live with him while you were here. Sure we want you to come to see us. It would make us right mad for you to come to Arizona and not come. I have always told you boys that this was your home and are always welcome to come home when ever you want to. Bryce and Albert are still here but Albert is going to start out on the Rodeo road again. He got his leg broke again in February this year. He is just barely cripping around. I have had lots of fun with two cripple men this Spring.

Everett is planning on starting to the Rodeos in July. He is far from being well but he has stayed along as long as he feels like he can afford it. We plan on going to Reno, Nevada for the 4th of July and from there I don't know. If ever you want to write us just address it to home because we have our mail forwarded often. I don't guess we will be home when you come out but will see you when we get home in November.

The train just went up and I want to go after the mail so will ring off for this time and don't let your letters be so far between. We are always glad to hear from you. Everett joins me in sending best regards to all the family.

Sincerely yours,

Lois and Family.

Top: Letter from Lois Bowman to John Gould.

Left: Sam, Charlie, Cole and Jake Gould, 7 Up Ranch, 1997.

Top: *Charlie Gould breaking colts to lead on the O RO Ranch, 1982.*
Above: *Sharon Gould roping at the Yolo Ranch.*

Facing Page:
Top: *Charlie Gould and Leonard Beatty, Avery's Cowboy Reunion, 1981.*
Bottom: *Scott Dieringer and Charlie Gould lion hunting.*

Above: Charlie Gould YP Ranch, Owyhee, Nevada. Photo © John Langmore.

Facing Page:
Top: YP Crew, Owyhee, Nevada, 2016. Photo © John Langmore.
Bottom: Charlie Gould sitting in a saddle house, Owyhee, Nevada, 2016. Photo © John Langmore.

The O RO

Doctor Ed Bert Perrin was born in Eutah, Alabama, in 1836 into a family of substantial means. As a young man he attended medical school, and when the Civil War broke out, he served the Confederacy as a doctor. He was with Beauregard at Gettysburg. The blood and misery he witnessed while he served in that capacity must have satisfied him because when the war between the states ended he never worked as a doctor again.

Doc Perrin gathered up what he could of what should have been his share of the family's estate and headed west. He had a flair for business, which for the most part surfaced in the form of acquiring large tracts of land. He also knew how to enlist investors who were willing to put their money in real estate ventures of his choosing. The West was opening up after the Civil War with a multitude of immigrants who were starved for opportunity and hungry for land. Arizona was one of the last frontiers. Doc Perrin had a brother-in-law occupying a high post in the Southern Pacific Railroad who had intelligence as to where the various routes of trains would be and prior acquisition of tracts of land along those prospective routes could be very lucrative. As a result of his use of this intelligence, Doc Perrin became one of the leading land holders from Parks, Arizona, west to Seligman.

With increased capital at his disposal, Doc Perrin purchased Luis Maria Baca Float Number Five in 1876 and a year later purchased another land grant in Southern Arizona known as San Ignacio Del Babocomari. The size and other legal issues concerning the Babocomari had never been settled, and Doc Perrin would spend the next twenty-five years in and out of court trying to put those issues to rest. They were very costly.

The Baca Float Number Five, or the Grant as it is always called locally, is fifty miles north of Prescott in Yavapai County. Doc Perrin got word of it being for sale and traveled to Prescott where he met with an agent who was qualified to show the doctor the property. The two men set out from Prescott in a buckboard traveling northwest on the old Simmons Road and then turned up the north fork of Walnut Creek on what was an established stage route going toward a place known as the Oaks and Willows that was located inside the Grant and was an established stage stop. They were just inside the Grant's boundary near a spot that would eventually be known as Seep Dam when the day got late, and the two men decided to make camp for the night. They unloaded the few supplies they had brought and made their beds and built a fire and cooked some supper. In the wee hours of the morning, one of the men got up and added some wood to the fire. A wind had come up, and a little before daylight, their campfire got away from them and took off, being pushed by the wind. In those days fire was not considered a bad thing, and the two men didn't give it much thought. The agent suggested they travel on toward the Oaks and Willows and an opportunity to view more of the property. Doc Perrin stood watching the fire burn and travel, and in answer to the agent's suggestion that they proceed, he answered, "No, any country where the grass is good enough to burn like that is great cow country! I don't need to go any farther—I'll buy it."

Doc Perrin's first wife passed away, and he remarried to Eliza McMullin whose father was John McMullin who served as a Texas Ranger and was captured by Santa Anna's army during the Texas war with Mexico and marched to a prison in Mexico City. When he finally got out of the Mexican prison he immigrated to Southern California and formed a partnership with George Washington Trahean and began trading for and selling cattle to gold miners. The McMullin-Trahean partnership was very successful, and the partners became very wealthy and established numerous ranches in the San Joaquin Valley, the principle of which was near the confluence of the Stanislaus and San Joaquin rivers. They were the first people to sell livestock to Henry Miller and Charles Lux who went on to form one of the West's largest cattle ranching enterprises.

The McMullin girl whom Doc Perrin married was named Eliza after her mother, and she was born in 1859. She went by the nickname Lilo, and she and Doc Perrin had a son born in 1890 who bore the name Lilo also. The doctor was more of a land speculator than a cowman and continued to trade and speculate as well as recruit investors in his numerous ventures. He was very mobile and lived out of a suitcase and hotel rooms as much as anywhere. His battle in court concerning the size of the San Ignacio Del Babocomari drew on and on, but he was a trooper and continued his speculating until his death in 1932. Hi son Lilo was forced to sell the Baca Float Number Five Ranch in 1934 due to debt the doctor had accumulated totaling $3,500,000, a lot of money for that day and time. Lilo Perrin, the doctor's son, kept a nice ranch in Coconino County and died there months short of his one hundredth birthday. He was a distinguished old gentleman and very well liked around Flagstaff and Williams where he lived.

One of the American West's most legendary characters was Colonel William C. Greene who started out with a small ranch in Cochise County Arizona. As a young man he got in a gun fight in Tombstone and killed a man who had threatened him, and the legend of Colonel Greene grew from there. He was even better at recruiting big money into his various endeavors than Doctor Ed Perrin, and beginning in the late 1800s, he developed copper and gold mines in Sonora that were the biggest in the world. He also built a ranch that ran on the south side of the international boundary going west from Agua Prieta to the San Pedro River and south of the town of Cananea where his largest mines were located. His Sonoran ranch was so large it was cut up into seven divisions and employed seven large crews of vaqueros to keep the cattle worked. He owned a beautiful ranch north of the

Mexican border in the San Rafael Valley south of Patagonia and another ranch on the San Pedro River west of Naco. He had his own stockyards on the American side on his ranch along the San Pedro, which amounted to owning his own international port of entry. At these stockyards on his Naco, Arizona, ranch, he crossed hundreds of thousands of his own cattle into the United States. There is a famous photograph that hangs in the office of the Shasta Livestock Auction in Cottonwood, California, that shows 5000 big steers being trailed into the Greene stockyards at Naco.

Greene Cattle Company, what the Colonel's ranching enterprise was known as, ran Hereford cattle in Sonora as well as Arizona and branded O RO on their cattle: one O being on the left shoulder and the RO on the left hip. They put an RO on the left hip of their horses.

Colonel Greene lived in a big house in Cananea Sonora, and one morning in 1911 he drove his nice coach from his home to his office in downtown Sonora. The wagon was pulled by a team of young and somewhat green horses. Upon remounting his wagon late in the morning, the Colonel ran his leg down between pieces of iron that held a step on the side of the wagon, and he fell; and as a result the team spooked and stampeded, dragging Bill Greene to his death while people on the sidewalk watched.

The colonel's widow eventually married her husband's general manager, a very competent man by the name of Charles Wiswall.

In 1934 Charles Wiswall and the former Mrs. Greene purchased the Baca Float Number Five Ranch from Lilo Perrin, and Greene Cattle Company's land holdings in Yavapai County began. Since that day the ranch has always been known as the ROs. The Grant, as it was called, was a block of land, all deeded, twelve miles wide and twelve miles long, a hundred forty-four sections of the most beautiful country in all the West. Two years later, in 1936, Greene Cattle Company purchased a neighboring ranch that bordered the Grant on the west side that was known as the Mohon Ranch. It was 157,000 acres in size. Now the Greenes had themselves a bonafide big outfit.

In 1958 Charlie Greene, the youngest of Colonel Greene's sons, took over the reins as the manager of the Yavapai County ranch. The family still had the ranch in Naco, Arizona, and the San Rafael ranch south of Patagonia in Santa Cruz County. 1958 was also the year the corrupt government in Mexico stole the Greene's extensive holdings in the state of Sonora, including their large cattle ranch. The Greene's built a large house a mile and a half east of the Oaks and Willows that was famous for having seven different large fireplaces inside its walls. Charlie, his wife, and daughter Terry spent most of their time there until 1973.

Besides the headquarters at the Oaks and Willows, the O RO Ranch had five cow camps scattered about the ranch. The camps were known as Sandstone, Triangle N, Mohon, Bear Creek, and Francis Creek; the latter being on the far southwest corner of the outfit. The ranch was always known among the cowboys who worked there as a rough country outfit because of the mountains and numerous canyons scattered all over from one end to the other. The ranch was very well watered with numerous springs and natural water holes in the bottom of canyons, and a good number of dirt tanks. There were only a few water wells and no pipelines.

The O RO Ranch in Sonora had been famous for raising good horses, and Charlie Greene kept that practice alive at the ranch north of Prescott. There were always two or three studs and at least thirty mares on the ranch, and between seventy-five and a hundred broke saddle horses.

In the '60s the O RO acquired the reputation among cowboys of being an old man's outfit, the main reason being the wagon boss, Whistle Mills, turned 70 in 1967; his jigger boss, Buck Smith, was ten years younger at 60; and the cook, Ralph Chapman, was Whistle's age. The Triangle N camp man, Coley Lyons, was born before 1910 and had worked for the Greenes from the time they had bought the ranch. In spite of the fact they were old, those four men made up the nucleus of the O RO crew for many years, and they held the outfit together. Had anybody been giving prizes away for such a thing, Coley Lyons probably would have won an award for being the hardest working camp man in the West. Whistle was as good as any cowboy at gathering bronco cattle in rough country. They were all exceedingly loyal to Charlie Greene.

The O RO under the management of Charlie Greene was without a doubt the old-timey-est cow outfit of its size in the United States. They branded in the spring and shipped in the fall, and in between roundups they packed a little salt. In the winter they would put out a little cake to the bulls—heavy emphasis on the word little. They bought what they considered to be good bulls, and they raised good horses. That was the extent of their management. The ranch was very rough, with an entire major mountain range within its boundaries, the Mohon Mountains, plus Mount Hope and several other major mountains besides, and numerous deep canyons. There were only two big pastures that the cow herd ran in year round: one of them being over 200 sections in size and the other a 100 sections, and another hundred sections of smaller holding pastures and traps. In some years they would ship 500 or so weaner steer calves in the fall but then left the rest of the calves on their mothers who would kick them off in the spring when new calves were born. During spring roundup a rodeer would be throwed together every day, and the yearlings would be cut out and driven to camp and a holding pasture.

After the yearlings would be cut out, the calves would be branded while someone held the newly separated yearlings, or perhaps they would have a small corral to hold them in during the branding. Driving the freshly separated yearlings away from their mothers and familiar surroundings required expert cowboying. It was a cowboy outfit. The wagon would be out eight to ten weeks in the spring and close to three months in the fall with no days off during that time, and it took all of that to come close to getting around the rough and primitive 257,000 acre ranch. When Charlie Greene sold it, the O RO was running about 3500 mother cows and the outfit was not severely overgrazed. It was a standard joke among Arizona cowpunchers that Whistle Mills thought cattle were still sold by the head and not the pound. Cole Moorhouse, a Texan, claimed he overheard a conversation between Whistle and Coley Lyons with Whistle presenting a question, "Coley, have you heard any news?"

"Well, last summer I read a newspaper when I was in Prescott."

"Yeah, well what did it say about the war?" Whistle continued.

"They're predictin' the North is going to win; at least that's what the paper said. Like sayin', I never thought the South could win."

Regardless how old and uninformed Whistle and his crew may have been, they understood cows and how to gather the rough old ranch. They seldom went to town and there was no television, transistor radios or cell phones on the ranch. The company would send tobacco out to the ranch by the case and deduct what you needed out of your check. The outfit wasn't known for high wages but was famous for providing good groceries. Ralph Chapman, the wagon cook, was the best.

In the summer of 1973, Greene Cattle Company sold the O RO Ranch in Yavapai County to the JJJ Corporation owned by John Irwin II and his son John III and daughter Jane. John Irwin II was born in Keokuk, Iowa, but claimed the State of Connecticut as home. He served as Under Secretary and Deputy Secretary of State under President Nixon, and then was Ambassador to France in 1973 and 1974.

The JJJ Corporation bought the ranch and all of the old men left with the exception of Coley. Whistle and Ralph had never married but had been friends for fifty years. Whistle was a reformed alcoholic who had been dry for about ten years. He was seventy-six years old, and everyone predicted he would move to town and drink himself to death, but he fooled them and stayed sober and lived another five years. Ralph didn't fare as well; he hadn't lived in town since the First World War and he didn't last long.

Charlie Gould had married a beautiful girl he had met in California named Susan Crabtree and in the spring of '75 was needing a job, and when he heard the O RO was hiring, he joined the outfit just as the spring roundup was about to commence. The wagon had moved to Francis Creek on the southwest corner of the ranch and was going to start the work there. The JJJ Corporation had plans on modernizing the old outfit and had hired an ex-BLM ranger to be the manager. He had no experience on a cow ranch, but he had a college degree, and he had worked for the government, which meant he knew how to spend money.

Tracy Dent had been hired to be the wagon boss, and Charlie's old friend Mike McFarland was also part of the crew. Charlie was told that the job would only be temporary because the cow camps were all occupied by other employees that had been on the payroll for awhile. Charlie was still excited and glad to have a chance to work on the famous old ranch.

The crew and the remuda got moved to Francis Creek, and the men began to set up camp across the creek from the camp house and barn and corrals. Charlie took his teepee tent and selected a spot that looked good with a minimum of rocks where the floor of the tent would be. He put his teepee up and put his bedroll inside and then went to the kitchen and found an old coffee cup in the chuck box and poured himself some coffee. He noticed the old metal cup had a rivet braided in the bottom of it, plugging an old hole. He laughed to himself about the oddity of a cup with a copper rivet in it, but it didn't leak so he used it in spite of its oddity.

Coley Lyons had been off doing something when Charlie set his teepee up, and about the time Charlie filled the cup with the rivet, he noticed Coley go walking by packing his teepee. In a short moment Coley returned to where Charlie and several men were visiting and drinking coffee. "Like sayin', I don't demand much around here, but who's got their teepee set up in my spot?" Coley said. He stood there, all 150 pounds of his old, six-foot, boney frame, and stared at everyone. Everyone stared at Charlie, and he realized he had committed a gross error.

"I guess that's me," he said. He stood up and walked back to where his tepee was, and Coley followed. Charlie tore his teepee down and then helped Coley erect his house in the same spot. Nothing more was said, and Charlie moved off a ways and put his teepee up on some real estate while Coley got his canvas house arranged just like he wanted it. At about the same time, the two men walked back to the cook's domain, and Charlie found the riveted cup where he had laid it and took a sip of coffee while Coley rummaged through the chuck box looking for a cup. Presently he stood over Charlie who was forty-five years his junior and said, "Like sayin', I don't ask for much around here, but nobody uses my cup."

Charlie looked up at the old cowboy who was staring at the copper rivet in the bottom of the now empty cup. "I'm sorry," Charlie said, and he got up and rinsed the cup with the copper rivet and wiped it clean and filled it with hot coffee and handed it to the old man who took it, looked at Charlie and nodded his head and then went and sat down on a stump and lit a Chesterfield cigarette.

The crew at that time consisted of Tracy Dent as wagon boss, Coley Lyons, Mike McFarland, Billy Murphy, Joe Chavez, Audey Echols, Todd and Joe Bob Browning, Jimmy and H.L. Green, Boots O'Neal, and Charlie; and Bob Haley was wrangling horses. The cook was an old codger named Lloyd Tenney, and he boiled everything including the T-bone and rib steaks.

On one of the first days of the roundup, they made a drive into a dirt tank north of Francis Creek named Wagon Tongue and threw a rodeer together and branded outside, and Charlie necked the calves and drug them to the fire riding a bay horse named Snapper. He would end up having a long relationship with Snapper.

Bob Haley was an old cowpuncher who had been raised around Seligman. His father had worked for the Three Vs and was well known. Bob had a serious speech defect and talked funny, and if you didn't know him, you might have though he was simpleminded, but he was anything but simpleminded. He could really rope. He was a scrapper, and when he was partying in town, he had been known to get into a fight. He wasn't necessarily tough, but he would fight anyway. After the crew had been working for several days, a couple young boys from Texas showed up, and Tracy gave them a job. The crew made a drive into Burro Mesa and gathered a lot of cattle, and Bob Haley showed up with a change of horses, and when everyone had a fresh horse, they commenced to brand and had a corral to pen the cattle in. Tracy asked Bob if he wanted to rope, and he answered that sure he would love to rope. Bob hadn't shaved in several weeks, and his hat was wore out, and his Levis were so dirty they were slick and shiny. His saddle was old and dried out.

Charlie was talking to the Texas boys when Tracy asked Bob to rope, and the two Texans mumbled, "Oh hell, with this old man roping, we'll be here all day." Bob Haley heard the remark also.

Charlie and Todd Browning were flanking on one side of the fire and the two Texans on the other, and Bob was dragging to both sides. Bob rarely missed, and he drug every calf to Charlie and Todd's side by two feet; but Bob purposefully roped the biggest calf available by the left hind leg and above the hock for the Texans. Charlie noticed Bob grinning with tobacco juice running down both sides of his chin as the Texans struggled flanking the calves; but they were too dumb to know what the old man was doing to them.

Charlie had gone to work for Tracy at the O RO with the agreement that if a situation came up on another ranch somewhere that included a house for his family to live in, he would take it and leave because at that time all the available houses for families were taken. After Charlie had been working at the O RO for several weeks, Gary Overson, who owned a very large ranch southwest of Las Vegas, Nevada, sent word that he would give Charlie a job complete with a house for his wife Susan who was about to give birth to their first son. Charlie loved the O RO and wanted to stay, but he needed a better situation for his family, so he left and went to work for Gary Overson in Southern California between Mountain Pass and Cima. Charlie's old friend Dewey Brown was there, and they were busy gathering and shipping cattle that Gary had partnered on with Ronnie and Hoss Dilday who were also at Gary's ranch helping with the work. Charlie had worked for Ronnie Dilday several years earlier in the San Joaquin Valley.

Cole Gould was born in Las Vegas, Nevada, on June 3, 1975, and then several weeks later, Tracy Dent sent word that the Bear Creek camp job on the O RO had become available. Tracy wanted Charlie to come back. The O RO and Bear Creek at 5000 foot in elevation looked a whole lot better than the desert at Cima, California, which is only a few miles from Death Valley at 120 degrees Fahrenheit; so Charlie, Susan and Cole headed back to Yavapai County, Arizona. They moved into the Bear Creek Camp in early July 1975.

Charlie and Susan got moved into Bear Creek, which was very near the center of the O RO Ranch. The camp itself sat on a plateau that is small in size (there are very few flat spots on the whole ranch) and only a short trot away from a series of rough, rocky and very steep canyons and ridges known as Jackass Basin. On the north end of Jackass Basin the towering and rough Mohon Mountains rise up making a landmark that can be seen for a hundred miles. The house at Bear Creek sits at 4800 feet in elevation, and Mohon Peak, a short eight miles away, is 7500 feet.

On the northeast side of the Mohon Mountains, sitting in the mouth of a shallow canyon, is Triangle N, the cow camp where Coley Lyons lived and worked for thirty-five years. It's north and about a ten mile trot from Bear Creek. On the second day Charlie was at Bear Creek, Coley Lyons came trotting up on a horse. Coley did not own a vehicle of any kind and possibly didn't know how to drive one. He had horses to ride and mules to pack at Triangle N, but no company truck. There was no two-way radio at his camp and no phone or electricity. When he wanted to visit with someone, which was seldom, he saddled a horse. He took care of himself and his part of the ranch and was very independent.

Charlie was barely unpacked and definitely not settled in when Coley rode up and dismounted. He got Charlie's attention and motioned for him to come and palaver. Coley knelt down and used the palm of his hand to smooth a piece of ground like a teacher erasing a chalkboard. He looked at Charlie and began to talk. "Like sayin', this here is my country," and he took a stick and drew a picture to illustrate his interpretation of the O RO Ranch. "And this here is your country," drawing a circle around an area south of what he called my country. He looked and made sure Charlie was paying attention. "This here is our country." Circling, with the stick an area in between my country and your country. Again he looked at Charlie and proceeded. "You can ride in our country, but you stay out of my country, but I will ride in your country all I want to, and you will see my horse tracks. Like sayin'—do you understand?"

"Yeah sure, Coley, I understand."

"Okay, I'll be seein' ya. Like sayin', tell the missus hello." He stepped on his horse.

"Why don't you come on in and have a cup of coffee?"

"Thank you, but, like sayin', I better be goin'."

The skinny old man rode off. He wore glasses and a silver belly hat with the crown stove pipe creased but brought to a point in front like Roy Rogers or Jim Shoulders. He had a pair of Ed Blanchard spurs that were famous. They had Chihuahua shanks and two and a half inch rowels made out of solid brass that were hand cut like a fancy snowflake. Each of the six spokes had a hole drilled in it, and you could hear the spurs ring from a mile away. Outside his saddle house door there was a pile of wore out horse shoes that would fill a pickup bed. His horses had sweat marks on them, and his mules had lots of white hair on their backs. He was up and gone long before daylight every day, and he knew every rock and badger hole on the O RO Ranch.

Six months went by, and Charlie put out a lot of horse tracks and packed salt all over his country and range branded big calves that had been missed and sewed up prolapsed cows and other undesirable chores. He made a hand. And as he prowled around, occasionally he would see Coley's horse tracks in his country; in other words, he knew Coley was keeping an eye on him. That was fine; he let the old man do whatever he wanted. He liked him and thought he was one of a kind. Unexpectedly Coley showed up one day. He rode up to the barn and horse corral at Bear Creek and said, "How ya doin'?"

"Doin' fine, Coley. Get off and come in and have a cup of coffee."

"No, like sayin', I can't stay long." Coley replied.

"No, come on in! Susan will make us some coffee, won't take long."

"No, like sayin', I just wanted to tell you that you won't be seeing my tracks in your country anymore, but you'll still see 'em in our country. But don't be ridin' in my country!" Coley sat on his horse holding a Chesterfield cigarette out on the tips of his fingers and grinning. He was happy, not jovial or loud, but happy. Charlie had passed the test, and it was his odd way of presenting a diploma of sorts or a plaque of recognition. The two men stared at each other momentarily connecting, and then the old man turned his horse and rode off north toward his country.

On November 11, 1976, Sam Gould was born to Charlie and

Susan, and after several days they brought him home to Bear Creek. The Oaks and Willows was at least sixty miles from Prescott and a lot of that is dirt, and Bear Creek Camp was another twenty miles past that, and that twenty miles, at least in those days, was rough, rocky and nigh impassable during a severe winter storm. Charlie and Susan had been home several days with their new baby when Coley came riding up. It was bitter cold and a little breeze was blowing. The old man rode up and sat on his horse and looked toward the house. Charlie walked outside to talk. "Howdy, Coley. How ya' doin'? Get off and come in, and we'll have some coffee."

"No. Like sayin', can't stay long."

"No, come on in and warm up for a minute. It won't take long to make a fresh pot of coffee."

"No. Like sayin', I heard that you and the missus have a new baby boy."

"Yeah, he was born five days ago."

"Well, go get him so I can look at him." Coley still sat on his horse.

"Darn, Coley, it's colder than hell out here! He's just a little guy, he'll freeze to death."

"Well, wrap him up. I wanna look at him."

"Get off and come in and have some coffee, and we'll let you hold him."

Coley struck a match and lit a Chesterfield. "I don't want to hold him, I just want to look at him. Go get him."

Charlie turned around and headed toward the house thinking Susan was going to kill him. After considerable conversation and preparation, Charlie returned to the shoulder of Coley's horse. The wind was blowing cold, and little Sam was wrapped up. Coley looked down while seated on his horse. "Well, like sayin', uncover his head, I wanna look at him."

"Jiminy crickets, Coley, the poor little guy will freeze to death."

"Like sayin', it ain't gonna hurt him none, let me see him!" Coley had a mouthful of straight teeth; he was grinning. He put a Chesterfield to his lips and waited.

Charlie pulled the blanket to the side and exposed little Sam's face. He instantly turned blue.

"Nice looking boy! Congratulations to you and the missus!" And with that, Coley turned his horse and rode north toward his country.

Charlie and Mike McFarland were close friends, and so several weeks after Charlie and Susan got moved into Bear Creek, Mike sent word that they should all go into Seligman on a Saturday night and attend a big street dance that was going to be held in conjunction with the town's annual Seligman Days celebration. The whole O RO crew was going to the big shebang, including Tracy Dent and his wife Betty. Tracy was a small man with white hair and a very quiet manner, and Betty was the perfect picture of a nice gentle country woman. You couldn't have made Betty Dent say something negative about anyone or anything if you stuck a Colt .45 in her face and threatened her. Everyone loved her.

While all this was brewing, there was other big doings being organized. John Irwin, President of JJJ Corporation and owner of the ranch, had only a year or so before served as the United States Ambassador to France. For obvious reasons, Mr. Irwin was well connected. On the very day of the Seligman street dance, Mr. Irwin traveled to Phoenix Sky Harbor International Airport and met an entourage of French nobility and dignitaries that he had become friends with while serving his country as ambassador. As soon as the French people, who were made up of people of both sexes, disembarked from their international flight, they loaded up in Mr. Irwin's private airplane and flew straight to the primitive airstrip at the ranch. As soon as they had landed at the O RO, the Irwin family and the European aristocrats got in Mr. Irwin's car and drove north to Seligman, thirty-eight miles to the north. The Irwins had told the French folks about the Seligman Days celebration and that the O RO cowboys were already in town taking part in the festivities.

The street dance was actually held under the canopy that covered the big door in front of the old Seligman Garage. Under the canopy was a cement floor that someone had scrubbed free of the oil stains from leaky crankcases, and cleaned and swept the place up a little. Next door to the east sat the Copper Cart Restaurant, and directly across the street was the famous Black Cat Saloon, a den of iniquity known for several hundred miles both directions. The street that lay between the Seligman Garage and the Black Cat was Main Street, but was also Route 66. This was before the interstate was finished, and ocean-to-ocean traffic went right down the middle of Seligman, only two narrow lanes wide.

The whole O RO crew was there, with the exception of Coley Lyons, and there was music and dancing on the motor-oil-stained cement under the Seligman Garage canopy. Everyone was having a great time, and when the Irwins arrived, they introduced the French nobility to Tracy and Betty Dent and all the O RO cowboys. After shaking hands with the French folks, Charlie walked across Route 66 to buy a case of beer. As he walked through the crowded saloon, he bumped the cue stick of a local boy named Birch who was known to be nasty and hard to get along with. The bump to the stick caused the boy to miss his shot, and there was money on the game. After Charlie purchased his case of beer, he walked by the offended pool shooter, and because of the crowded conditions, they touched each other a second time, perhaps unintentionally.

Charlie crossed through nationwide traffic and reached the canopy and was handing a cold Coors to a wealthy Frenchman when the pool shooter hit him from behind and knocked him down and proceeded to mount him like a bronc, with his fists stroking instead of his spurs. Betty Dent screamed, "You can't do that!" And Charlie's wife moved forward thinking she might see if Charlie was still alive. Charlie's wife, Susan, had beautiful long wavy brown hair, and when she got near the fracas, the pool shooter's woman braided her fingers into Susan's long beautiful hair and went to shaking her about. "You can't do that! You can't do that!" Betty Dent demanded. The place erupted, one of the O RO men got Susan freed from the human curry comb that was molesting her, and some more O RO hands drug the pool shooter off of Charlie. Now the fight started in earnest, and

Charlie commenced to teach the pool shark how to fight. Mike McFarland was swinging his fists, and eventually the fight ended when Jimmy Green punched a local Seligman boy and knocked him into the radiator of an oncoming diesel semi that was trying to transport freight to Los Angeles. The traffic came to a complete standstill. When it was over, no one knew who won. The O RO boys were pretty beat up, and the Irwins and their French guests had disappeared.

Charlie and Susan stopped and spent the night with Mike and his wife Billy Jo at the Oaks and Willows, and about sunup the two cowboys got up and dressed. They looked in the mirror as they washed up and surveyed the damage which consisted of black eyes, fat lips, and bruised cheek bones, as well as bloody knuckles. Charlie had worn a brand new shirt that Susan had made for him with her bare hands, and it had been ripped off and destroyed.

"Well, what do you say we go down to the bunkhouse and drink some coffee?" Mike suggested.

"Yeah," Charlie replied, "and maybe pick up our paychecks. I might'a got us all fired."

"Well, now that you mention it, I was thinking the same thing. Mr. Irwin probably isn't too proud of us right now. Better go face the music." They entered the bunkhouse kitchen and everyone was pretty quiet. Jimmy Green had a black eye. Tracy Dent, the wagon boss, sat in a chair trying to hold a coffee cup steady, but his hands were trembling due to the effects of a severe hangover. His skin was pale and his demeanor ghostlike. The atmosphere was apprehensive to the point of gloomy.

Suddenly, without warning, a car pulled up and stopped abruptly in front of the bunkhouse and out stepped Jane Irwin, John Irwin's daughter, whom everyone knew would someday own the ranch. She was a couple years older than Charlie. Jane was very well liked, but still, she was the owner's daughter. She burst into the room with enthusiasm. The men sank into the chairs and hid behind their coffee cups. "Man you guys put on a show last night! Our friends from France thought that was the most spectacular thing they had ever witnessed. It was the real wild West! They loved it! They loved it."

Mike McFarland had worked at the O RO several times previously to when he and Charlie worked together starting that spring of 1975. On those earlier terms as an O RO cowboy, he had worked for Whistle Mills when he was wagon boss and Greene Cattle Company was the owner. Mike knew the ranch well, and he knew how Whistle had gathered it and the style and method of Whistle's leadership. He was a disciple of rough-country cowboying and the art of working with a holdup. When the JJJ Corporation bought the ranch from Greenes, a great deal of that technique was lost or abandoned. Whistle retired and moved to town, and the new management and new wagon boss did not follow Whistle's method of operation to any large degree. They weren't acquainted with the canyons and mountains and the limitless escape routes and hideouts available to a wary cow that didn't want to be gathered by a crew of cowboys. The drives, or circles, got bigger, and holdups farther apart; and, subsequently, a bigger percentage of cattle went ungathered.

Then in the early winter of 1976, Tracy Dent decided to leave, and the ranch manager promoted Mike McFarland to the wagon boss position. For several years the O RO roundups had been what could be called a little loose, at least in comparison to the Greene Cattle Company days with Whistle at the helm. Because drives had been bigger and faster, and the use of the holdup had been abandoned, or whatever reason, a noticeable amount of unbranded bronco cattle had accumulated all over the ranch and needed to be cleaned up before the situation got out of hand.

The spring of '76 was a roundup to remember for those who were at the O RO. Mike McFarland acquired an all-star crew: Charlie Gould, Ben Fancher, Clay Tyree, Audey Echols, Andy Garcia, Cole Moorhouse, Todd and Joe Bob Browning, Coley Lyons, and old Lloyd Tenney who still boiled the T-bone steaks. Mike reverted back to Whistle Mills' techniques, gathering the rough country by making smaller, tighter drives that went into a holdup where men had controllable cattle waiting to be used like padding to help stop the wild ones. He worked slower and methodically, searched and pried out the bronco cattle from their lairs, and with his stellar crew, they pursued the outlaws and caught them. The men were all aware of the positive changes that were made, and they stayed at the top of their game from start to finish. By roundup's end they had gathered over 300 unbranded cattle a year old or older that had been scattered all over the ranch.

The ranch manager, who was Mike McFarland's boss, had been talked into capitalizing on the reputation of the O RO horse program, and he hired Twister Heller, a well-known Nevada horseman, to take over the management of the horses. Twister could make a horse slide and spin and things that were impressive to watch but, perhaps, not applicable to gathering cattle in the brush and trees. To replace some good cow horses that were sold, in order to get the new horse program advertised and recognized, Twister went north to Elko County, Nevada, and bought a bunch of broncs from Willis Packer who raised hundreds of horses on his ranch near Tuscarora. The horses were hauled to the Oaks and Willows, and Twister and an assistant put a few rides on them and then sent them to the wagon for Mike to distribute to his crew. It was an awkward situation. Traditionally the wagon boss would have been the man running the horse program, or at least having considerable influence over it. The gathering and working of cattle would have been the main reason to have the horses. In this case, the wagon boss and his opinions and the needs of the cowboy crew took a backseat to the art of selling fancy horses and all of the magazine articles, glitter and hype it took to promote the sale of O RO horses to dudes, team ropers, or anyone with a pen and big checkbook. The Willis Packer horses were a disaster. Not a single one of them was good to punch cows on in the rocks and brush, and to top that off, several of them were bonafide buckers. The three Packer horses that were the worst to buck were a big Thoroughbred-looking bay named Bomber, a sorrel named Red Bird, and a gray horse called Gray Eagle.

Gray Eagle was particularly counterfeit and would wait until he had you in some comprised position and then take to you.

One day the crew was trailing a herd of cattle down a canyon between Jolly and Bear Creek, which was their destination. Charlie was up on a point and in the lead of the cattle, and Clay Tyree was back toward the drags riding Gray Eagle. Clay rode the gray horse near a tree, and the horse purposefully crashed into the tree and managed to scrape Clay off onto the ground, and then he ran off. The gray horse came stampeding down the side of the herd, and Charlie tried to get him stopped but didn't. The cattle were skittish and wanting to stampede, and Charlie had to make a hand and keep the cattle held up or chase the horse, and he chose to stay with the cattle. After getting the cattle stopped, and when everything was under control, he left the herd and set out in pursuit of the loose horse, thinking he would find him down the trail a short distance; but instead the horse's tracks continued on all the way to Bear Creek three or four miles away. When Charlie got to Bear Creek, he saw, by reading sign, that the horse had run up to a large dirt tank full of water that was divided by a barbed wire fence going across its middle so two pastures could make use of the water. The tracks showed that the horse had bailed off into the deep water

Charlie got the cattle stopped and when everything was under control...

and swam out over the division fence in the middle of the deep water, and then reaching the other side, the horse continued south.

Charlie tracked the horse for miles going south and down in elevation through the rocks toward a place known as Wagon Tongue. He tracked him for several hours and finally came to a dead end, not being able to pick up any tracks going in any direction. By now he had been gone for several hours and was eight or nine miles south from where he had left the crew. He doubled back to Bear Creek where the men were going to stop for the night and caught a fresh horse, and Clay Tyree borrowed a saddle from someone and got on a fresh horse, and he and Charlie went south toward Wagon Tongue again and trailed the horse to the same spot but could not find where the horse had gone from there. It was very rocky and in a particularly rough and craggy piece of country, and they were scratching their heads trying to figure where the outlaw Packer horse had gone. Suddenly they heard the outlaw knicker, evidently wanting the company of the horses the men were riding. He was hidden down in a rocky crag where it was impossible to see a track. Clay's saddle was still on him, although both bridle reins had been jerked off and lost; but Charlie had found them laying on the ground while he was tracking the horse.

Charlie and his family were camped at Bear Creek for close to two years, and Charlie found a little known trail west of camp that descended down into Jack Ass Basin. It was in a place not commonly known and was very steep and winding. Charlie showed Ben Fancher the trail, and Ben named it Sneaky Trail, which fit its various attributes. One day Jimmy Green was riding Gray Eagle and was with Charlie in Jack Ass Basin, and Charlie led them to the bottom of Sneaky Trail and started up the steep rocky incline with Jimmy Green following. Right when they reached the most treacherous place, Gray Eagle blew up and bucked Jimmy Green off, and he landed in the sharp rocks, and Gray Eagle danced on top of him for a while and then ran off. Charlie went and caught the outlaw and led him back to Jimmy who was standing in a rock pile licking his wounds, which were bloody and numerous, "Here's your horse," Charlie said as he handed Jimmy a bridle rein, the other having been broke off and lost as the outlaw ran off dragging them.

"Thanks a lot," Jimmy replied.

The summer of 1977 started out really dry on the O RO, and Charlie was staying at Bear Creek and was getting some rain on his country and, because of that, was having little trouble taking care of business. Audey Echols and his wife were living at Sandstone in the middle of the Grant and east of Bear Creek where Charlie and Susan lived. Audey was having lots of trouble. It was not raining on the Grant and the dirt tanks were drying up and cows were bogging down, and Audey was working from dark to dark trying to keep cows pulled out of the mud, and life for him was miserable. He and Charlie talked, and Charlie offered to trade camps with him, and Audey agreed. Mike McFarland approved of the change, and so the two families traded camps; and as soon as Charlie moved into Sandstone, it went to raining everywhere, and he had very little trouble. Sandstone Camp and the Grant were his favorite places.

Range branding calves that the wagon crew missed during roundup is a thing often talked about by cowboys. On most outfits the bosses frown on range branding because they think it makes cattle wild. Charlie asked Mike if he could range brand any calves he found on the country he was taking care of, and Mike gave his approval. Charlie had several good dogs that would hold cattle up, and the dogs would obey Charlie's commands enabling him to rope the calves in as easy a way as possible, sneaking a loop on them by getting them in a corral or tight spot of some kind where they could be caught without being run for a half mile. He was good at it, and Mike noticed the cattle were no wilder as a result, plus a good many of the calves got branded. Charlie would make the O's in the brand square and you could recognize the calves that he had branded.

The JJJ Corporation got its name from John Irwin, John Irwin Junior, and Jane Irwin, the latter two individuals being the son and daughter of John Sr. In the fall of 1977, John Irwin Junior asked Mike McFarland if he could have a job as a cowboy on the fall roundup crew. The question both puzzled and amused the wagon boss who thought one of the owners of a ranch and corporation asking one of his employees for a job was odd. Mike couldn't imagine saying no; after all, it was his ranch. "Hell no! I don't want a gunsel like you on my crew," would hardly have been an appropriate response. The fact is, Mike liked all of the Irwins, young and old; and if the young man, who was about twenty-two years old at the time, wanted to work with the cowboy crew, he thought it would be a good thing.

The roundup commenced just after Labor Day, and John Irwin Junior took his place among the men. He slept in a canvas teepee tent like all the rest and was up as early as any man and willing to go hard all day. He had pluck but no skill or natural aptitude. Everything was foreign to him to the point of being downright hard. He was not a good rider, being tall and gangly, and he owned a sorry, ill-fitting saddle with stirrups that were adjusted way too long. Charlie Gould and Clay Tyree tried to give him advice. Every day they would tell him, "John, why don't you shorten your stirrups up a little? It will be much more comfortable." He would answer them back very politely but firmly, "I like my stirrups just fine the way they are. Thank you." After dark Charlie and Clay would slip out and change the adjustment on John Junior's saddle, making the stirrups shorter the way they thought would benefit him the most. After going aways the next morning, John Junior would let them back out to where they had been, and then late at night Charlie and Clay would sneak out and shorten them again. Finally, after a week, John Junior came into the cook tent early in the predawn morning where men sat hunkered down drinking coffee out of metal cups. "I've an announcement to make," he declared and then continued, "would whoever is changing my stirrups, please leave them alone!" Charlie and Clay gave up and watched him ride humped over with his toes barely reaching the stirrups the rest of the fall.

After the roundup had been going for about two weeks, John Junior received a message from New England from some large corporation that was offering a very good position: an opportunity he thought he couldn't turn down. He apologized to Mike McFarland while explaining the situation, saying he must leave and take advantage of the offer. He was gone about ten days and then reappeared at the wagon. "I was wondering if I could have my job back?"

""Well sure, John, if that's what you want. What about your other job?"

"I wasn't happy there; this is where I want to be right now." So he took the ill-fitting saddle with the long stirrups and threw it on a horse named Captain and rode off with the men. Captain had been one of Whistle Mills' favorite horses. John Irwin Junior worked the rest of the fall with Mike McFarland's crew that included old Ben Fancher, Audey Echols, Huck and Eldon Sandsness, Billy Murphy, Clay Tyree, Cotton Elliott, Jimmy Green, Joe Chavez, Coley Lyons and Charlie Gould. John Junior didn't ask for any favors or special treatment or extra time off, and everyone on the crew respected him, long stirrups and all.

The people above Mike McFarland were making lots of changes to the ranch in the name of improvements. There was very little conversation about any of these so called improvements between the man who had the company checkbook and Mike McFarland, or any of the other cowboys who knew the ranch such as Coley Lyons or Charlie Gould. The company was spending money like it grew on trees, building fences and cross fences, running heavy equipment all over the ranch, building roads in places where nobody wanted to ride in a car. They were building horse barns and stalls that the cowboys weren't allowed to use and buying horses out of Nevada that bucked and couldn't stand up in the rocks like the good old O RO horses. There was lots of glitter and splash. Times were changing.

In the winter of 1977-'78, Mike McFarland left the ranch for another job, thus ending the tenure of who, some say, was the best O RO wagon boss after the Whistle Mills' days. Charlie Gould and his family left the outfit a short time later.

Fall Roundup on the
Double O Ranch

Charlie's good friend Larry Leist had gone to work for a big operator by the name of Bob Rufenacht, who was running yearling steers all over the Western United States, had big ranches leased and some purchased and for awhile owned more cattle than anyone west of the Mississippi River. A good man named Larry Titsworth was Rufenacht's manager. Titsworth could fly an airplane as well as ride and rope. He knew how to work cattle and had the aptitude to have fun all the time regardless what he was doing. Everyone liked him. Titsworth knew Charlie and Larry Leist were good amigos so he offered Charlie a job and promptly sent him to California to help take care of some yearlings the outfit was running there.

John Ivory was the Rufenacht outfit foreman in California but was still under Larry Titsworth who had failed to call Ivory and tell him he was sending a cowboy from Arizona to help him. The ranch where John Ivory lived was called the Silver Creek Ranch and was east of Hollister. Charlie drove into the Silver Creek Ranch with his wife Susan and sons Cole and Sam, who were two and three years old. John Ivory was obviously surprised. "Who are you?" he asked Charlie.

"Well, I'm Charlie Gould, and I'm here to help you take care of some steers."

"Oh really? Said who?"

"Well, Larry Titsworth and Bob Rufenacht sent me out here."

John Ivory looked at Charlie with a sideways glance and lifted an eyebrow. "Wait here a minute," he instructed Charlie, and he disappeared into the bowels of his home and a telephone. After a few minutes he returned saying, "Well okay, they say you're alright, but they never told me anything about you coming."

Charlie and John Ivory got along well after their rough start, and they had hundreds of steers to care for. John had been a top professional saddle bronc rider and had come from a well-known cowboy family in Oregon, and he had lots of good cowboy and rodeo stories to tell.

Charlie's wife Susan was from California, and Charlie's brother Skeet and his wife Diane lived not far away, so the pair were in familiar territory and were happy.

While Charlie worked for John Ivory at the Silver Creek Ranch, Larry Titsworth and Larry Leist were tearin' it up in Arizona. Larry Leist owned a colt that was wilder than a March hare and was bad to run off. The two cowboys were down by Apache Junction between Mesa and Superior gathering steers off of a big desert outfit called the Pollock Ranch. They were down to the point where there were only a few head of remnant cattle left, and they were driving around the ranch in a pickup hooked to a gooseneck trailer with their saddled horses in the trailer. Larry Leist had the runaway bronc in the trailer, and Larry Titsworth had mentioned earlier that morning that he thought the horse was sure-enough good looking, but he had never seen Larry Leist ride him. "Man, I like that horse. How about sellin' him to me?" Titsworth asked.

"Oh, you wouldn't like him; I better just keep him." Larry Leist said while thinking to himself, If you ever saw this son of a gun run off with me, you wouldn't be braggin' on him. But he kept the horse's bad habits to himself and nothing more was said for awhile.

They drove down a sandy desert two-track road that led through saguaro and cholla cactus scattered amongst palo verde and mesquite trees and were not seeing any tracks. Then abruptly as they rounded a bend in the two-track road, they spotted three big Mexican steers that weighed about 700 pounds. They weren't short over a half dozen so seeing three in a bunch was going to cut the remnant in half.

They got excited, and Titsworth slammed on the brakes and jumped out to unload his horse, which was a good one. The slamming of the doors and trailer gates squeaking got the steers stirred up, and they took off running through the cholla. Titsworth was the first to get his horse unloaded, and he pulled his cinches up tight and got on and took off in a dead run in pursuit of the Mexicans, leaving Larry by himself to deal with the bronc. The excitement had the bronc stirred up, and he wouldn't stand still but kept whirling in a circle as Larry tried to get a toe in the stirrup and slip up on the outlaw. Titsworth had disappeared into the maze of cacti headed in a northerly direction. Larry Leist was wishing that his compadre had waited long enough to stand by the bronc while he got on but was going to have to deal with the situation by himself. He wasn't happy. Finally he got a toe in a stirrup, and he slipped up on the whirling outlaw, and the horse grabbed his hind end and took off through the cactus going east at a very high rate of speed.

Larry Leist's hat brim was turned straight up in front because of the screaming wind blowing in his face. The bronc could not be turned or slowed down, and Larry's bridle reins were as tight as a guitar string, when suddenly directly ahead Larry Leist saw that they were approaching a sand wash that was a lot deeper than the ground he and the bronc were traveling on. Larry's body stiffened out of fear of what he saw coming. A six-foot cliff, the result of erosion on the banks of the sand wash lay directly in their path, and when he and old runaway reached its edge, the bronc never slowed down.

As Larry Leist sailed through the air, he looked to his left and saw Titsworth running hard in his direction in the bottom of the wash, and no more that six-foot away from where the runaway landed in the sand was one of the three Mexican steers who were now running south down the bottom of the wash. Titsworth had run after the steers and managed to turn them down into the wash, and he was behind them fifty yards and running fast. He saw Larry Leist's runaway bail off of the cliff and land behind the big black Mexican. Larry Leist had a loop built and was tied hard-and-fast to the saddle horn. When the runaway landed in

Larry Leist's hat brim was turned straight up.

the sand directly behind the Mexican, Larry took one swing and roped the steer deep around the middle and immediately forked a palo verde tree on the east side of the wash, and he, the steer, and the runaway bronc came to an abrupt halt.

"GEEMANY CHRISTMAS, I NEVER SAW ANYTHING LIKE IT! I NEVER SAW A HORSE RUN TO A COW LIKE THAT! WHAT DO YOU WANT FOR HIM?"

"Twenty-five hundred," Larry Leist said drily.

"I'LL BUY HIM! NEVER SAW ANYTHING LIKE IT IN MY LIFE!"

Larry Titsworth had a Cessna 182 airplane, and he flew it around to Bob Rufenacht's ranches tending to his business. He flew the airplane like he rode his horse. One time he and Larry Leist were in the air, and they flew into some severe wind turbulence, and the plane suddenly dropped a hundred feet in altitude and bucked and floundered like a bronc. Larry Leist turned purple and started looking for a sack to puke in, but Titsworth hollered, "Yeehaw! Powder River, let 'er buck!"

Larry Leist lived on the Denny Ranch twenty-three miles west of Seligman and three miles east of the Grand Canyon Caverns where there was a motel and landing strip. From time to time, Titsworth would fly his Cessna airplane to the caverns and land and would get a room at the caverns motel while he helped Larry

Leist work cattle on the Denny. One afternoon he landed the Cessna, and Larry Leist drove to the airport in a ranch pickup to get him and then drove over to the motel where Titsworth was going to rent a room for a couple nights. After acquiring a room, they were going to drive on down to Larry and his wife JoAnn's house to eat a good supper. JoAnn is very famous for her cooking. Larry Leist pulled up to the motel and stopped, letting the pickup idle while Titsworth went in to get a room. Working behind the counter in the motel lobby was a very homely and skinny old man named Louie. He had long gray hair and was always closely shaven. He dressed funny. He was the local Seligman gay person.

After several minutes of waiting, Titsworth came out of the motel slapping his leg and laughing. Larry Leist watched him and wondered to himself, "What in the heck has got into him now?"

Titsworth got into the passenger door, and Larry Leist took off before Titsworth got the door shut. He was laughing and slapping his leg, "You shoulda seen it. The ugliest old gal I ever saw was working in there, and when she checked me in, she propositioned me!" He roared with laughter.

"Yeah," Larry Leist replied, "that was Louie. He's homosexual."

"Stop this ^%#@%^&* truck; I'm gonna kill him! I'm gonna kill him!"

Larry Leist laughed but kept driving toward home while Titsworth swore he was going to commit murder.

Bob Rufenacht had cattle scattered all over the West, and after a while he and Larry Titsworth started talking about moving Charlie around to various ranches in several states to help gather, ship, sort or doctor steers; whatever needed to be done at one ranch and then another, maybe a thousand miles away. He was going to be sort of a traveling top hand, handyman, troubleshooter, and boy-Friday all wrapped into one. Everyone involved in Rufenacht's enterprises liked Charlie, and he liked them, but he didn't want to be on the road constantly. He needed a home for his family, so in October of '78, he quit Rufenacht Ranches and went back to Arizona looking for something more permanent.

Dave and Gene Ericsson, along with Ben Fancher and Jack Fuller's help, had dreamed up the idea to have a rodeo and reunion for real ranch cowboys. They partnered up with a fellow in Flagstaff named John Avery who owned a bar and steakhouse on the north side of town. John had built a rodeo arena just outside his steakhouse with the idea that people could eat, drink and watch a rodeo all at the same time. The Ericssons and Avery promoted the first Arizona Old-Time Cowboy Reunion, and it was held on October seventh and eighth in 1978. Charlie, Susan, Cole and Sam showed up at the reunion looking for a job.

Charlie's good friend Dewey Brown had been running the Double O Ranch that was south of Seligman and lay between the O RO and the Diamond A. Joe Mendiburo, who was from California, operated the Double O, and he also had other ranches. He had decided to move Dewey Brown to New Mexico to run his ranch over there, and he put Mike Landis to running the Double O in Dewey's place. Mike needed to hire a man to take care of the Hs Camp on the west side of the Double O, and while he and Charlie were both attending the big reunion, they talked, and Mike hired Charlie.

The Hs Camp is about eighteen miles southwest of Seligman on the main road that goes south toward the Oaks and Willows, the O RO headquarters. The Double O Ranch is close to the same size as the O RO but not as rough, and although it's a fine ranch, it is not as good a ranch as the O RO, but few are so it's an unfair comparison. The Double O is high plateau country with some malpai hills as well as limestone rims. There are lots of cedar trees, and in some places, especially on the ridge between the Double O headquarters and the Hs Camp, they are very thick. The ranch has abundant gramma grass everywhere when it rains and lies at 5000 feet in elevation and higher.

Joe Mendiburo operated the ranch as a steer outfit and would, for the most part, stock it with steers of his own, although he might partner on some with men like Phil Stadtler, John Roen or others. Most of the cattle would be shipped off in the fall, and then the ranch would be restocked in the spring, although some might be left to winter there, depending on feed conditions or the market. Joe was a good man and had the reputation of being good to work for.

Most of the steers had been shipped off of the Double O when Charlie went to work there, with the exception of a few steers that were running in some of the rougher and brushier parts of the ranch. There was a handful of big steers, three- and four-year-olds, running on the brushy mountain north of the Hs Camp that had eluded Mike Landis for several years, and another bunch of about the same number running in a rocky brush-thicket south of camp between there and the Anvil Rock place.

Charlie had some dogs that he had used off and on for several years on the O RO and the Diamond Bar north of Silver City where he had worked for a spell before going to the O RO. They were holdup dogs, trained to go to the head of a cow and stop them, using force if necessary. In other words, they would get ahold and bite a critter if that's what it took to stop them. Charlie could, however, control his dogs and stop them if he wanted to. Mike Landis saw the dogs when Charlie moved into the Hs and told Charlie that he didn't like to use dogs while working cattle, but nothing more was said.

Not long after moving into the Hs, Charlie went prowling up on the mountain west of Red Lake and north of camp. He jumped a bunch of four big steers, all of them full grown. The steers took off running downhill toward the east and Red Lake Flat with Charlie and his dogs following. He kept the dogs in check and just followed the steers until they reached Red Lake and open ground, and then he siced the dogs on them. The steers were big and tough, and the dogs got aggressive, and for awhile Charlie just watched them. The steers ears and noses got chewed up a little, but after a while they got tired of the biting and barking and gave it up.

It took awhile, but Charlie drove all of the steers to the Hs and put them in the corral without having to rope any of them. Then he went down into the rocky brush thicket south of the camp and gathered what he could find in there, with things going about the same way. The steers got chewed up a little but were deposited into the corral without roping any of them.

Charlie sent word to Mike that he had the steers gathered, and he could come and haul them off. The ranch did not furnish the Hs camp man a pickup.

When Mike came to pick up the steers, he expressed great surprise at Charlie's good luck gathering them. The steers were very big and had been very elusive. And then he saw the evidence of teeth marks and a little blood on their heads. "By golly! I told you I didn't want you using them dogs!" Mike said.

"Well, yeah you did, but I used them anyway."

"Well, by golly, what are we going to do about that? I told you not to use them dogs. I don't like dogs around my cattle."

"That's right, you did, Mike; but the cattle are in the corral, and I didn't have to rope any of them."

"Well, by golly, I don't want to use dogs around here." Mike was having a hard time elaborating further on the subject because he was mad.

"Mike, the steers are in the corral. They have been getting away for years. What's the problem?"

"Well, by golly." Mike said as he stomped off to his pickup and proceeded to back his gooseneck trailer back up to the chute. Nothing more was said about Charlie's dogs.

Joe Mendiburo sent a load of saddlehorses to the Double O from California in the summer of 1979. The ranch was in bad need of horses to ride, especially good ones; in other words, the outfit didn't have any good ones. Clay Tyree was working for Mike Landis also, and he and his wife Sandy lived at the Double O headquarters. Clay and Charlie both were getting outside horses to ride and making extra money doing it, and if it had not been for that, everyone would have been afoot. So the truckload of California horses showed up, and they were a welcome sight. A fellow named Jack Turnage delivered the horses. Jack had worked at the Double O several years earlier and was well known around Seligman. He and Mike were acquainted but were not fond of each other. Among the horses that Jack unloaded was a chunky built gray horse that stood about 15 hands and weighed 1150 or 1200 pounds. Mike looked at the horse and asked Jack, "What about that gray horse there?"

"Oh, he's a good one." Jack said no more and climbed into his truck and headed back to Bakersfield.

Nobody touched the gray horse for several weeks or thought anything about him. Then after the fall roundup began, Joe Chavez came to work, and the outfit was camped at a place named Soto about ten miles west of Seligman. Mike gave Joe Chaves about five horses to ride, and he took a day or so to shoe them. Among the bunch was the chunky gray horse. When Mike roped the horse out of the remuda and led him up to Joe who had a halter in his hand, he said, "He's a good 'un," and then walked off. It was noontime, and after catching horses, Joe set out to shoe the gray horse while everyone else laid down in their teepees to take a nap, which was a daily ritual to Mike Landis. Mike laid on his bed inside his teepee reading a Louis L'Amour book and fell asleep with the open book laying over the bridge of his nose. He was snoring and the breath coming out of his nose ruffled the pages of the book as he slept.

Suddenly there was a huge explosion down at the round corral made out of cedar pickets and about a hundred yards east of everyone's teepee tent. A great cloud of dust rose up and the loud crashing and cursing sounds woke everyone up, and they stared eastward in wonder at what in the world had happened. Finally, coming out of the cloud of dust walked Joe Chaves. His hat brim was broken and torn away from the crown on the left side of his head. His eye glasses were bent, and one lense was missing. There was blood coming out of his nose, and his knuckles were bleeding. In his hands he was packing what was left of what had been a bridle. The bit, a replica of a US Calvary bit made by Ed Hollis in Beeville, Texas, was bent with one of the checks being mangled to the point of being broken. Both bridle reins were missing.

"By golly, Joe! What the hell happened?" Mike said as he stood up and exited his teepee.

"You told me that *^$#@^&* was a good horse!" Joe looked

at Mike through the mangled eye glasses.

"Well, by golly, Jack Turnage told me he was a good horse, Joe."

"I quit!"

By bragging on the horse, Jack Turnage thought Mike Landis would saddle him up and attempt to ride him, and therefore get even with him for some offense previously committed. Poor old Joe Chavez received the brunt of the joke and forever after blamed Mike who was totally innocent. Heck, he was in his teepee reading a Louis L'Amour book.

While staying at Soto during that same time, Charlie stepped on a bronc that he was riding, and the horse blew up and went to bucking wildly and jumped into a gate made out of barbed wire. The bronc became entangled and fell on top of Charlie with razor sharp barbed wire tangled into his legs. While everyone else watched, Clay Tyree sprinted a hundred feet and got ahold of the horse and kept him from kicking Charlie to death or cutting them both to pieces. Charlie was grateful to have a friend who could think and move fast enough to come to his rescue.

Mike Landis was famous for his fetish of letting cattle string out and walk when trailing them from one place to another. Regardless of how far it would be in between members of his crew, he didn't want the cattle to be stopped.

That fall, 1979, the crew, after Joe Chavez quit, consisted of Mike Landis, Charlie Gould, Clay Tyree, young Eldon Sandsness, and a young Mexican cowboy whose name has been forgotten. The crew worked for several weeks putting together a large herd of steers, all Mexicans, that they gathered off of the Double O country that lay between Interstate 40 and the Aubrey Valley. One morning they left Camel Well with the herd of Mexican steers that numbered 2101 head. The five cowboys were headed toward the Daggs shipping trap twenty miles away, all of it through rolling country with numerous cedar thickets.

"By Golly, don't stop them cattle! Let 'em walk, them Mexican steers will walk like saddle horses all day if you don't stop them." Mike said in a serious tone as he instructed Charlie and Clay to take the points of the herd and head them toward Daggs. Eldon and the Mexican boy would be on the flanks, one behind Clay and the other behind Charlie with Mike bringing up the drags.

They took off, and the cattle walked and strung out, and at first it was a beautiful sight with the cattle strung out two or three abreast and marching right along. There is a considerable amount of open country within a mile or so of Camel Well, but as they progressed down the trail, they encountered thicker cedars and limestone ridges and an occasional trail or road that went cross-grained to their intended destination. Charlie and Clay let the cattle walk on, and the herd stretched into a mile in length and then two miles. Charlie and Clay as well as Eldon and the Mexican had to do lots of loping up and back along the herd's flanks to keep the steers moving correctly. By midafternoon, when the leaders reached the freeway, the drags were all the way back at a water known as Limestone four miles distance. Charlie and Clay discussed their plan of action. Mike had given orders to let the cattle keep walking; besides if they stopped them, they knew the cattle would begin to graze and slowly scatter. The cattle were gentle, but everyone's horse was now given completely out because of their constant need to go back and forth along the flanks of the herd. Neither Charlie nor Clay had seen Eldon or the Mexican for over an hour.

They opened the gates allowing the cattle to walk under the freeway through the huge cement culverts and then drift on toward the gate going into the Daggs Trap. When 500 steers had walked to the other side of the freeway, Charlie and Clay crossed under the pavement also. Whether it was a miracle or a result of the men's expertise, the cattle kept walking toward the gate several miles in the distance.

Mike had given Clay instructions to count the steers as they walked through the gate. When the first steer reached the gate, the two point men finally saw Eldon and the Mexican come into sight north of the freeway, but they had no idea where the drags of the herd was. For most people who are good at counting big bunches of cattle, it is easier to count if the cattle are going by at a good steady clip, but this herd was so strung out it took Clay an hour and a half of steady counting before the drags and the last steer finally walked through the gate. It was slow and monotonous, and Clay's mind wandered. It was the worst scenario, but he had worked hard at doing a good job. The last steer walked by and Mike said, "By golly, how many was there?"

For an hour and a half nobody had spoken, and Clay had worked hard at concentrating, but the sudden loud question that broke the silence also broke his concentration. He forgot what the final count was. He stared off in the distance, gritting his teeth, mad at himself for forgetting the number, and mad at Mike for asking the question.

"Two thousand one hundred and one," Clay said picking the number out of the sky. He had no earthly idea how many he had counted, but he wasn't going to admit that to Mike. The next day they gathered the Daggs Trap and loaded twenty-six semi-trucks with the steers they had trailed into Daggs the day before. The final tally for that day's shipping was 2101 head.

The following year, 1980, began more or less like the year of 1979. During the months of December and January, Charlie and Clay Tyree stayed busy gathering remnant, and by February the outfit was cleaned up with all the remnant steers shipped and gone.

In March Joe Mendiburo started shipping in a new set of steers that were for the most part Mexicans. Phil and Dan Stadtler and John Roer owned 1500 or so of the new steers, and Joe Mendiburo owned the rest. By the time all of the new cattle had been received, they totaled about 7000 steers; of that total of 7000, about 5000 of them were horned Mexicans that were so common in those days. By modern standards they would have been called number one ropers: The kind that thirty years later would be hard to find.

On the first of July, Clay Tyree quit the outfit and moved on to greener pastures, and I hired on at the Double O and with my family moved into the house at the Double O headquarters that Clay and his family vacated. That summer, 1980, would end up being one of the driest in Northern Arizona's history. On the Fourth of July weekend, a big summer front moved in, and it clouded up and all the old cowboys and ranchers in the northern half of the state rejoiced and said that it looked like the good old days when it, according to legend, always started raining around the Fourth of July. There was one huge storm that dropped as much as four inches of rain in places along Cataract Creek, most of which were on Babbitt's W Triangle Ranch, but it didn't rain very much anywhere else. The W Triangle grew a summer's worth of feed off of that one storm but all the other ranches in Northern Arizona languished in drought and depression. The Double O Ranch and its 7000 steers suffered like everyone else.

On the first of August, a big crowd of Arizona cowboys congregated at John Avery's Kowboy Kountry Klub Bar and Steakhouse and participated in the third annual Avery's Old-time Cowboy Reunion. Charlie, his wife Susan, and Cole and Sam loaded up and went to the reunion, as did me and my wife Jean Ann and our two sons Everett and Clay. Everyone camped out in the pine trees in back of the arena sleeping in teepee tents or in the back of stock trailers. No one who came and participated owned a big aluminum living quarters trailer or expensive bus. Most of the horses that cowboys rode and competed on were fresh off a ranch somewhere, and few had ever been in a roping arena of any kind.

Wayne Tallent was the stock contractor and brought most of the bucking horses and roping cattle. Charlie, Larry Leist and myself served as pickup men without pay, and all the other work around the arena was done by cowboys who pitched in and made a hand wherever it was needed.

The stock contractor, Wayne Tallent, was a rodeo hand and a good arena roper but was not a ranch cowboy. He was big and had a reputation for being a tough guy and did a lot of screaming and hollering at cowboys, giving orders and cussing people out for not doing things the way he thought they should be done. For the most part everyone ignored him. He took to hollering at Larry Leist during the bronc riding, not being happy with the way Larry did something while picking up a bucking horse. Charlie and I figured that Larry would punch his lights out, but nothing happened. On Saturday night a big crowd had assembled in the building that overlooked the rodeo arena and housed the steakhouse and bar. Wayne Sunday-punched young Tommy Hafley and knocked him to the floor, but Tommy got up and took to Wayne and gave him a thorough licking, including a good black eye. The fight ended with Wayne laying on the floor. As he got up with no fight left in him, he remarked, "Darn, I'd a never hit 'em if I'd a knowed he was that tough!"

Mike Landis hauled the gray horse that had bucked Joe Chavez off the fall before and asked to have him put in the bronc riding draw, and Clay Tyree drew him and won the bronc riding on him. Wayne Tallent traded Mike a sorrel horse that had quit bucking for the gray gelding.

Charlie and I met a cowboy who was about our age named Howdy Fowler who had drove down from Nevada to enter the rodeo. He was a nice fellow, and we took a liking to him, and so all three of us teamed up and entered the wild horse race. Our plan was that I would be the anchor man, Charlie would mug, and Howdy would do the riding. Charlie's wife Susan made all of Charlie's shirts, and she was very good at it. Our team won first in the first performance with Howdy doing a great job riding, and Charlie attacked the bronc and mugged him to a standstill but got his brand new homemade cowboy shirt ripped to shreds in the process. We won the second go round also, and Charlie ruined another new homemade shirt. On the third day we placed second, but Charlie managed to destroy another new shirt, but we figured it was worth it because we were sure we were going to win the average and belt buckles. When it was time to give all the awards away to the event winners, they gave the wild horse race buckles to the team who won the third go round. Charlie asked John Avery and the rodeo secretary, "Hey, what about us coming in first in the first and second go rounds? Shouldn't we get the trophy buckles?"

"No! The first two go rounds don't count, just the third go." The secretary waved us all away, her gesticulations hinting that she was very busy.

A bunch of cowboys were sitting around our camp on Saturday afternoon talking and telling stories. Among the bunch was Leonard Neal who was in his late seventies, and Mike Landis,

Charlie Gould and me plus some other cowboys that I can't remember. Everyone talked about the drought and the hard times that were coming if it didn't rain soon. Leonard Neal had probably had a drink of two, and perhaps we were passing a bottle around, but I don't remember, but Leonard was in a story-telling mood. Leonard liked cowboys, and although he was one of the wealthiest men in Arizona, he would have rather sat around a camp and visited with some cowboys than been in the company of a bunch of Hollywood stars and stockbrokers. He was on a roll telling one yarn after another, and we were all laughing. A big thunderhead had built up to the east over Mount Eldon five miles away, when suddenly a loud crack of thunder erupted out of the distant cloud. "What's that?" Leonard jumped up off of the pine stump he was sitting on and gazed to the east with a terrorized look on his face.

"That's thunder, Leonard!" Charlie said loudly.

"By golly, I don't think I ever heard that sound before," Leonard said with a grin.

Everyone roared with laughter because he had pulled the feigned surprise off with perfect timing.

In those days the bronc riders saddled their broncs out in the middle of the arena while cowboys held them snubbed up to saddle horses. Then the bronc rider had to ride the horse until he quit bucking, regardless how long that was. I blew a stirrup at the last jump my horse made and therefore was disqualified. Howdy Fowler, Charlie and I won a couple dollars apiece for our efforts in the wild horse race, which the judges determined was somewhere below first. Charlie owned three shirts less than when he left the ranch, and so we all loaded up and went back to the Double O Ranch south of Seligman.

The drought continued all over Northern Arizona, and the 7000 steers on the Double O Ranch walked through the malpai rocks and cedar trees searching for nourishment in the form of green grass but found little. The cattle were healthy and their frames got bigger and bonier but they gained very little weight.

In early October Mike got word to start gathering the outfit and get the cattle loaded and gone. He hired an old alcoholic from Kingman known as Goat Blair to be the wagon cook. He acquired the moniker "Goat" because his family had been goat ranchers in Mojave County when he was a boy, and he had grown up herding goats.

Mike talked all of the time of his days working on the JAs in Palo Duro Canyon and the upper and lower Matadors. He loved to expound how the outfits were fun, and everyone who worked there was a top hand, the likes of which didn't exist anymore. According to his memory, the men on those outfits cared about nothing but riding bucking horses and roping wild cattle, and something as mundane as eating was only done because of necessity. Therefore, a good wagon cook and something good to eat was almost taboo to talk about in Mike's presence. Besides, good groceries cost money, and in the forefront of Mike's management philosophy was never spend any company money. Therefore Goat Blair was a fine specimen to make a cook out of, at least in Mike's mind.

Another one of Mike's management paradigms was, "Good horses don't need no hay or grain. Well, by golly, those JA horses never saw a flake of hay or morral full of oats in their life!" The fact that every cowboy at the JA Ranch in 1949 probably had a dozen or more horses in their string never entered Mike's calculations. The Double O Ranch was sorely short of horseflesh, and Mike didn't believe in buying horse feed.

Charlie and I both rounded up a bunch of broncs to ride from neighboring ranches, which made us both some extra money and kept us mounted better than anyone else on the crew. Had we not been fortunate enough to acquire those horses to ride, the cattle might not have got gathered.

Along with the cook, Goat Blair, Mike hired Joe Hall, a nineteen-year-old kid with big knuckles and very thick bones in his forehead, and a boy from New Mexico named John Eby. Joe Hall would eventually become famous in the Southwest, and his quest for that fame began on the Double O Ranch in the fall of 1980.

We all congregated at the Double O headquarters around the first of October to shoe up the remuda and load groceries and supplies into the chuck wagon. Mike had put a gray horse in Joe

Hall's string that was five years old but very green. Joe's outfit consisted of an old basket-stamped Hamley bronc saddle and some batwing chaps made out of twelve ounce latigo leather. His spurs had very large rowels. As Charlie and I watched, Joe put the Hamley saddle on the gray horse's back and a very heavy rawhide bosal with a steel cable core on the horse's face. He then led the horse out into the driveway south of the big stone barn. Joe gathered up the braided nylon reins connected to the heavy bosal and put his size eleven boots deep into the oxbow stirrups and stepped on the very breedy and hot-blooded horse who immediately flipped over backwards driving the saddle horn and high cantle down into Joe's midsection. The horse jumped up and stood over Joe as he lay on the hard ground groaning.

After a minute or so, Joe scraped himself up off the ground and adjusted his glasses that were encased in heavy black rims. He rubbed various body parts, scrubbing pieces of pea gravel out of his hide and then prepared to mount the gray horse who had not moved an inch. He pulled tightly on the braided reins putting lots of pressure on the large bosal. The horse stood still like a rock until Joe's fanny hit the saddle, and then he jumped straight into the sky and flipped violently over backwards. This time the saddle horn and Hamley four inch cantle crashed down into Joe's pelvis.

"AAAhhhhhhhhooooooommmmmmiiiii, AAHH!" Joe screamed as Charlie and I looked at each other. The gray horse stood directly over Joe looking down at him in horse wonderment.

"Joe, you want some help?" Charlie asked.

"No, I'm about to get him, I think." Joe answered as he stood up rubbing his hips and thighs.

He straightened his glasses and pulled his cinches tighter and stuck his left cowboy boot all the way into the left oxbow stirrup, and when he got his seat, he lifted both legs and deposited both spurs, large rowels and all, into the horse's chest cavity. This time when the horse came over backwards, he got a lot of air between ground and sky and came falling downward driving the cantle of the saddle into Joe's temple, breaking the rawhide and knocking the cantle loose from the bars of the saddle tree.

"AAAHHOOOUUUCCCHHHH!"

"Joe," Charlie intervened, "let's try something different."

"Okay, I'm ready. What should I do?"

"First thing," Charlie said, "loosen your cinches a little bit and lead that son of a gun around for awhile and wait while I go saddle a horse. Keep moving him around until I get back." Charlie ran to the nearby horse corral and caught a horse and saddled him up real fast and led him out to where Joe was leading the gray around. Joe's glasses were permanently twisted, and he was bleeding out of numerous orifices.

"Keep leading him around for a minute while I whip on him." Charlie took his rope down and swatted the gray horse on the behind while Joe limped along in front of him. Finally Charlie said, "Okay, get on him without pulling on his head and keep your spurs out of him, and maybe he'll move out without falling on you again."

When Joe got mounted, Charlie rode by the gray horse in a trot and kept riding west in a straight line, and the gray horse fell in behind Charlie's horse traveling in a long swinging trot. The cantle on the old Hamley saddle was knocked loose, and Joe was a little bloody and his eye glasses bent, but he had survived. Actually, he was unaware that his life had been in danger.

After several leisurely days the remuda was shod and the chuck wagon loaded, and we were ready to go to work. The remuda consisted of perhaps thirty-five horses including seven or eight that Charlie and I were being paid to ride by and for other people. I had six outside broncs that were old enough to ride hard and use. I had been given five company horses to ride, but at least two of them were unsound, and Charlie was in the same shape, but we were better mounted than anyone else. Mike Landis had, of course, the best of the horses that the ranch owned, a total of five or six, and he owned a personal horse or two so he was mounted well; and he had the quality of being able to ride a horse without hurting them. Joe Hall and John Eby were not much better than afoot, but neither man knew the difference, so it didn't matter.

We had 7000 steers to gather that were scattered about over close to 400 square miles of country, a great deal of which was cedar thickets. Joe Mendiburo wanted the cattle gone by mid-November, six weeks off into the future. We pulled out of headquarters and moved to a place five or six miles west of Charlie's camp, the Hs, and started the roundup there. The campsite was named the Pickett Corral, and Charlie stayed in camp at night because Mike didn't believe a man should ever go home when the wagon was "out," meaning roundup was in process. A married man going home wasn't "Western" and went against Mike's beliefs. Married men on the JA and Matador in Texas never went home according to his memory. According to him, very few of the old-time cowboys he wanted to emulate were even married. Actually, in Mike's psyche, at least in those days, there was very little room for the opposite sex. One wonders if the continuance of the human race would have ended had it been left up to Texas cowboys.

We would roundup the Mexican steers and deposit them in traps, and when part of the ranch had been gathered, the cattle that had accumulated would be moved to other holding pastures close to the shipping corrals. Most of the shipping was done at a place known as Daggs, which was in the bottom of Chino Wash up the creek northwest of the Double O headquarters five miles.

Between the west half of the ranch and places known as the Hs, Pickett, EL, Number Six, and Red Lake was a high malpai ridge that ran more or less north and south for many miles and was from two to five miles across going east and west. The shipping point, Daggs, was located on the east side of this dividing ridgeline, and so throughout the fall we would trail several big herds of steers from the western half of the ranch to Daggs. The first of these herds we trailed from Charlie's camp, the Hs, across this cedar-infested mountain to the Daggs pens. We made this drive after working for several weeks around Pickett, EL, Anvil Rock and Red Lake.

Going east from the Hs, there is a canyon jutting up into the west side of the dividing ridge that goes generally eastward and climbing altitude until it reaches a divide, and then a trail leads down a canyon on the east side of the divide, and finally reaching a gate in the backside of the Daggs shipping trap. The distance across this trail from the Hs to this gate is ten or twelve miles, all of it being overgrown with cedars, pinion pine, and different species of brush. In places, with the exception of the trail itself, it is a dark jungle where visibility is as little as a hundred feet.

We had a couple thousand steers deposited in a trap at the Hs, and one crisp October morning we gathered it and commenced to trail them across the divide to Daggs. Mike always put Charlie and me on the points, and he remained in the drags, with John Eby and Joe Hall left to ride flank. When we started gathering the trap at sunup, Mike gave Charlie and me our orders, "You two fellers point 'em across to Daggs, and we'll bring the rest of 'em along. Don't be stoppin' them ^*(%$#@)** Mexican steers! Let 'em go! They'll walk across there like saddle horses."

We gathered the trap, which wasn't very big, and Charlie and I rode up to the gate, and he stepped off of his horse and opened it and threw it wide open. He took the right point and I took the left, and we gave the steers plenty of room, and they filed out the gate and went to walking. Mike was right, the cattle moved like a remuda, and soon the leaders were a half mile ahead of the drags.

Mike loved Joe Hall and considered him to be a very good prospect to make a top hand. Joe was Western, a term Mike used a great deal. Joe always wore a big black wild rag hanging loosely about his shoulders and a very large black hat. A great deal of the time, Joe and Mike rode along together in the drags swapping tales of the old West.

In contrast to Joe Hall, John Eby was the quintessential gunsel. He had a cheap factory-made roping saddle and tight chaps with zippered-up legs and dime-store spurs. His hat was the cheapest generic model that could be bought in a Western store. He told no stories about the old West because he had none to tell. John was short on experience but was, in fact, very intelligent, and Charlie and I enjoyed his company. He had a quick wit and good humor. He attempted to talk about ranch management to Mike Landis, a thing Mike resented. Mike had very few opinions about ranch management with the exception of never spending any company money. He didn't like John Eby at all.

By the time the leaders of this trail herd reached the divide, about halfway between the Hs camp and the gate going into the

Daggs shipping trap, the herd was strung out for about a mile and a half. Charlie and I would try to stay as close to the leaders as possible to assure they remained pointed correctly, but that became increasingly harder to accomplish because we also had to make constant forays back along the flanks to keep steers that wanted to branch off on a different route thrown back into the herd. Occasionally we might see John Eby, who was trying to make a hand, but we never saw Joe Hall, who was usually engaged in conversation about the old West with Mike.

The cattle were strung out way too far, and Charlie and I both knew it and wanted to stop the leaders but had been given strict orders to, "Let them go." Then when the leaders stepped over the divide and started downhill, they walked even faster. About the time the middle of the herd topped the divide and the leaders were long gone, a small bunch of wild burros that lived on the ridge came running down from a southerly direction and crashed through the cattle causing great havoc. The first problem was the herd was now split with the drags of the lead bunch hurrying on in a run and the leaders of the drag end being turned around and running the wrong way. The second problem was, not a few split off and went running north toward a natural rock hole known as Green Water Hole. Charlie was the only one anywhere near the burro incident and saved the day by racing through the timber and rocks gathering wayward steers and whipping the confused herd into order. John Eby finally showed up after a spell and provided Charlie with some assistance, and the column was thrown back in order. Charlie's horse suffered much during this drive because of the constant going back and forth keeping the flanks of the herd moving, and the violent rush through the rocks keeping the burro intrusion from ending in total disaster. I was not aware that anything had taken place because I was a mile ahead near the leaders, and Mike Landis and Joe Hall were also ignorant of any facts concerning the burro incident as they rode along in the cool breeze telling stories. When we put the last steer through the gate into the Daggs shipping pasture, Mike looked at Charlie's horse and remarked, "By Golly! Your ole pony's had quite a workout."

"Yeah, Mike, he has." And with that answer from Charlie, we

rode on to the north and Daggs where our cook, Goat Blair, had moved the wagon and set up camp while we trailed cattle. Goat had been drinking whiskey, and the roast he put out for supper was so cold that the grease in the roaster was hard and the meat close to inedible, so we ate stale bread that had been made the day before and drank coffee.

The Double O headquarters was only five miles down Big Chino Wash, and I thought that Mike might suggest that we make a quick trip down for the night to see our families, which had not been visited for several weeks. But that was not the way real cowboys in the old days had done it, so we stayed in camp. Charlie had not seen his wife and two sons any more than I had seen mine, and we were running out of clean clothes. In the fall of 1973 I had worked for Mike at the Diamond A Ranch and had witnessed him wearing a new unwashed and unshrunk pair of Levis all the way through the roundup from first day to last without changing or washing them, so I knew Charlie or me getting some clothes washed wasn't on the front burner of his stove.

We shipped several thousand Mexican steers at Daggs over a two or three day period, and then without delay we picked up camp, including Goat who was getting dirtier and drunker, and moved to a place known as Black Tub out on the west end of the ranch near Cross Mountain and the road to Fort Rock.

Dave Ericsson had a big contract with some wealthy animal lovers who were trying to save all the wild burros in the Grand Canyon from destruction because the US Park Service had announced that the burro population was out of control. A famous television and movie critic had gathered a group of city slickers willing to finance the humane removal of burros out of the canyon, and Dave had been given the contract. A great many of Northern Arizona's best cowboys were employed by Dave and rode down into the depths of the canyon where they would rope the burros and tie them up and then roll them into a net so they could be lifted up with a helicopter to a corral on the south rim. Among the cowboys who helped Dave in this exciting enterprise were Ben Fancher, Tim Lange, Chuck Lange, Jim Marler, Billy Roer, Hank Roer and a few others.

On the south side of Black Tub where we made our wagon camp was a little rocky mountain where there was always a bunch of wild burros running. Dave contacted Mike Landis and asked him if he could come with some help and perhaps capture some of these burros and add them to the number he had captured out of the Grand Canyon. Of course Mike answered in the affirmative because he and Dave were old friends, and the burros were a nuisance anyway.

So a day or so after we set up our camp and started rounding up the steers in the area, Dave and Ben Fancher pulled into camp with several new Ford pickups and big gooseneck stock trailers, with plans to capture some easy burros. Within several hours of their arrival, a big pickup hooked to a flatbed trailer with California license plates showed up. Strapped down onto the trailer was an old-style Bell helicopter with a glass bubble for a cockpit and an open steel frame that made up the tail. Gas tanks on both sides hovered above and behind the open doorways that led into the cramped cockpit. The flying machine was untied and Ben Fancher got into the cockpit with the pilot, and they flew off on a scouting expedition looking for wild burros on top of the mountain.

For several days we gathered steers and put them in a trap located right at our campsite, while Ben and Dave worked at roping burros that the helicopter chased to them. Several times they made trips at night depositing burros into the corral at the Grand Canyon.

One afternoon Charlie, John Eby, and I rode east of camp several miles to Markham Well to take a much needed bath. Mike and Joe Hall didn't accompany us because real cowboys out in the West don't usually bathe. There was a handmade rock water storage at the foot of the windmill tower that was rectangle in shape, about thirty feet in length and twelve feet wide and perhaps six feet deep. The water coming out of the ground at this well had the perfect mineral content (unknown to us) that kept the water crystal clear all the time. There was absolutely no algae or moss polluting the water, and you could see every grain of sand in the bottom of the storage. The east bound lane of the newly completed Interstate 40 was a few feet higher and perhaps sixty-foot distance from the storage, but we undressed and swam and waved at the cars driving by with tourists staring at us. We figured that they probably had never seen men as manly as us, and beings no one showed up to arrest us, we didn't care what anyone thought. It was an abnormally warm Indian summer day, and we had a wonderful time, and as we rode back to camp, we discussed the possibility of some Hollywood director showing up at the wagon wanting to hire the three men with Tarzan physiques. No one showed up.

The fact that it was very dry and the country was short of feed helped, and after four or five days, we had gathered close to 2000 steers, and on the last day we were camped at Black Tub, we trailed all those cattle east seven or eight miles and penned them in a corral surrounding a big dirt tank known as Forks in the Road. It is at this spot that the old dirt road forks with one road turning south toward the Hs and on to Anvil Rock and eventually the O RO Ranch, and the other fork continues west to Black Tub and on to the Fort Rock Ranch. When we got our big herd of steers penned, we made a quick running circle south of Forks in the Road and gathered several hundred more steers and penned them with the others in the big water lot corral. Then we returned to camp and prepared to move camp the next morning and go back to Daggs where we planned on shipping all of those steers.

When we got back to camp we discovered that the pilot of the California helicopter had crashed and destroyed the bird about 400 yards from our camp. He had flown too close to the ground chasing burros, and the blade had hit a cedar tree which subsequently sucked the big machine into the malpai rocks and dirt with two men aboard. Neither man was hurt but were badly shaken, and there was a great deal of conversation about who was liable for paying for the helicopter that was nothing but mangled steel and broken glass.

Goat Blair got extra drunk that night to celebrate all of the excitement and the fact that we were moving camp the next morning. There was very little to eat for supper. Before sunup we had our teepees and beds rolled and Goat poured into the pickup pulling the wagon, and we set him off on an easterly course toward Daggs sixteen miles away, and Mike, Charlie, Joe Hall, John Eby and myself headed toward Forks in the Road with plans to move the herd now numbering in excess of 2200 steers on to the Daggs shipping trap, a trail of about eight miles.

When exiting the corral we needed to put the cattle on the old county road that went eastward toward Seligman, and after five miles or so, we would need to turn to the southeast and point the cattle down into Big Chino Wash towards Daggs. The corral surrounding the Forks in the Road Dirt Tank was only a hundred yards south of the interstate highway, and then the road we were to take the cattle down was immediately adjacent to the freeway and the highway right-of-way fence. The country was rolling ridges and canyons and lots of thick cedar and pinions, and the dirt road was going generally downhill especially after a mile or so. When we got to Forks in the Road, Mike gave us our orders, "Charlie, you and Ed point 'em down the country, and by golly don't stop 'em, let 'em walk. These Mexican steers will walk like saddle horses."

"Okay, Mike, whatever you say," Charlie replied. There was only one narrow gate coming out of the wire corral, and it was on the south side of the corral, but we needed to point the cattle east by northeast. Charlie positioned himself on the east side of the gate and that put me to the west, and we waited outside a hundred yards distance.

Mike, Joe and John rode to the north end of the big water lot to get behind the steers, and the leaders boiled out of the gate running south. Charlie rode hard into their necks and bent them around eastward toward me, and I rode fast and kept them turning until they were running straight north where they hit the highway right-of-way fence, and there the leaders stopped. "Just right," I thought to myself. I knew if we didn't get ahold of the cattle at the start we would never be able to control them.

When I got the leaders settled down and stopped on the fence, I rode as fast as I could back southward and tried to help Charlie who was running back and forth keeping the cattle bent back towards me. When only half the cattle were out of the gate, both of our horses were lathered up and sweating while the other three men had barely got out of a walk. Several times I stampeded back to the right-of-way fence and held the leaders up in hopes we could still have the cattle in a bunch when the last steer came out of the corral.

When about 1700 steers were out of the corral, it became very hard for Charlie and me to control them while Mike sat on his horse inside the corral visiting with Joe. It was nip and tuck, but I thought that we were going to be victorious when I ran for the fourth time and stopped the leaders from taking off. In the distance two hundred yards, Mike saw me stopping the cattle, and he stood up in his stirrups and screamed at the top of his lungs, "LET THEM SORRY *^%$#@&%*^ cattle go! What the hell are you doing—LET 'EM GO!" Charlie was still south of the corral running a good horse to death in an attempt to turn the cattle my way. Mike, John and Joe took an extra two minutes getting the last ten steers out of the corral, and by that time the leaders were a mile away and running downhill, and there was nothing I could do to slow them down.

Charlie could do nothing but make a hand and continue turning the cattle eastward as the other three men chased a half dozen steers around inside the water lot. It might not have made much difference, perhaps the two of us couldn't have kept them slowed down anyway, but if John or Joe would have rode up to help us and three of us stayed up in front, we could have controlled them, but that opportunity had now passed.

In one of those Kodak moments that will forever be etched in my memory, Dave Ericsson and Ben Fancher drove by me traveling eastward toward Seligman on the freeway. The leaders had run downhill several miles and were nearing a place known as Twin Buttes. I had managed to get out in front of the cattle and was running as fast as my tired horse could go. The steers were six or eight wide, and I almost thought the steers were laughing as they ran. They knew that they had won the battle; I knew that I had lost the battle, and Ben Fancher and Dave Ericsson watched as they drove by. Ben was waving at me with a silly grin on his face, and Dave was pounding his fist against the steering wheel, and I could see both of them roaring with laughter.

Soon after Ben and Dave drove past, I slowed down and rode off to the right side of the herd and let them go. My horse was as wet as if I had just rode up out of a river that we had swam across. His sides were heaving as he sucked in as much air as possible, and his legs felt unsteady. Hundreds of steers ran past me as I rode along dejected.

I rode slowly along for another mile and reached the edge of Big Chino where I stopped and unsaddled my jaded horse. After awhile Charlie rode up and stepped off close by and unsaddled his horse who was in as bad a shape as mine. We stood there for a long time watching hundreds of steers scatter out between where we were and Daggs and points beyond. After a long time Mike, John and Joe rode up following several hundred dink steers that made up the tail end of the herd. Their horses had never sweated a drop.

"By golly! Where are the cattle?" Mike demanded.

"They're out there." Charlie and I replied in unison and we pointed toward Daggs. We were mad enough to fight, and nothing more was said until we had thrown our saddles back on our jaded horses and cinched them up. Then very gently Mike suggested that maybe we could spread out and gather some of the cattle that had gotten away. When we finally counted what we could find and deposit into the Daggs Trap, we were 400 short.

We shipped several thousand steers at Daggs with the mood being depressed because the cattle were much lighter than anyone expected, and it was cold and windy. Because of the need to use the telephone, Mike and I drove down to headquarters for a night, and then we were moving camp again, this time to Soto on the north side of the freeway and on the south edge of Aubrey Valley.

Goat Blair's cooking had got steadily worse, and he was dirty beyond description. By some quirk of nature, Mike did not seem to care about Goat's failure to produce something decent to eat or his filthy personal habits. Perhaps one reason for his non-commitment to feed his crew was the fact that he himself was very conscience about his weight, and he had a distinct dislike for overweight people. He prided himself in his slim waistline so he successfully curbed his appetite. But it was a mystery why Mike put up with the lack of cleanliness in Goat's kitchen.

One afternoon after Mike's habitual naptime, he got in his company pickup and drove to headquarters to use the telephone, or something else, and did not invite me or anyone else along. He told Charlie to catch horses for the next day's circle and said he would see us in the morning. Goat was passed out on top of his bedroll, and the filth he lay in was indescribable. Charlie tried to roust him up so he could fix some supper, but he refused to be motivated, so Charlie and I set out to fix the crew something to eat, and then Goat got up and on the fight, telling us we had no right to be in his kitchen.

"You're fired old-timer," Charlie declared.

"Hell, you can't fire me, you snot-nosed kid," Goat replied.

"I just did. Get your stuff throwed together; we're taking you to town."

"You can't fire me." The old man shook his finger at Charlie as he stood swaying and trying to look defiant.

There was another old pickup at the wagon that would barely run, and I started it and backed it up to the wagon, and Charlie and I shoveled what belongings Goat had and dumped it all in the bed of the pickup like it was refuse as the old fella staggered around cursing. Joe Hall and John Eby stood off in the distance acting like they were witnessing Fletcher Christian cast Captain William Bligh into the open water. When we had what little Goat Blair owned thrown into the truck, we threw him in the cab and got in with him, Charlie behind the steering wheel and me riding by the passenger door, and we drove to Seligman. We unloaded Goat and his outfit in the parking lot of the Black Cat Saloon where he seemed content enough to be.

Where's my paycheck?" Goat demanded.

"You don't deserve one." Charlie told him and we drove back to Soto.

When we got back to the wagon, Charlie and I dove into the kitchen on wheels with a vengeance and went to scrubbing away the filth while Joe and John looked on in fear. Among other unspeakable artifacts, we found seven porcelain roasters that had half-eaten beef roasts or other cuts of meat that had turned to green mold floating in putrid grease. We scrubbed and scoured, and after several hours we went to cooking. Charlie fried some steaks, and I found some canned cherry pie filling and make a couple of pies. When the food was ready, we invited John and Joe to eat, and they approached warily as if they were afraid to dine with convicted felons. They obviously thought that Charlie and I would soon be looking for employment elsewhere. We weren't so sure that they weren't correct in their estimation.

The next morning way before sunup, Charlie and I were up making breakfast when the headlights of Mike's pickup approached. He parked the truck and then walked into camp and saw us cooking. "By golly, where's Goat?"

"Goat's gone, Mike."

"Gone? What do you mean, he's gone? Where is he?"

"He's in town, the last time we saw him. I fired the filthy old rascal and we took him to town." Charlie stood looking at Mike, holding a spatula in his hand.

"What do you mean, you fired him? I'm runnin' this outfit! You can't fire him. What the hell are you talkin' about?"

"The filthy old coot couldn't get out of bed to cook supper, and when we tried to cook for ourselves, he got on the fight so I fired him and took him to town and dumped him out in front of the Black Cat! If you don't like it, I'll leave, too," Charlie said.

"So will I," I added.

Mike stomped off and sat down on a stump and stared into the campfire where Joe and John sat also. Goat Blair was never talked about again.

We stayed at Soto for several days gathering cattle and putting them into a shipping trap on the far northwest corner of the ranch. Then we moved camp to some shipping pens at the spot which is on the south side of the railroad tracks at Pica.

One day Charlie and I were riding toward camp down through the Pica shipping trap. There were several thousand Mexican steers in the trap, and almost all of them had big wide horns, and the cattle averaged about 575 pounds in weight. Charlie and I were both riding colts that we were being paid to ride by people who were not affiliated with the ranch in anyway. We decided to rope a few steers on our broncs. After roping a few and having great fun, we coiled our ropes up and meandered on toward camp. As we rode along we came upon a big Mexican with wide horns standing all by himself. "I'll bet you can't rope that steer before he gets to the cedar tree over there." Charlie said pointing to a lone cedar tree about ninety yards distance. He looked at me and grinned.

I didn't even answer such a dumb statement. I took down my rope and tied it to the saddle horn and built to the steer who stood innocently a third of the distance to the tree. Me and the colt took off like a flash, and I got within a rope's length away as the tree approached at lightning speed directly ahead. The colt was very green, not much past the gee haw stage. I threw and roped the Mexican clean around the horns and went left, and me and the Mexican forked the cedar going all out. I figured I might be dead, but I sure wasn't going to pass on a Charlie Gould challenge. We all survived, including the tree, but Charlie almost died laughing at me as I leaned out onto my left stirrup contemplating bailing out of the wreck. Our colts were a lot better broke when we unsaddled than they had been when we threw our saddles on their backs.

Joe Hall talked Mike into giving him a day off. None of the rest of us had been given a day off for close to six weeks. Joe convinced Mike that he needed to go see a friend who was a dude wrangler at the Grand Canyon.

Joe's friend at the Grand Canyon had a very beautiful wife whose name was Chris, and Joe showed back up at the wagon with Chris. Mike Landis preached from morning to night every day about the rules and regulations of old-time cowboys and cow outfits. He bragged about running an outfit that was correct in all things pertaining to cowboy etiquette and the Code of the West. Well, according to the Code Book, Chapter 3, Paragraph 7: No Girlfriends of Wagon Hands Will Be Allowed to Spend the Night in a Teepee in the Middle of a Camp Full of Celibate Men.

Charlie and I were never offered a pickup to go home and see our families, and Mike didn't like his wife so he wouldn't go home to see her, and he considered any cowboy who wanted to visit home occasionally to be second rate. To top it all off, the beautiful girl was Joe's best friend's wife.

Mike Landis laughed and giggled when Joe brought her into camp. Nothing was said about the Code of the West. He put his blessing on her and Joe's foray into the teepee: Well, after all, it was too late to take her home 160 miles away. We sat around the fire telling stories while Joe and Chris tied the teepee's canvas door shut, and then Joe lit a lantern so Chris, who was unaccustomed to undressing in the dark, could prepare for bed. The bright light of the lantern cast the profile of her shapely figure onto the canvas wall of the teepee while the rest of us sat around the fire and listened to Mike's stories about the JA Ranch in Palo Duro Canyon.

Several days later after Chris had been returned to Joe's best friend, we were sitting around camp. Joe Hall was in a particularly pensive mood sitting off by himself. He wore a white shirt that was dirty and a black vest. His wild-rag was black and big enough to wrap a beef up in. His spurs hung just right off of his Paul Bond boots with eighteen inch tops. The rowels in his spurs were big enough to be spokes in a wagon wheel. And his chaps were made out of twelve ounce latigo. All things considered, he cut a striking figure.

"What's the matter, Joe? How come you're so quiet?" Mike asked.

"Oh, I was just dreamin'."

"Well, hell, tell us what you're dreamin' about."

"Well," Joe stared at a far distant hill as his soliloquy played out, "me and Chris are stayin' in a log cabin in a high mountain meadow. I can see little snowflakes fallin' down outside the window as I sit in my easy chair puttin' new silver conchos on my headstall, and I look over into the kitchen and Chris is standin' there makin' biscuits. And I can see a white handprint on her Levis' pocket because I went over there and got my hands in the biscuit dough and then patted her on the fanny."

We had the last big shipping of the fall at Pica, and Joe Mendiburo, his son George, as well as Phil Stadtler and John Roen were there for several days. They were all very nice men and treated all of us cowboys in a friendly manner. Phil Stadtler was especially entertaining to be around because he was quite a cowboy himself, and he dressed and acted more like a real cowboy than the other men. As Mike introduced Phil to all the cowboy crew he would say, "Oh! I know you." It was his way of trying to make humble men feel important.

The talk among the men who owned the cattle was negative because of the drought, the bad cow market, and seven thousand steers that didn't weigh much more than when they had arrived at the ranch six or seven months earlier. But no one blamed us for events that were out of our control. Because we did not have a wagon cook, Joe Mendiburo told Mike to take the wagon crew up the highway to eat supper at a café that was located at the Grand Canyon Caverns. Mike didn't like this idea because it was not old-timey, and something like that would never have happened at the JA or Matador ranches in Texas. Joe gave strict orders to Mike to do it whether he liked the idea or not.

One night when we got done with supper at the caverns' café, Charlie talked Mike into stopping at a saloon that was between the café and our wagon camp. We went into the joint, and it was pretty empty except for some locals who probably worked at a nearby mine. Joe Hall was feeling pretty manly, perhaps because his testosterone level was boosted by the memory of Chris, so he picked a fight with one of the locals who promptly cleaned his clock. As we were standing against the wall watching the fist fight, a friend of Joe Mendiburo's who happened to be with us pulled a Smith and Wesson .357 magnum pistol out of his coat pocket and told Mike, "Nobody better mess with me." Charlie and I talked Mike into leaving real fast before someone went to shooting.

On one of our trips to the caverns' café, a bottle had been purchased, and we sat around the fire and drank it after we got back to camp. I went to bed and then Charlie showed up and drug my bed out of my teepee wanting to wrestle, which didn't seem like fun to me, but we wrestled anyway and finally went to sleep with Aubrey Valley sand in our beds as well as in our underwear.

We finished the roundup around the third week of November, and we all took a few days off and then we set about gathering what remnant cattle were left on the ranch. By the middle of December we were having trouble finding tracks or live cattle anywhere so Mike, Charlie and I slipped over to the neighbor's ranch to look for some Double O cattle. I suppose Mike called the neighbor and told him what we were going to do, but I'm not sure. Anyway, we rode around in the cedars at the foot of Cross Mountain on the north side, and we finally found two Mexican steers that belonged to Joe Mendiburo. It was the first Double O cattle we had found in several days.

The two Mexican steers were very gentle, and we could have driven them down the slope to a corral where we had left our truck and trailer in an hour, but Charlie and I were bored. "Did you ever neck two wild steers together and drive them?" Charlie asked.

"By golly, lots of times and it sure works good, too," Mike replied.

"Well, what do you do? Do you just tie their heads together with a piggin' string?"

"Yeah, it's best if you tie the biggest critter around the horns and the lighter of the two around the neck. There's little tricks you need to know to make it work right, but it sure works good; the cattle can't scatter on you as you drive 'em."

"Well, why don't you show me and Ed how to do it. We've never seen it done before." Charlie looked at me and grinned.

"Well, by golly, we got to catch 'em first." Mike shouldn't have said that because Charlie and I weren't much good for anything besides roping.

We got the two gentle steers tied down on their sides and proceeded to tie them together with a piece of nylon rope. The biggest was a brown steer with big wide horns, and we tied one end of the rope around the base of his horns. The lighter one was a dopey-acting yellow steer, and we tied the other end of the rope around his neck, and then we let the two steers up and pointed them east toward our destination. There was a road from the start of our adventure to our destination about three miles distance. On both sides of the primitive road was a cedar thicket of colossal proportions. Mike claimed that steers tied together in this fashion, about three feet of slack in between them, would drive very well even in timber, so we took to the cedar thicket instead of the road.

For four hours we wandered around like drunken sailors as we followed the two unassuming brutes and watched them fork every tree in their path. "Well. By golly, this usually works real good."

On the first of January, Joe Mendiburo's lease on the Double O Ranch was up, and he decided not to renew it. It had not rained all year, and the winter of 1980-81 proved to be one of the driest in Northern Arizona history, so Joe was tired of the Double O. Everyone on the outfit was out of a job. Charlie was offered a job at the O RO, and he took it. I was offered a job on the Babbitt Ranch north of Flagstaff, and so Charlie and I separated, but we didn't lose track of each other.

So You Want to be a
Jigger Boss

When Charlie and Susan moved back to the O RO Ranch, Charlie became the jigger boss under Pat Cain. The term "jigger boss" is somewhat of a conundrum, or at best an ambiguous position and job description. Usually a jigger would be someone who is considered to be a top hand and someone who knows the ranch well and because of that is capable of leading drives and riding point during a trail drive and other such high profile duties. Sometimes he may be a better cowboy than the wagon boss. But historically jigger boss positions, at least on Northern Arizona ranches, aren't always loaded with authority or reward. Many a jigger boss on a big Northern Arizona ranch has complained saying, "I'm nothin' but a pissin' post." One cowboy who was Frank Banks' jigger boss on the Babbitt Ranch north of Flagstaff was quoted as saying as he whipped his horse down the hind leg because the horse had tried to stop and have a bowel movement, "Poop a runnin' you sorry *^@#$%^&, that's what I gotta do!"

Around the first of December in 1982, Ray Lambert set out on the trail that goes from the Triangle N Camp on the O RO and skirts around the north side of the Mohon Mountains to the Mohon Camp, a distance of about seventeen miles. Ray had been given the job of staying at and taking care of the country around the Mohon Camp and planned on staying there through the winter or until the spring roundup started in April.

Triangle N was the camp that Coley Lyons had taken care of for over thirty years but had recently been occupied by a Texan named Waymon Vessels. Staying with Waymon at Triangle N was a younger and much greener cowboy named Rance, but Waymon was definitely the older of that pair, and the one possessing years of experience and therefore more seniority.

Ray Lambert had been deposited at Triangle N with all of the supplies he would need for a lengthy stay at Mohon, and Triangle N served as a staging point for his expedition to Mohon, and he spent one night there with Waymon and Rance. Early in the morning Ray began packing supplies on three mules, and with Waymon and Rance's help, he set out on the trail at midmorning. Ray had the three mules tied head to tail and was leading them, and Waymon and Rance brought up the rear leading Ray's three extra saddle horses.

The country that the Triangle N Camp man is responsible for lies on the east side of the Mohon Mountains, and the Mohon camp man's country is on the west side of the mountain with the dividing line being a deep rocky canyon known as Pine Canyon that flows north off the top of the mountain. There was no road into the Mohon Camp until the late 1960s but that road is a very long and rough trail that is far greater in length than the mountain trail that a horse-backer would use. The old camp house at Mohon was built in 1948, and all the lumber, cement and other material used to build it was packed in on the backs of mules. The Mohon Camp is about as isolated a place as you could find anywhere in America. The country is rough, steep and rocky, and there is no way to get in or out of there, unless you fly in a helicopter, in less than several hours of hard riding.

The trail to Mohon leaves Triangle N going north and passes by a large dirt tank known as Midway, and there the trail turns westward and rises up onto a high ridge between Midway and Pine Canyon. The three men rode along this route with Ray and his mules leading the way, and Waymon and Rance following with the horses. They topped out on the high ridge and started down into the depths of Pine Canyon and came to a place in the trail that was very steep with a dangerous slope off the right side of the trail. Here at this spot Ray got into a serious wreck. Things had been going nicely, and perhaps Ray had lowered his level of awareness. Perhaps he took the lead rope that was attached to his lead mule and dallied several times around his saddle horn making it hard to get loose. No one knows all of the details for certain, but the lead rope got jammed up tight under the tail of the horse Ray was riding, and the horse went to bucking and spinning, and he couldn't get loose from the lead rope, and the wreck reached epic proportions; all of it taking place in a most dangerous setting. In the end, Ray was thrown from the horse and went sailing downhill off of the steep and rocky incline and finally came to rest in the arms of a very large prickly pear cactus. Landing on the cactus helped cushion his fall and probably saved Ray's life.

Waymon and Rance jumped off and hobbled their horses and walked down the steep incline to where Ray was laying; he was delirious, being partially conscience, and possessed the look of a man who was seriously injured. He was bleeding out of his nose, mouth and ears and was impaled with sharp cactus spines everywhere his skin was exposed, including his head and face.

No one knows all of the details...

Some of the thorns had penetrated his coat and eventually came to rest in his body.

Waymon and Rance observed the injured man and determined that he was very near death. They went back up the trail thirty feet above and caught Ray's horse and the mules and took Ray's bedroll off of one of the mule's backs and drug it downhill and lay it on the ground next to the cactus, but they did not pick Ray up and put him on or in the bed, but instead left him laying in the middle of the prickly pear, not being sure if Ray was aware of his surroundings or not.

The two men then went back to the trail and unpacked the mules and tethered them out on the ends of their lash ropes to several big rocks along the edge of the trail. The lash ropes were between twenty and thirty feet long. Then they got all of the horses and turned around and started back to Triangle N, six miles away, leaving Ray and the mules at the scene of the accident.

Until John Irwin bought the O RO Ranch, there had never been radios or any kind of communication system installed in any of the five cow camps. Camp men like Coley Lyons would go for days and weeks with no communication with anyone. People did not check on these men on any kind of a regular basis, and no one thought anything about it. But the Irwins had installed two-way radios in the cow camps and a base unit at the Oaks and Willows.

Waymon and Rance got back to Triangle N about midafternoon, and Waymon went into the house and radioed the headquarters. Dick Jagels, the ranch manager, and Pat Cain, the wagon boss, were both gone and unavailable; so Charlie Gould, who was the next man in the chain of command was given word that he needed to get into the house where the radio was located, an urgent message was waiting for him.

"Charlie, this is Waymon at the Triangle N," the conversation began.

"Waymon, this is Charlie. Can you hear me?"

"Charlie, Ray is hurt really bad. Got bucked off going down into Pine Canyon. I think he might be dead."

"Waymon, when did he get bucked off? How long ago?"

"About three hours ago, we were helpin' him pack everything back into Mohon when his horse got rim-fired by a lead rope and threw him downhill in a really bad spot. I think he might be dead."

"Waymon, was he conscience when you last saw him?"

"Well—kinda, but kinda out of his head. He's bleedin' out of his ears and mouth—ain't makin' no sense."

"Did you leave Rance there with him?"

"No, he come back here with me; we brought the horses."

"You left him there by himself?"

"Hell, Charlie, there ain't a damn thing we can do for him. We left his bedroll there with him, but there ain't nothing we can do for him."

"Did you put him into his bed?"

"No! He's in a cactus, and he is kinda out of it, kinda delirious, so we just left his bed layin' there. There wasn't a damn thing we could do, Charlie."

"Listen to me, Waymon! Tell me exactly where Ray is."

"Well, we was just past Midway where you top out on that high ridge and start off into Pine Canyon, right where the trail gets slick and steep. His horse threw him down that steep spot just past the top, and he landed in a big cactus about thirty feet below the trail."

"Listen to me, Waymon. You guys get back over there and help him. I'm going to try and get a helicopter, but by the time it gets there, it might be dark so you need to build me a great big fire so the chopper will know where to land."

"Hell, Charlie, there ain't a damn thing we can do for him. He's dead or soon will be."

Charlie interrupted and hollered into the radio, "Waymon, you get your ass over there and try to help him and build a big fire on top of that ridge—you understand?"

"You don't need to get huffy with me, Charlie; there wasn't a darn thing we could do."

"Go back over there and try to help the man. Do something, and build a fire."

Charlie got on the ranch's only telephone, which was in John Irwin's house, and started trying to locate a helicopter that would respond to the emergency. The Arizona Department of Public Safety helicopter was unavailable, so he called the Yavapai County sheriff's office, and they said they couldn't respond until he had been turned down by three private facilities, so he called the Phoenix Baptist Hospital, and they told Charlie they would get in the air immediately. It was now close to four o'clock.

The dispatcher at Phoenix Baptist asked Charlie, "How can we find you?"

"Fly to Bagdad and go north about thirty miles, and there will be a big cone-shaped mountain sticking up all by itself. That's Mount Hope. About six miles east and a little north of there, I will have a big fire built that you'll be able to see. That's the ranch headquarters. Land there and I'll get in with you and take you to where the injured man is."

Charlie gathered up the crew consisting of several men who were staying at the headquarters, and they went out north of the shop and built a big bonfire in an open spot. From where their fire was located it was a straight shot to the top of Mount Hope six miles away.

The sun had slipped away below the western horizon when the helicopter arrived from the Phoenix Baptist Hospital. The chopper touched down, and Charlie forced his way inside quicker than the pilot or nurse approved. "Let's go, we got a long way to go and a short time to get there! Fly this thing straight west." The faint shades of daylight were growing dimmer as they flew west toward the canyon and cactus where Ray Lambert lay waiting. "I've got men waiting where we need to go, and they've got a fire built to guide us in to a landing spot," Charlie told the pilot.

From the Oaks and Willows, where Charlie got on board, to the ridge where Ray got bucked off is only thirteen miles as the crow, or helicopter, flies, but on the ground following the existing primitive road, it's about twenty-five miles and a two hour trip. In less than ten minutes the helicopter was over the spot where Ray had last been seen, but there was no fire. Through the hazy shadows of dusk, Charlie could make out the lay of the land, and he told the pilot where to land, but the pilot was reluctant. It was completely against procedure and all laws of common sense to land a big helicopter on top of a boulder strewn ridge when it was dark except for a faint lavender glow that was quickly vanishing from the horizon. Charlie was forceful, even insistent, and he talked the pilot down on top of the boulder pile.

Charlie jumped out and started running toward the spot where he thought Ray might be. As he ran down the trail, he made out the form of Ray's mules standing in the darkness, and then he tripped and fell down onto the rocks, his legs being jerked out from under him by some hidden trap. As he picked himself up out of the rocks, he realized that he had been tripped by one of the ropes that the mules were tied with. It was so dark that you couldn't see the ropes laying on the ground like hidden snares. The helicopter pilot and male nurse were unloading a gurney and medical bag out of the helicopter, and Charlie hollered to them, "You guys need to be careful, there are some mules down here, and you might trip over their lead ropes!" The two men from the hospital listened but could not imagine what this wild cowboy could be talking about.

From that spot Charlie slid downward through the slick rocks to where he could make out the dark form of something the size of a refrigerator and something pale in color that was on the ground next to it. It was the big prickly pear cactus and Ray's bedroll laying on the ground next to it.

At some point after Waymon and Rance had abandoned Ray, he had managed to crawl, with no one's help, out of the cactus and into his bedroll, and that is how Charlie found him, laying in his bed and covered up by the bed tarp and heavy blankets, being full of cactus spines and caked with blood, but alive.

As Charlie pulled back the bed tarp covering Ray's bloody head, a loud commotion erupted above Charlie and Ray about fifty feet away. As a man screamed, "AAAAHHHH," something came crashing down the hillside bouncing through the rocks. The male nurse had tripped over a mule's lead rope and dropped the gurney and medical bag he was carrying.

Ray was conscious and somewhat coherent and related to his rescuers that he had a horrible headache and felt like he had broken ribs and other broken bones. He was terribly thirsty and cold. He was surprised that Charlie was there because he had determined that it was his time to die.

The pilot, the nurse and Charlie got Ray transferred out of his bed and onto the gurney that had been flung down the mountainside, and then they made the arduous trip up the hill and then down the trail meandering through the maze of snorting pack mules and lead ropes laying across the ground like guywires. While the pilot and nurse prepared to load Ray, Charlie turned the pack mules loose knowing they would by instinct go back to the Triangle N. They strapped Ray securely in the helicopter, and then the pilot fired the machine back up and got it airborne. It was now pitch black, and they flew east toward the faint glow of the huge bonfire at the Oaks and Willows thirteen miles away.

The chopper pilot didn't bother to shut the engine off when they landed and kicked Charlie out at the O RO headquarters and almost immediately the machine was airborne again and flying straight to Phoenix with very little fuel to spare. Charlie informed the other inhabitants of the ranch headquarters of what had taken place and what little knowledge he had of Ray Lambert's true physical condition. After a short conversation he went to his home and went to bed.

He was up at 3:00 a.m. eating a quick breakfast, and then he got in a pickup and headed to Triangle N reaching that camp about 5:00 a.m. Waymon and Rance were up drinking coffee and staring blankly into space. A half empty whiskey bottle was on the table. Neither Waymon nor Rance had any knowledge of what had taken place in the late afternoon of the day before.

When Charlie walked into the Triangle N house, Waymon offered him a cup of coffee, which he accepted. "Why didn't you guys go over there and build a fire like I told you to?" Charlie asked.

"Hell, Charlie, we didn't figure there was any use. We didn't figure you'd get a helicopter anyway, and there wasn't a darn thing we could do for Ray," Waymon said.

"Well, I did get a helicopter and had to land it in the dark because you didn't build me a fire."

"You got a helicopter in there last night?" Waymon asked. Rance looked on as if he was in shock or he had seen a ghost.

"Yes, I got a helicopter, and you guys weren't there, and there was no fire."

"Is Ray dead?" Rance asked sheepishly.

"No," Charlie replied. "Ray is in the Baptist Hospital in Phoenix, and you guys are fired. As far as I'm concerned, the ROs doesn't need you."

Charlie drove back to the Oaks and Willows and sent two men back toward Midway and Pine Canyon to gather up Ray's belongings that were still scattered about the ridgeline where they had been unloaded off of Ray's pack mules.

Within a few hours both Dick Jagels, the ranch manager, and Pat Cain, the wagon boss, showed up at the ranch. They had been in town doing business on Whiskey Row, and they soon heard the details about Ray getting hurt and Charlie calling a helicopter. Details about Ray's condition began to filter back up to the ranch. He had numerous broken ribs and a broken collar bone and a severe concussion. Bruises began to surface all over his body, but his injuries, now that he was safe in a hospital, were not considered life threatening.

Dick Jagels and Pat Cain discussed Ray's accident and its aftermath with Charlie. They wondered if calling the helicopter was necessary. They expressed concern over the Irwin family's reaction to getting the bill requesting payment for the use of the helicopter.

"Look," Charlie told them, "I get a message late in the afternoon that Ray Lambert had been bucked down off the side of a mountain, and he was dying. I was told that he had blood coming out of his ears, nose and his mouth. They said that Ray wasn't making any sense. Waymon told me that in his opinion Ray wasn't going to make it. You two guys weren't here, and everyone was looking at me, wanting me to make a decision, so I called a helicopter, and if I had it to do over again, I would call a helicopter."

"No, you're right, Charlie, you're right." Dick Jagels answered apologetically. "I suppose we are just going to have to pay for it."

"Yes, you're just going to have to pay for it. I'll bet the Irwins can afford it."

"Well, I've heard that you and the boys at Triangle N aren't seeing eye to eye about what happened," Pat interjected.

"I fired both of them."

"Charlie, you can't just fire men every time things don't turn out the way you want," Pat said.

"They left Ray laying in a prickly pear cactus, didn't even help him get into his bed. I ordered them to go back and stay with him until help arrived, but they didn't do it. I told them to build me a big fire so the helicopter could land safely, but they sat around camp doing nothing, so—yeah, I fired them."

"You did your best, Charlie! You did your best. You were in a tough spot, but you can't go to firing people for no reason." Pat ended the conversation. Waymon and Rance stayed on the payroll.

At the same time the Ray Lambert incident was taking place, the JJJ Corporation was in negotiations with Victorio Land and Cattle Company, who were operating the Diamond A Ranch, to purchase 7000 mother cows that were running there north of Seligman. The cows were all crossbred cows, the majority of which were Brahman crossed, a good many of which were big tiger-striped cows, the type that were very popular in those days especially in the Southwest. The cows were purchased at a fair price across the board, considering the fact that they were not uniform in type.

The cows were sorted at the Diamond A Ranch according to breed, type and condition and sent from there to several locations. Some of them went to a ranch in California that the JJJ Corporation owned, and a large portion of the big tiger-striped Brahmas went to Phoenix where they were advertised and sold at an auction. It had been raining a lot, and Arizona was enjoying several wet years in a row and the tiger-striped cows all sold at a premium.

After all of the sorting was done, the JJJ Corporation had 1700 English-cross cows left over that they intended to bring down to the O RO Ranch. The fact that the other cows had sold so well made the 1700 English-cross cows a pretty cheap buy, making it a very successful piece of cow trading. But now they were presented with a new problem. It was storming a lot, and the roads were in horrible shape making it impossible to bring the cows down to the Oaks and Willows in trucks. Dick Jagels and Pat Cain were scratching their heads wondering what to do. Victorio Land and Cattle Company wanted the cows to be off the Diamond A, the sooner the better.

"Why don't you just trail the cows down here?" Charlie told Dick and Pat.

"Charlie, you can't just trail 1700 cows down here, that's a big bunch of cows. It's too far. It would be awful hard to do," Pat Cain said.

"It wouldn't be that big of a deal, just go right down through the Double O. It would take a few days but it could be done," Charlie argued.

"But, Charlie, Mike Landis wouldn't want us to trail a big herd like that through the Double O. You can't just go trailing a herd like that across other people's property," Dick Jagels said.

"Mike Landis would love it! He loves things that are Western and old-timey; he would think it was great. I'll guarantee it," Charlie continued to argue.

Dick and Pat looked at each other skeptically. A long pause continued as the management team weighed its options, which were almost nonexistent. Finally Dick Jagels said, "You think you could do it?"

"I know darned good and well we can do it. It's not that big a deal. We need to go talk to Mike Landis and ask his permission, but after that, it's just a matter of doing it.

Again Dick and Pat paused in deep contemplation. They looked at Charlie and then at each other and finally Pat Cain said, "Okay, Charlie, it's your deal. It's your responsibility, and you put it all together. Tell us what you need."

Charlie drove north to the Double O headquarters and visited with Mike Landis and explained the situation to him. As Charlie expected, Mike agreed to let Charlie bring the herd across the Double O Ranch and gave him permission to use the several corrals he would need to pen the herd at night. Mike was in total agreement that driving a large herd the old-fashioned way, trailing them horseback instead of using cattle trucks, was the better plan. Charlie thanked Mike and went back to the Oaks and Willows and prepared for the trail.

For a crew Pat Cain gave Charlie Billy Grossman, Marty Elmore, Lynn Beatty, and Waymon Vessels. He was also provided another man who would have a pickup to use to haul the men back and forth from Seligman where the company would buy them motel rooms to sleep in at night, and they could buy their meals at a café in town. It was now mid-December and very cold and wet, and the plan to travel back and forth from Seligman was an easy fix compared to moving a whole camp outfit around, especially because of the fact that the whole trip was planned and executed with only a day or so to prepare.

The five cowboys were hauled to the Pica Camp on the Diamond A Ranch twenty miles northwest of Seligman where they unloaded their horses and took possession of the herd of 1700 cows. From Pica they went south three miles and crossed the herd over the top of the pavement on old Route 66 and then continued south three miles to the Santa Fe Railroad.

They crossed the herd over the top of the railroad tracks and on a mile or so and put the cows in a holding pasture for the night. They kept their horses in the Double O shipping pens that were on the south side of the railroad tracks. The men only had one horse to ride, and Charlie had told them to choose a tough one because there were no plans on changing to a fresh horse until midway through the trip.

On the second day of the trail, the men took the cows to a big dirt tank with a very large corral around it known as 21. It was only a six-mile journey, but there was a considerable amount of trees and brush mixed in with the draws and ridges, all country that you wouldn't call wide open. The cowboys day-herded the cattle along, allowing them to graze as much as they wanted because they were going to be penned up without feed all night. They made the trip uneventfully but did not pen the cattle until late in the afternoon.

The second day was cold and overcast, and they pointed the herd south and a little west across what is known as the 76 Plains, named after the 76 brand, owned by the Fancher family who had grazed cattle there before the Taylor Grazing Act of 1934. Along the way Waymon Vessels began to drink from a bottle of whiskey that he had acquired while staying in Seligman the night before. By midday he was quite drunk and had ceased to be any help but instead needed to be pushed along as if he was one of the cows; but the whiskey bottle was quite large, and he drank on and began to lean over in the saddle. There were still 1700 cows in the herd but now the crew had been reduced to four men and a loose horse with a drunk on his back.

They day herded the cows across the 76 Plains allowing them to graze, and when they were close to the south end of the plains, Charlie rode way up in front of the herd to stop the leaders who were wanting to walk on. After some time being way in front of his crew, he loped back along the flank of the herd and could see only three other men. He asked the first cowboy he came to, "Where's Waymon?"

"Oh, a mile back there he stopped and hobbled his horse and went to sleep under a cedar tree."

Charlie took off in a trot and rode until he spied Waymon and his hobbled horse. He rode up and looked down at the man who was unconscious. "Waymon, get up!" Charlie hollered at him, but he didn't respond but lay asleep hugging his bottle. Charlie stepped off of his horse and unsaddled Waymon's horse and laid the saddle and bridle on the ground and lay the saddle blankets on top of Waymon and then rode south leading Waymon's horse, and when he reached the herd he turned the horse loose with the cattle, and the crew drove onward toward Black Tub.

Before reaching Black Tub and the corrals where they would pen the cattle for the night, the four cowboys had to cross all 1700 of them under Interstate 40, pointing the cows through large culverts that went under both the east and west bound lanes. They not only had to coax the herd into the culverts but then keep track of and control them once they had made it through to the south side of the big highway. This was no small feat for a four-man crew, and had Waymon stayed sober and been present to take part in the action, he would have been appreciated.

When the last cow was followed under the blacktop, the herd was pointed toward the corrals at Black Tub a mile and a half away. Pat Cain drove up pulling a gooseneck full of fresh horses about the time the cows were penned for the night. "Well, it looks like you're short a man, Charlie," Pat remarked.

"Yeah, I guess so."

"What happened? Where's Waymon?"

"Well, the last time I saw him he was asleep under a cedar tree back there on the edge of the 76 Plains. He was hugging a whiskey bottle."

"And you just rode off and left him?"

"Yeah, I guess so."

"Well, you can't just go off and leave a man stranded out under a cedar tree." Pat acted astonished.

Charlie thought about Ray Lambert laying bleeding out of his ears in the midst of a prickly pear cactus. "Yeah you can, and I just did."

"Well, we gotta go get him, show me where he is."

The two men got in Pat's pickup and started back to where Waymon had been laying asleep. It took them a half hour to get there, and finally they found him sitting up under the same tree. It was almost sundown and was very cold with a wind blowing. Waymon's bottle was empty, and he sat on the shady side of the tree not having the wits to soak up what little sunlight was left. His face was making a sucking gesture, as if he had been eating lemons, and his eyes were enlarged and bugging out of his head resembling a lemur staring into a flashlight. His body was convulsing in uncontrollable shaking and shivering. His countenance was as a man who had resolved to face death in a frozen meat locker with no handle on the inside of the door. Pat and Charlie scooped him and his saddle up and deposited them into the pickup, and they drove back to Black Tub in silence.

At Black Tub, Pat and Charlie got out of the truck. "So what do you want to do with him, Charlie?" Pat inquired.

"I'm done with him, don't want him around." Charlie replied. So Pat left Charlie and his crew of three men with a fresh horse apiece and took Waymon back to the Oaks and Willows.

The next morning the four men turned the cows out of the corral and pointed them south toward Pickett, six miles to the south. For most of that stretch they followed a big open draw that was bordered by cedar-filled ridges on either side, but in some areas they had to go through places where cedars grew close enough to limit visibility. By now the cows were quite trail-broke and gentle, but their sheer numbers kept the four cowboys on their toes, and there was no riding along holding hands and singing cowboy songs. They allowed the cows to graze as they walked along, and a grazing herd will scatter, although slowly, more than a herd that is walking as if on a mission to reach its destination. The men had their hands full.

They held the cattle overnight at Pickett and then walked them on to Anvil Rock the next night, and then finally on the sixth day of the trail drive, the herd filed through a gate on the north end of the Grant and entered the O RO Ranch. Charlie and his men watered the cows out at Franks Tank in the North Steer Pasture and pointed them onto the slope on the south side of the big dirt tank and turned them loose. There was lots of grass, and they were full of water so Charlie figured they would not scatter too far during the night.

That night the men slept at the Oaks and Willows feeling good about getting the cows into the O RO boundary fence. The following day, the seventh day of trailing, they moved the herd farther south and turned it loose at the Muddy Windmill, west of the headquarters, and from there the cows were trailed in smaller bunches and scattered all over the big ranch; some of them eventually reaching Francis Creek, another four days drive to the southwest.

In that day and time, the O RO remuda was still basking in the limelight of a reputation for being the best cow horses in Arizona. That heritage of good horses was started on the huge O RO Ranch in Sonora, Mexico, that Colonel William C. Greene built up beginning before 1900. The Colonel would buy stallions that could be purchased in the United States and take them south to Sonora for his ranch where hundreds of Steeldust-type horses were bred.

When John Irwin and the JJJ Corporation bought the O RO Ranch in Yavapai County, the remuda was made up of the foundation stock descending from the Sonoran O RO horses. One of the most prolific and influential bloodlines was perpetuated by a stallion named Hijo Del Rey, nicknamed Rastus. Rastus died at the Oaks and Willows not long after the Irwins bought the ranch; he was in his late twenties. His sire was a stallion named El Rey who was an own son of Peter McCue who was born in 1895 and died in 1923. Peter McCue is considered to be one of the great foundation sires of the Quarter Horse breed, and so, incredibly, cowboys at the O RO Ranch were riding geldings at the O RO Ranch as late as the 1990s that were great grandchildren of a foundation stallion born before 1900. El Rey was one of the last colts sired by Peter McCue, and Hijo Del Rey was one of the last sons of El Rey.

In one of the last colt crops sired by Rastus was a filly whose name has been forgotten who was the dam of a dozen horse colts in a row. These twelve geldings were the cream of the O RO remuda, one of which was a dark brown gelding named Hershey who was a famous cutting horse broke and ridden by Mike McFarland. Hershey was sired by Medicine Man, a black O RO stallion sired by Lightning Bars. But it didn't matter what stallion the Rastus mare was bred to, the resulting offspring rose to the top. After a string of twelve impressive sons, the Rastus mare had a filly who would become known as Stitches, and she, like her mother, was a producer of great geldings.

The trailing of 1700 cows from Pica to Muddy Windmill, west of the Oaks and Willows, was a feat that had not been reproduced in Northern Arizona by anyone in Charlie Gould's generation. Dick Jagels and Pat Cain, both of whom were much older than Charlie, would have never attempted it by themselves. The fact that Charlie accomplished it with only three men helping him made it even more impressive. Charlie had gone to great pains making sure Mike Landis had no bad feelings about the big herd crossing the Double O Ranch. Actually, Mike thought it was a great idea and gave Charlie his blessing from start to finish. Trailing the big herd across the country instead of trucking them was "Western" so Mike heartily approved. Charlie was grateful and felt like the O RO Ranch owed Mike something in return.

Charlie knew the O RO remuda better than anyone with the exception, perhaps, of Coley Lyons who was an expert on the history of the O RO horses. For many years when the Greenes owned the outfit, Coley had been responsible for registering the colts with the American Quarter Horse Association, and that had been a duty that Coley took immense pride in. So Charlie, with a little advice from Coley, picked out what he considered to be the very best yearling stud colt the ranch owned. It was a brown colt out of Stitches which also made him a nephew to Hershey and a dozen other of the very best horses that had ever been on the O RO Ranch. Charlie told Pat Cain and Dick Jagels what he was doing, and they approved, so he loaded the colt in a trailer and hauled it up to the Double O headquarters and presented him as a gift to Mike Landis.

For several years Mike Landis had been raising horses for the Double O Ranch, which was under new ownership since 1981. Mike had purchased a bunch of mustang mares that Dave Ericsson had caught in Southern California at a place known as China Lake. The China Lake mustangs were line bred and members of a very small gene pool because of the isolated area where they ran, and they were famous for their small bodies, big heads, and propensity to be totally incorrigible. They had the same intellectual traits as inbred cats possessing six toes and two heads and no hair. The China Lake mares were the start of Mike Landis's Double O horse program, which in fact became legendary in the 1980s and '90s.

When Charlie unloaded the brown O RO colt and presented him to Mike, he was beaming with pride. The two cowboys had a good visit. Charlie had known Mike a long time, and Mike had worked for Charlie's dad almost fifty years before. They hashed over old times and talked about cowboys and horses from the North and the South. Mike smoked Bull Durham cigarettes, and they drank several pots of coffee, and then it was time to go.

"I thought that brown colt might make you a stud for your mare band, Mike. He's related to the best horses the R0s ever raised," Charlie said as he was walking out the door.

"Well, by golly, I hadn't thought of that. I'll have to take a good look at him. He oughta make a good pony one way or the other." The two men shook hands, and Charlie climbed into his truck and headed back to the O RO Ranch.

Not long after that, Mike and a cowboy who worked for him roped the brown O RO colt around the front feet and jerked him down on his side and tied him. With a very sharp knife, Mike castrated him; and then in the spring, he turned a China Lake mustang stud weighing 850 pounds into the Double O mare band, and as a result the China Lake gene pool escaped contamination from the likes of Peter McCue, Lightning Bars and Hijo Del Rey.

In 1981 and '82, Charlie, Susan and Cole and Sam lived at the Oaks and Willows. Coley Lyons had moved from the Triangle N Camp where he had lived for thirty some years, batching the whole time and wearing out a large pile of horse and mule shoes every year. Coley had gotten old and felt like he couldn't take care of his country as good as he had been, and he had too much pride to think of himself as second rate so he humbled himself and moved into a room in the headquarters bunkhouse. He had some privacy which was appreciated and a necessity after living in a remote cow camp most of his life. He kept three of his favorite horses and prowled through several of the pastures around headquarters, the north and south steer pastures and the heifer pasture.

Coley had used bulldog tapaderos on his saddle for as long as he could remember, but he became weak, and his saddle became too heavy to throw onto a horse's back, so he took the taps off to decrease the weight. That worked for awhile, and then he began taking his flank cinch off when he threw his saddle on to take a few ounces off, and then when he got the saddle on, he would put the flank cinch back on. Eventually Coley rode his horses with only one cinch, and he quit packing a rope, all in an effort to keep the weight of his saddle down to a minimum. He would not let anyone help him saddle his horse. Coley let Charlie shoe his horses, and as time went on, the two men became very close friends.

Coley had worked for the Three Vs before he went to work for Charlie Greene on the O RO. He had a shoebox full of old Kodak photographs taken on the Vs in the old days, the '30s. They weren't quality photographs, but they did show numerous old-time cowboys and life on the famous cow outfit. They were valuable because photos of the Vs are very rare. Charlie spent hours going though the photos, and as Coley told him who and what was in each photo, Charlie would label them. Coley offered to give Charlie all of the pictures, but he postponed accepting them. "No," Charlie said, "I want them, but I want you to keep them for now.

"Okay, but I'm giving them to you."

"I understand. I want them, but you keep them for now."

Coley owned a pair of Ed Blanchard spurs that had been custom made for him many years before. The spurs were famous. They had Chihuahua shanks and big snowflake-shaped rowels cut out of solid brass. They were silver mounted with the suits of cards—spades, clubs, hearts and diamonds—mounted on the heel bands. He owned one old grazing bit that he used on all of his horses. He gave the spurs and bridle to Charlie, but like the pictures, Charlie told him to keep them until a later date.

Charlie and Susan and the boys moved to the Sandstone Camp early in 1983, and so they didn't see Coley quite as often but still kept tabs on him. One day Susan drove to the headquarters and was going to make it a point to check on Coley. She knocked on the door to his room but he didn't reply. She looked out in the barn and horse corral and walked all around the headquarters. No one was around, or so it seemed. Finally she knocked on the bathroom door in the bunkhouse but got no response, but she felt something was on the other side of the door. She pushed the door open and there Coley was laying on the cold cement floor.

Coley was conscious but trembling with chills and fever, obviously suffering from double pneumonia or something similar. He told her to leave him alone. He said he wanted to die there. He did not want to be helped. Thinking that she was doing the right thing, Susan drove to the "mansion" several miles away and called for help, and when help arrived an hour or more later, Coley was hauled into Prescott.

The wagon crew was camped out in the middle of the ranch branding calves, but the word spread and the men heard that Coley was sick and in the hospital. They worked on, and several days went by with no word; and then one night Pat Cain, the wagon boss, went home to headquarters for the night. When he returned at four in the morning, Charlie and Cole Moorhouse and several more men were up drinking coffee. After visiting awhile about the work they were going to do that day, Charlie asked Pat, "How's Coley? Have you heard anything?"

"Oh, he's dead." Pat said it as if a horse had died, or maybe an old dog.

They had a service for him in Prescott at an old funeral home south of the plaza several blocks. The funeral wasn't well attended. Coley didn't have a lot of close friends. He had never been the life of the party and he wasn't charismatic. He was a loner, a bachelor; he was glue. He had worked his butt off for a lifetime packing salt, sewing up prolapsed cows, moving cows with muddy legs and muzzles away from dried up dirt tanks; and when everything was falling apart, he held the outfit together. He was very opinionated but for the most part silent. The people in management didn't ask him for his opinions, and didn't bother reading his obituary.

Charlie, Susan, Cole and Sam, along with Charlie's parents, John and Margaret, walked to the funeral home from the Western Bar on Whiskey Row. Cole Moorhouse was with them and several old cowboys who knew Coley's worth. No member of Coley's family, all of whom lived in Texas, was present at the funeral as far as anyone knew. There was only a nephew and an old sister still living. Coley hadn't been to Texas in so long no one remembered when it might have been.

Someone who didn't think Coley was important enough to attend his funeral, thought his stuff was valuable enough to lay hold of. The Blanchard spurs and old bridle and all of his pictures disappeared.

Helping the Goswicks

Charlie went through some hard times and found himself single and living alone in 1986. He needed some place to be and a way to make a living, and George Goswick, the old patriarch of the Goswick family, offered Charlie a small house to live in near the Goswick Ranch headquarters on the banks of Big Bug Creek between Mayer and Dewey, and on the north slope of the Bradshaw Mountains in Yavapai County.

The Goswicks were old-timers in Arizona and had owned that particular ranch since 1928. They were descendants of Lowland Scots who in the Old Country three and four hundred years ago had been famous for their skills as horsemen and their ability to pursue and kill wolves with the use of hounds. Hunting has been a Goswick family tradition for centuries.

The Goswicks who landed in America fought their way through Appalachia to Kentucky, pausing for a while, and then moved on to Missouri. Then as Arizona was being settled, they migrated to central Arizona and camped at the confluence of Tonto Creek and the Salt River. They always had dogs, and when they first settled in Arizona, a great deal of time was spent in the pursuit of stock-killing bears as well as lions. In the pioneer days when lion and bear hunters were common, the Goswicks were known as some of the best.

The Goswicks had a little cow work to offer Charlie as well as the old house to live in that lay on the banks of Big Bug Creek; the whole setting being a boulder pile in a brush thicket with few flat spots. Charlie went to advertising for broncs to break at $350 a month with Charlie supplying the feed and horseshoes, and he had plenty of people bringing him colts to ride. But there were really no horse-breaking facilities at his camp with the exception of a good number of big trees to tie horses up to; so that's how he broke them. He would tie an unbroke colt to a tree and from there he would sack them out, saddle them, and get on and ride them without the luxury of a corral of any kind, just get on 'em and go. There was lots of timber, thick brush and boulders in every direction, and from camp a man couldn't ride far without reaching the steep incline of a mountain. But he rode and broke lots of them under those conditions, somewhere around sixty head in a couple years. He also helped the Goswicks in their cow work as well as other ranchers in the area.

Because the Goswick Ranch was extremely steep mountainous country and covered with heavy brush thickets and trees, the Goswicks rode lots of mules. Charlie started to break a big sorrel mule for George Goswick. The mule had some age on him and was stout. About the time Charlie was going to mount the big mule for the first time, George Goswick rode up and observed the big mule saddled and tied to a big tree by the edge of Big Bug Creek, which was a boulder pile of epic proportions. "What the heck are you going to do, Charlie?" George asked.

"Well, I'm fixin' on gettin' on your mule."

"Right there? Under that tree?"

"I don't have a better place."

George rolled himself a Prince Albert cigarette and surveyed the situation. Charlie stepped on the mule, and the wreck commenced much to George's amusement, but Charlie and the mule survived.

The next day no one was around, and the mule got Charlie under a tree and Sunday-punched him and bucked him off. He caught the mule and stepped on him again, and as they began to cross over the bottom of the boulder-strewn creek bottom, the mule bucked Charlie off again, and he landed head first onto a huge boulder. The one-point landing split Charlie's scalp wide open and he began to bleed profusely. He was addled and

...George rode up and observed the big mule saddled and tied to a big tree...

staggered up to the Goswicks' barn a quarter mile away. George, Mark and Brian were there when Charlie walked up acting funny with his hat setting on his head in a crooked fashion.

"What the hell happened to you?" George asked.

"Oh, that sorrel mule bucked me off." Charlie took his hat off, and a cup full of coagulated blood fell out onto the ground in a lump.

"We need to take you to the doctor," the three Goswicks said in unison.

"No, I ain't goin' to the doctor, but you might help me catch that mule."

They helped Charlie round up the mule and then went down and observed the boulder that Charlie had landed on. They christened it the Charlie Gould Rock, and the name and the rock are still there.

Charlie rode the mule for a day or so with no trouble, and then on about the fifth ride, he stepped on the big mule, and after going a ways, he started up a mountain trail; and after traveling upwards a short distance, the mule spooked at a big rock that was laying in the middle of the trail, and he whirled and stampeded down the country and stopped under the tree where he had been tied for a week. Regardless at what Charlie did to urge the mule away from the tree, he would go nowhere. No amount of whipping, spurring or pleading did any good. The mule would only wring his tail and stomp his feet against the ground, but would go nowhere.

Charlie took his rope and tied one end of it around the mule's throatlatch and tied it tight with a bowline knot. He then took the rope and threaded it through both rings on his snaffle bit and then threw the rope over a very stout limb of a tree on the edge of the creek. While sitting on the mule's back, he pulled the rope tighter and tighter until there was no slack at all. The mule had to lift his chin upward to get any relief from the tight rope that Charlie had tied hard and fast to the tree limb. He stepped off of the mule and walked away leaving him saddled and hanging from the tree. It was about ten o'clock in the morning when Charlie walked away from the mule. He then went about his business and spent the rest of the day riding several other colts that he had tied to numerous trees around his camp. Along in the middle of the day, George Goswick rode by and observed the mule hanging with his tiptoes barely reaching the ground. "What are you doin' to my mule, Charlie?"

"Teachin' him to hate that tree," Charlie replied.

George rolled himself a cigarette and lit it and blew Prince Albert smoke sideways out of his lips. "I'll be darned, let me know how that works," George said and he rode off shaking his head and laughing.

A half hour before sundown, Charlie went down to the tree and stepped on the sorrel mule and reached up and cut the rope around the mule's neck, and the big beast took off in a dead run seeming to be very happy to go anywhere as long as he wasn't near that certain tree. Charlie got the mule broke and the Goswicks kept him until he died.

While Charlie was living on Big Bug Creek, the Goswicks sold their ranch, but the new owners didn't buy the cows so the Goswicks and a few friends spent most of a winter gathering the outfit. The gentle cattle were not hard to gather and that part of the roundup didn't take long, but gathering the remnant took a few months to accomplish. Charlie helped George, his son Rink, and grandsons Mark and Brian on these cow hunts. Other friends and neighbors also helped including Scott Dieringer, Jim Marler, Steve Hampton and Tom Johnson.

Because the Goswicks were lion hunters, they always left camp with some hound dogs. Scott Dieringer was also a hunter and was accustomed to cowboying with hounds. The hounds would hit a lion track and take off following it but would also go to the head of a wild cow or bull and bite and bark and help hold cattle up. The Goswicks rode mules most of the time and were always packing firearms; most of their friends had a gun of some kind when they were part of the Goswick crew. One day someone who didn't understand the lifestyle or what the men were about observed the Goswick crew, including Charlie Gould, and commented, "What exactly are you guys doing? You've got all these mean looking dogs, and you've all got guns and ropes tied all over your saddles, You look like a bunch of outlaws or maybe a lynching party or something."

George held his Prince Albert cigarette between his thumb and finger and answered dryly, "Well, you see, with these dogs and ropes and guns, we are ready for anything. Whatever we start chasin' with these dogs will either get shot or roped. Don't really matter to us, we're always ready for whatever happens." That was about as long a statement as George Goswick ever made about anything to anybody.

That part of the Bradshaw Mountains is very thick with brush and trees as well as very steep. One day George and Brian and Charlie jumped a small bunch of cattle that ran like race horses, and the cattle were soon out of sight. The men trailed them for a while, and it seemed to Charlie that catching up to them was hopeless. George simply rode along following tracks and gazing off at various landmarks saying almost nothing. Finally Charlie could stand it no longer. "George aren't you worried we can't find them?"

"Oh, hell, Charlie, cattle don't have wings! They can't fly, they gotta leave tracks, we'll find 'em." George paused and rolled a Prince Albert cigarette and struck a wooden match against the leather on his chap leg. They rode on at George's pace. Before sundown they had the cattle caught and tied up.

Charlie observed George act the same way toward several lions they were chasing. He knew every trail and mountain pass for fifty miles or farther. They would be chasing a lion who seemed to be uncatchable. George would stop and gaze around and point at some landmark off on the horizon and say, "I'll bet that son of a gun is headed toward that pass over there." They would follow the dogs and tracks, and more often than not the lion would take them on the course George had predicted.

George acquired a brown horse from Charlie's old friend Dewey Brown, and he gave the horse to Charlie. They called the horse Bomber, and when Charlie started riding him, he was a little cranky to ride but Charlie really liked him. George, Brian and Charlie jumped a small bunch of cattle, three or four cows running with four maverick bulls a year to three years old. The bulls soon separated themselves from the cows, and Charlie was in the spot to pursue them, which he did. The bulls ran down into Nemo Basin, finally reaching a spot that wasn't completely vertical, and Charlie roped all three bulls, one at a time, and tied them down all within a quarter mile. George and Brian finally showed up trailing the cows and found Charlie sitting next to Bomber whom he had unsaddled so he could cool off. George spied a bull laying on his side with his hind legs tied. "Well, you got one of 'em, huh, Charlie," George said.

"Yeah, and there's one over there, and another over there, and the other one is tied to a tree down the canyon a couple hundred yards."

George said nothing but grinned, and he held the bunch of cows while Charlie and Brian tied the other bulls to trees where they would spend the night and then be led out the next day.

The day before Christmas in 1987, Charlie was with the Goswick crew gathering cattle up in the mountains at a place known as Little Wolf Creek, and a day or two before that, Charlie had roped a bull weighing about a thousand pounds and tied him to a tree. The tree that the bull was tied to was located on the edge of a very steep and treacherous slope, being close to vertical, and not a place where anyone with good sense would lead a wild bull down off of. George gave Charlie and Brian Goswick orders to ride up on top of the high ridge where the bull was tied and untie him and turn him loose and point him downhill. "I don't want you boys leading that bull down that hillside, it's way too dangerous; you'll get killed. Just go up and untie him and try to point him downhill, and we'll catch him again when he hits the bottom." Waiting at the bottom of the steep incline with George were his son Rink, his other grandson Mark, and Jim Marler who lived on a neighboring ranch. They all watched Charlie and Brian creep their way up the hillside to where the bull was tied up.

Charlie and Sharon, his old sweetheart from grade school in Tempe, had just got married, and Sharon had given Charlie a bright red wild rag for Christmas, and he was wearing it tied around his neck. He and Brian reached the tree where the bull was tied, and they heeled him and pulled him down, and Charlie took off his new red scarf and tied it around the bull's horns like a Christmas decoration. The two cowboys turned the bull loose and got him pointed down off the mountainside. The bull crashed downward through the brush and trees, and George and his crew could hear limbs breaking and rocks rolling and then they heard the sound of Charlie's voice hollering, "Merry Christmas you sorry ^*@#$%^!'"

"What the hell is that goofy son of a gun doing now?" Jim Marler remarked when he heard Charlie's Christmas greeting, and then the bull came bursting out into the open wearing a bright red wild rag. Jim got lucky and was the one who got to rope the bull.

Early one morning George Goswick and Charlie set out together with plans to attend the Yavapai County Cattlegrowers annual calf sale held at the Hays Ranch near Peeples Valley. The calf sale was a big annual event that had been taking place every year for over fifty years and was as much a social event for ranchers and cowboys as it was a venue to sell livestock. There was going to be a lot of ranch people there to visit with so George and Charlie were looking forward to the day's events. On their way through Kirkland, the pair got sidetracked when they stopped at the Kirkland Bar to have a drink. They ended up staying at the bar all day, and some of the people who had been at the calf sale started showing up late in the afternoon.

George challenged Charlie to a game of pool, and they agreed to put up their cowboy hats as a wager, and Charlie lost and had to give his black hat to George who laid it neatly on a table. And then another cowboy in the bar bet George that he could beat him in a game of pool, and George beat him and laid his hat on the table. After an hour or so, every cowboy in the joint was bareheaded, and George had a stack of cowboy hats on the table, but he ran out of victims so he sat down and gazed at all his friends who were hatless, and he laughed and said, "Well, you boys can all have your hats back, I think I'll go home." He got up and left the bar and got in his pickup and headed toward Prescott without Charlie who had decided to stay at the bar for awhile.

Charlie got home by himself, and the next morning he saw George, "What time did you get home last night, George? You left Kirkland pretty early. Where did you spend the night?"

"I stopped by the fairgrounds and could see lights in the posse building, so I stopped to see what was happening. They were having a big poker game, so I sat down to play with them. Doc Fletcher was there and Matt Butitta, the Savionis, Jim Giler and Del Hubbard. We had a good time."

"Did you win any money?" Charlie asked.

"Well, only five thousand."

Kelly Butler is a good Texas cowboy who migrated to Arizona in the early '80s and worked on some ranches including the O RO where he and Charlie became good friends. While Charlie was living at the Goswick place on Big Bug Creek, Kelly came to see Charlie, and he brought along his new bride. They had been married several days.

It was on a weekend, and Charlie was in the mood to relax and enjoy the company of his good friend, so they were sitting around the house telling old cowboy stories. And drinking whiskey.

Charlie owned a particularly large and beautiful Siamese tomcat who was a good mouser. The cat's downside was the fact that he possessed a very obnoxious personality, and he had a loud tomcat voice. "Meow, meow, meeoow." The cat continuously interrupted the two cowboys as they swapped stories.

Charlie possessed two very comfortable old arm chairs with cushions stuffed with ingredients that modern chairs don't have: things that make a chair comfortable like the arms of a good dancer or the embrace of a lover. And draped over the comfortable cushions were several layers of old Navajo saddle blankets. It was a setting that only a cowboy could create. It was comfortable like the interior of Charlie Russell's studio. Off on the far side of the room sat Kelly's bride in a straight back chair smiling and marveling at the wit and humor breaking forth out of her newly won Prince Charming's mouth. The two conversing cowboys could see the sparkle in the young bride's eyes.

Presently, as Charlie was in the middle of one of his favorite stories, the Siamese tom jumped into Kelly's lap and curled himself up in a catlike position and went to purring. And then, about the time Charlie got to the punch line, the cat cut loose with a loud, "Meeooow, meeooowww."

"Darn, Charlie, why do you keep this old cat around?" Kelly asked.

"Well, he's a good mouser."

"Golly, this son of a gun hasn't shut up since I got here!"

"Meeow, Meeoow."

Charlie talked on and then a light came on behind Kelly's eyes. Charlie could tell his friend was on to something.

Kelly laid hold of the cat with his fists, firmly enough the cat could not easily escape but soft enough to not create alarm in the cat's brain. "Let's cut this son of a gun, Charlie." Kelly whispered.

"Oh leave my cat alone."

"No, Charlie, let's cut him. I'll hold him."

"You can't hold that cat while I cut him. No way!"

Kelly had become excited. He was known as a man who thrived on excitement. "No, Charlie, I got him. Let's cut him."

"Well, if we cut him we better stuff him down a boot top."

"No, Charlie, I got him, I got him. He cain't get away!"

The bride smiled at her new husband.

"Okay," Charlie said, "but you better get ahold of him or he'll scratch your eyes out."

"I got him, Charlie, I got him!"

Kelly's grip tightened around the cat's abdomen and he shoved him down between his legs and squeezed. The cat's head was upstream and his tail was near Kelly's knees. The sharp blade of Charlie's Case pocketknife had been unfolded, and Charlie approached the cat's backside with his knees on the floor in front of Kelly's legs.

"Hold on, Kelly." Charlie commanded.

"I got him, Charlie! I got him!"

The blonde giggled from across the room.

Charlie grabbed the cat's tail with a hold similar to the grasp of a professional bareback rider's grip on his rawhide riggin' handle. His fingers squeezed the Siamese scrotum and the razor sharp blade slashed into the interior of the sac exposing what was inside. "Meeeooow, Yeeeeoowwwo, RRarrhh."

The cat's entire body stiffened as if he had been plugged into a light socket.

"YYAAAHH, CHARLIE, HE'S GOT ME! HE'S GOT ME!" Kelly jumped up screaming in mortal agony, and as he jumped out of the chair, his knees knocked Charlie backward and rolled him across the floor. The sharp pocket knife flew through the air and landed in the kitchen. The bride jumped out of her chair staring at her husband who began twisting in a circle.

Kelly spun faster and faster. "CHARLIE, HE'S GOT ME! GET HIM, CHARLIE! GET HIM! AAAHHHAAGGGH!"

"Charlie, get him off of my husband," the girl screamed.

Charlie rose up off of the floor as the cat's body sailed past.

"GET HIM, CHARLIE, GET HIM, AAAAGGGHH!"

The cat's rotating body came flying toward him, and Charlie reached out and grabbed the cat's hind legs and held on. The tearing sound of 16-ounce denim mixed with the vibrations of shredded flesh went through the chaotic room as the cat hit the screen door running, not to be seen for several weeks.

The room fell silent as Kelly staggered toward the bathroom. His wife followed her bridegroom holding onto his shoulders to steady him as he struggled along. The two newlyweds entered the bathroom and shut the door behind them. "AAAHH, Charlie, you gotta help me!" She had opened the door and was screaming and waving her arms for Charlie to come look.

Charlie picked himself up off of the floor and walked to the door and peeked inside the small room, and there sat Kelly on the commode with the lid down. His head was leaning backwards over the water tank and his face had turned to the texture and color of wax paper. The muscles in his jaw and neck were twitching uncontrollably and his hands were shaking. Shock had obviously set in.

Charlie's gaze went downward from Kelly's face toward the location of the wound, and he quickly turned his gaze away thinking, "The honeymoon is over."

He walked toward the back door of the house as Kelly's wife followed pleading with him, "Charlie, we've got to do something."

"No, you've got to do something," Charlie answered, and he went outside to feed his horses.

The Goswicks leased some pasture northwest of Prescott at the Rancho Moana, and when it came time to haul the cattle back to the Goswick Ranch on Big Bug Creek, Charlie helped them. They were hauling them in gooseneck trailers and made multiple trips back and forth.

As they drove down the Contreras Road on the west side of Granite Mountain, they drove by a huge man as he walked out from under a big culvert situated where the road crossed a creek. The man was packing a sack of stuff and had the appearance of a homeless vagrant, what people used to call a hobo. He was very dirty. "Wow, look at that crusty looking character!" Charlie remarked to George as they drove on pulling a load of George's cattle. George made no comment.

Several hours later they came driving back down the same road on their way to get another load of cattle, and they drove past the big hobo again. "Man alive, that's a scary looking son of a gun." Charlie remarked as George blew Prince Albert smoke out the pickup window.

They drove on up the road ten miles and loaded another gooseneck load of Goswick cattle that had been penned at the corrals at Rancho Moana and then started out toward home pulling the heavy load. A mile or two south of where they had seen the bum earlier, they spied him again standing by the roadside holding his bag of plunder. He was so dirty the dust on his hair and skin shone from reflecting against the sun. He had long hair and was unshaven and stood about six foot six inches tall and was very husky.

"Damn, that's a scary looking dude! How would you like to meet up with him in a dark alley, George?" As the question came out of Charlie's lips, George stopped the pickup. They were out in the middle of nowhere several miles from the nearest ranch or residence of any kind. George had said nothing. He dug down into his Levis' pocket and pulled out some paper money that was all wadded up, and he handed all of it to Charlie and said, "Here, go back there and give this money to that guy."

"Are you serious?"

"Yeah, I'm serious. Walk back there and give him the money."

"Why?"

"Because I told you to."

Charlie took the wadded up bills from George's hand and opened the pickup door and walked toward the giant who stood by the roadside fifty yards behind the truck. As he walked along Charlie counted the money, and it totaled fifty dollars: a twenty, a ten, a couple fives and some one dollar bills. It was all that was in George's pocket. Charlie approached big man and handed him the money while the giant eyed him warily, and then he walked back to the truck and got in, and he and George drove off toward Prescott.

"Why did you give the bum that money?" Charlie asked.

"Charlie, we don't know anything about that guy, but he has a story. Just like you have a story, and I have a story. The fellow needs some help and sometimes we ought to help people. You need to start learnin' stuff like that, Charlie."

Cowboy Heaven

In 1988 Charlie and Sharon moved to the AY Ranch which is near Cleator, Arizona. Cleator—which amounts to nothing more than several old clapboard buildings, one of which is a saloon—is a sister city to Bumble Bee, Cordes, and Crown King. All of these metropolises are remnants of old Arizona mining days when men bored holes all over the Bradshaw Mountains in search of precious metals. As the crow flies, Cleator is about twenty miles southeast of Prescott, thirteen miles south of Mayer, and sixty miles northeast of Wickenburg; but to put all of that into perspective, you should consider the fact that to travel on horseback from Cleator to any of those destinations would tire a very tough horse out. From Wickenburg to Cleator in a straight line would take several days of very hard riding, that is, of course, if you went over the top of the Bradshaws, otherwise you should add several more days of travel time.

Historically the Bradshaw Mountains and Yavapai County played an important role in Arizona's story. It was here, traveling up the Hassayampa River in 1863 on the south and west side of the mountain range, that Joseph Walker and his crew of explorers first discovered gold; and the area was inundated with fortune seekers and with them the first cowmen. Some of the best cowboys Arizona ever raised gathered cattle on the slopes of these mountains. The Goswicks, the Champies, the Lanns, the Langes, and the Clines being among them, along with a host of others. Because of the extreme ruggedness of the terrain and the elusiveness of the cattle, the style with which these men worked was akin to the methods used by the stockmen on the San Carlos and White River reservations where Charlie lived as a young boy. Even if they had never met, men like John Gould, Mack Hughes, Pat Hughes, Wheeler and Duane Reece, Giles and George Goswick, Lawton Champie, John Cline, Burl and Alvin Lann, Walt Lange, Whistle Mills, Travis Heckel, Ed and Clifford Koontz, and the Bowman brothers, Everett, Ed and Skeet; all knew of each other and they spoke the same language. They were comfortable on steep mountain slopes and brush thickets where cattle are difficult to handle. These men and these places were Charlie Gould's heritage.

The AY Ranch in size is not very big and is almost all made up of federal lease land. The facilities there—house, corrals, etc.—were better than what he had used on the banks of Big Bug Creek. He had a corral to ride colts in if he wanted, instead of being forced to ride them off of a tree limb.

Charlie continued to take in colts to break for anyone who would haul them to him, and Sharon became good at hazing for him when he would go outside in open country for the first time, which was usually within the first couple rides. He wasn't much for staying in a corral very long but wanted a bronc to have room to go and move out in open country.

Jim Marler, whom Charlie had known since the night Chili Beach had deliberately stabbed himself in his wooden leg, was running the Triangle M Ranch north of the AY, and the man who owned the Triangle M also owned the AY. There was a good number of bronco cattle on the AY, and Jim made a deal with Charlie to gather them.

The AY pasture land ran in a basin along Crazy Basin Creek and Poland Creek and rose steeply upward to the west reaching the heights of Crown King and near a notorious cow hideout known as Hells Hole. It was very steep and rugged country with almost no limit to the places and trails where cattle could escape.

Charlie had always owned a dog or two, but over the several years previous to moving to the AY, he had accumulated several more. His good friends, the Goswicks, Scott Dieringer, Bobby

Sharon was a constant help to Charlie.

Reeves and Clay Tyree were dog men, using them to hunt lions as well as cattle, and they had all given or traded Charlie some dogs.

With his dogs and Sharon as a crew, he ascended up into the eastern slopes of the Bradshaws. The dogs were not like so many that people brag about claiming there isn't a cow anywhere that can escape from them, but in reality the dogs they brag about and the cattle they are chasing are both out of control. Charlie had a "handle" on his dogs, and if he turned them loose, they would pursue and "get aholt" of a wild cow or bull with a vengeance; but he could also call them off and make them get back when he wanted. He and Sharon would ride and find a bunch of cattle, and Charlie would let the dogs bark and work them over for awhile; and more often than not, they would eventually be able to trail the cattle down off the mountainside and get them into a corral without roping them.

As time went on Charlie became more and more appreciative of Sharon's help, and she became a good right hand or girl-Friday, but at first situations would arise that she didn't know how to handle. She was a good rider and experienced with horses, but extreme rough country and wild cattle were foreign to her. On one of their first outings, they got several head of cattle held up, and among them was a mature bull with very sharp horns and an outlaw attitude. Charlie could tell the bull wasn't going to stay with the rest of the cattle for very long, but Sharon didn't have the experience to read him. The bull looked outward from his circle of running mates as the dogs surrounded them barking, but the bull had reached the point where the dogs weren't bothering him; instead it was the two humans ahorseback that he didn't like. "Sharon you need to watch that bull!" The bull had blood in his eyes, and he stared menacingly at Sharon who was closer to him than she should have been. The bull charged and Charlie hollered, "Sharon you better get the hell outa the way!" She moved, but almost too late, and the bull let her live another day; but he took off down the mountainside with several dogs pestering him as he went. Charlie nicknamed Sharon GTHOTW, abbreviation for Get the Hell Outa The Way.

Charlie and Sharon lived at the AY for several years all the while breaking horses, day-working for ranches in the area and, when time permitted, continuing his pursuit of the bronco cattle, all of which he eventually gathered.

In 1993 Charlie and Sharon went to work for Mike Oden who hired Charlie to run the 7 UP Ranch west of Prescott. The 7 UP had belonged to Mike's grandfather, Sam McElhaney, who bought the outfit in the late 1940s. Sam McElhaney had started and operated the McElhaney feed yard near Wellton, Arizona, which became one of the largest cattle feeding operations in the world. The 7 UP Ranch was actually made up of several individual ranches that had touched each other being combined to make one large ranch. These were the 7 UP, the Triangle HC, Johnny Lovelace's ranch in the bottom of Burro Creek, and Hardy and Bertha Schell's homestead in Conger Canyon, a tributary of Burro Creek.

About half of the ranch ran up on top and out of Burro Creek on its east side, and the west side of the ranch was below the canyon rim and took in a series of deep canyons and ridges that flowed off westward into the deep Burro Creek Canyon.

These canyons and ridges were called the White Hills by old-timers who were familiar with the area. Most of those old-timers were cowboys: men like Whistle Mills, Travis Heckel, Wallace Harper, and Ed Koontz. In modern times very few people know the White Hills and the head of Burro Creek because of locked gates and bad roads; there is very little access into the area. It is very remote and extremely rough country with elevation changes in some places of over a thousand feet in less than a mile. On the east end of the 7 UP Ranch, the elevation is several hundred feet above six thousand, and sixteen miles to the west at John Lovelace's old ranch, the elevation is about 3500.

If you ride upstream from the Lovelace Place seven miles, you come to the south end of the Grant and the O RO Ranch. Near that boundary line between the 7 UP Ranch and the O RO, Burro Creek Canyon comes to an abrupt halt at the foot of cliffs hundreds of feet high, and upstream from those cliffs, the Burro Creek drainage is of a gentler nature, everything flowing downhill from north to south. About half of the huge O RO Ranch drains down into Burro Creek Canyon and the ranch that Mike Oden now owned and where Charlie and Sharon moved and became responsible for. The cow camp that Charlie and Sharon moved into was called the Halfway House, its name being derived from the fact that it was about halfway between the Seven Up headquarters to the east and the Lovelace Place to the west. About a mile west of Halfway House, you come to the rim of the White Hills and Burro Creek proper, and from that spot and others like it, you can see for miles out across the canyon and ridges and eventually all the way to the west side of Burro Creek and the far southwest corner of the O RO and places like Francis Creek, Burro Mesa, Goodwin Mesa on the old Bogle Ranch. The Aquarius Mountains that rise up between Francis Creek and the Big Sandy River can also be seen way off forty miles, and if you turn north, you can see the Mohon Mountains and Mount Hope that rises up in the center of the Grant. From Halfway House it's only fifteen miles straight north to the Sandstone Camp on the O RO where Charlie had lived with his family, and about six miles northeast of that sits the Oaks and Willows. The neighboring ranch to the south of the 7 UP and Halfway House was the Yolo Ranch where Charlie had worked with his brother Skeet twenty-six years before. As far as Charlie was concerned, the 7 UP Ranch was as close to cowboy heaven as you could get.

When Charlie and Sharon moved to Halfway House, there were cattle scattered all over the ranch from one end to the other. Traditionally the cowherd would be turned out down into the White Hills and Burro Creek late in the fall after the calves had been weaned, but for whatever reason that practice had not been implemented in several years. At the same time that Charlie took the job to take care of the 7 UP, Mike Oden was in the process of buying a very nice ranch north of Williams that bordered Babbitts' W Triangle Ranch on its south side, and the details of taking possession of that new ranch and cattle was consuming all of Mike's time, so he told Charlie, "It's all yours." And he went north to his new ranch. Charlie was unfamiliar with the 7 UP and didn't know where the cattle were, but he went to work weaning calves sorting and moving cows and figuring things out for himself. Sharon, his youngest son, Sam, who was in high school, and Jimminell Cook who had been raised at Halfway House were his crew; and they got the work done.

When he and his crew got all of the cows throwed off into the canyon, Charlie started spending a lot of his time camped down in the bottom at the old Lovelace Place. From Halfway House to the Lovelace camp is about eleven miles and a drop of at least 2000 feet. Wallace Harper, who had worked for Sam McElhaney for twenty years, had used an ancient D6 dozer to build a road down to the Lovelace Place. You could get a four-wheel drive pickup or jeep down there, but the eleven mile trip would take several hours. In places the roads that Wallace built with the old dozer are cut through rim rocks and sheer cliffs hundreds of feet high and are truly an engineering marvel, especially when you consider the primitive equipment he used. The dozer had a cable lift instead of hydraulics and was World War II vintage.

One of the trails that Wallace Harper built with the old cable lift D6 dozer was particularly steep and treacherous and became known as Harps Boulevard. When you left Halfway House on the main trail going off into Burro Creek and the Lovelace cabin you went by a dam and dirt tank known as McElhaney Tank. Building that dam was one of the first things that Sam McElhaney did when he bought the outfit in 1948, and it was a valuable and lasting improvement to the ranch. McElhaney tank was about four miles west of Halfway House and probably 500 foot lower in elevation.

The main road that Harp built went by the dam on its north face and continued west for a quarter mile or so and then tuned left and fell off into a deep canyon that drained more or less west and dropped a thousand feet or more before it reached the bottom of Burro Creek. About the place where you make that left turn, there was a fork in the road giving you the choice to go right and down another road into a canyon that also fell off into Burro Creek. This canyon drained perhaps a little in a northwesterly direction. In between the two trails, or roads, although they hardly deserve the description of being a road, there is a very long and narrow mesa that runs several miles going west and finally ending in an impressive promontory overlooking the creek below, a distance of a thousand feet or more. It was this right hand fork that became known as Harps Boulevard.

In historical records there has been only one trip made by a human in a motorized vehicle down to the bottom of the canyon traveling down Harps Boulevard, and it was made by a well-known and well-liked character that we will call John.

John showed up at Halfway House with a friend who was a resident of Prescott by the name of Dan. John explained that they wished to drive off into the canyon to do some quail hunting. Charlie really liked John and figured if he wanted to risk life and limb, besides a good truck, and drive off into the abyss that was fine with him. John was known to be risky and wild and a true outdoorsman, and he had been in the canyon many times.

So John and Dan drove west, and just below McElhaney dam they turned right. No one knows for sure, but there could have been some liquor in the truck. As soon as you turn right and tip off the rim rock, the road bed slopes to at least 50 degrees and for about one hundred yards it is nothing but crushed malpai boulders the size of a cantaloupe one on top of another being pushed there by Harp's old bulldozer. It has the consistency of a loose shale bed but finally the bottom becomes more stable, but it is not less scary. To the left the face of the cliff the road had been cut into is almost vertical. Even riding down Harps Boulevard horseback, one wonders if a falling rock might crush you at any moment. And then after a half mile or so, there is a switchback turn that is as tight as 20 degrees, and the road is never wider than ten feet and continues to fall very sharply in elevation. Somehow the two quail hunters reached the bottom and found they had a spot about fifteen-foot square to turn around in.

It was in the bottom that John heard a snapping sound, and then suddenly the steering of his Chevy truck became very difficult and the brakes became hard and ineffective. The two men stopped momentarily for refreshments and then popped the hood to have a look. Upon inspection they found that the metal bracket that held the alternator secured in place had broken and because of that no tension could be put on the fan belt that besides turning the alternator also turned the power steering pump and other important engine components.

They looked upward past the towering cliffs and calculated that they were at least eight miles from Halfway and about 1750 feet lower in elevation. It was very hot and they were not young men anymore. They broke for more refreshments and surveyed the situation, and John came up with a plan.

He took a hatchet that he always carried and cut a good stout limb off of a young cedar tree growing nearby, and he and Dan wedged one end of the limb under the engine block and then put the other end across one side of the alternator, and by leverage they applied enough pressure to make the fan belts tight. John fired the engine up and tested everything. The alternator seemed to be charging, and the power steering worked, and he had good brake pressure.

They decided that under the circumstances they needed to get out of the canyon. They would hunt quail some other time. They had some more refreshments.

Beings it was John's truck he needed to drive, so that left only one option for Dan. He would have to ride on top of the engine applying pressure with his tree limb to keep the belt tight. Also, because the engine hood would have to be up, he would have to holler directions to John whose vision would be severely hampered.

"GO TO THE RIGHT," Dan would scream over the roar of the engine and the rolling rocks below. "GO LEFT! GO LEFT! DAMN IT, I SAID GO LEFT!"

Occasionally the truck would bounce, and Dan's head would be slammed up into the hood. The threat of being wounded by the spinning engine fan was always present not to mention touching the red hot radiator.

They bounced and creeped upward, and when they reached the switchback, John had to gun the engine and run the right front tire up onto the bank hoping that when it fell backward and off it would cause the front of the truck to slide to the left. This tricky maneuver had to be repeated numerous times before the corner was negotiated, and each time, Dan's head was slammed into the hood while he screamed, "Whoa, that's enough." And then past that, they had to crawl upward through the shale at 50 degrees, until finally they reached McElhaney dam. They were still four miles of very rocky road from Halfway House.

The two men never did shoot any quail on that trip, but no one else ever drove a pickup to the bottom of Harps Boulevard.

Once in a great while, Charlie and Sharon would take a large load of supplies down the main road in a vehicle, but usually they would pack what they needed down into the canyon on pack mules. Charlie would go down and stay there for long periods of time packing salt, fixing fence, clearing trails through the brush with a saw and hatchet, or just prowling around.

The ranch owned a good-sized pasture out on top of the west side of the canyon on what is known as Burro Mesa. A quarter of a mile from the Lovelace camp, there was a trail built by Wallace Harper going straight up the sheer cliff of the canyon's west wall and ending on the floor of the mesa above. The trail is less than a mile in length but is a 1000-foot change in elevation. In the fall cattle would need to be trailed up that trail to spend the winter in that pasture, and then in the spring they would be brought down and trailed east and out on top to spend the summer with all the rest of the cattle that wintered in the canyon.

Sharon was a constant help to Charlie because a great deal of the time they had the whole outfit to themselves, and it was more than one man could handle. She would bring Charlie supplies when he was staying at the Lovelace cabin, more often than not leading pack mules down the eleven mile trail with groceries, dog food, salt or tools and anything else that would be needed. Sometimes she would stay there with him for a few days, but usually there was too much to take care of at Halfway House to be absent for long.

The first winter Charlie was there, he began noticing maverick cattle scattered up and down the canyon bottom, mostly young stuff from weaner size to yearlings and two-year-olds. For the most part the cattle weren't real wild, just ignorant about the ways of men because nobody had ever tried to gather them. Charlie would ride and when he found a bunch of cattle that wanted to run off, which usually included some unbranded stuff, he would turn his dogs loose on them and let the dogs hold them up barking and pestering them. He would allow this to go on long enough that they would get used to his presence as he sat on his horse a short distance away. Many times this would happen in a spot that was so steep or choked with boulders and brush that it would have been impossible for a man to run horseback and go around and hold a bunch of cattle up, so the dogs were a big help to him.

Charlie spent the winter playing with bunches of cattle up and down the bottom of Burro Creek and its many tributaries and the ridges and mesas that lay between them. He did not run and chase the cattle including the unbranded ones. He did not put up with a dog that wouldn't mind, and he could call them off anytime he wanted to. In the spring he and Sharon gathered Burro Mesa and Burro Creek by themselves, trailing all of the cattle out on top on the east side of the White Hills and through a drift fence along the rim of the top country. In all they gathered well over 600 head of mature cows plus seventy or eighty head of mavericks, some of them two-year-olds and several older. They never roped anything to get it out of the canyon bottom and waited to brand the mavericks until they were branding calves in a corral that was up and out of the canyon itself. For the first time in a number of years, the canyon had no cattle left in its depths that would be seed for unbranded and therefore unaccounted for assets.

There was lion sign everywhere, and nobody had been hunting in the area for years with the exception of an occasional hunter who might make a pass on the outskirts of the ranch. The bottom of Burro Creek, the White Hills, and the upper Burro Creek drainage, which included most of the O RO Ranch to the north and west, was prime mountain lion habitat; and the lions had been living unmolested for a number of years. As a result the calf crop on the 7 UP Ranch had been hovering at 45 percent for a long time. Charlie was in a place to use the experience he had gained while working with George Goswick, Scott Dieringer, Bobby Reeves and others; and he and his dogs went to work, and they were successful. The second year Charlie and Sharon lived at Halfway House, the calf crop rose to 85 percent and was never lower than that the entire time they lived there.

Charlie loved being in the canyon and spent long periods of time there, which was evident when three years in a row on Christmas Eve or Christmas Day he followed his dogs who were in hot pursuit of what he thought was a mountain lion. Each time the chase started at a different place but ended up near a place known as Cooksies Garden. He would chase, climb and drag himself up through the brush and boulders and end up finding the hounds barking at a coon who had ran up a tree. "What a way to celebrate Christmas," he would tell himself. It didn't matter, he wasn't even mad at the dogs for chasing coons, he was happy. He wondered if it was the same coon but never figured that out.

When Mike Oden got himself established at the Freeman Ranch north of Williams, he asked Charlie to run the roundups there also, and for seven years Charlie lived at the 7 UP and took care of that ranch with Sharon's help; but in the spring and fall, he would go north of Williams and boss the roundups at the Freeman also. He would put a big crew together and get alot of work done fast, but because he always had good hands helping him, the work went easy. Among the cowboys who worked for him on these roundups were Clay Tyree, Gary Halford, Mark and Brian Goswick, Cole Moorhouse, Jimmy Rogers, Steve Rafters, Stan and Dewey Brown, Pat Prosser, Bud Watson, Don Hambrick, Jim Marler, Mike McFarland and others. They could and would get it all done in five days in the spring and eight in the fall. The rest of the time, he stayed at Halfway House and the 7 UP, and many of the same men would help him during the cattle works there.

Charlie continued to collect good dogs where he could get them, and at one time or another, all of his lion hunting friends gave him one. One of the best dogs he ever had came off the Cross U Ranch which is between the 7 UP and Prescott. He was there at the Cross U helping, and a cowboy there had a Shepherd cross dog that he declared was worthless. The dog, according to the man, was uncontrollable and a trouble causer. He asked Charlie to do him a favor and eliminate the dog. "He's no good, Charlie, dispose of him for me."

Charlie looked at the dog and thought that, yes, he probably was no account. The first strike against him was he was some kind of Shepherd mix, a true mongrel. Dogs like that don't usually have a good enough nose to be lion dogs. The second strike against him was the fact that he was uncontrollable, and Charlie really disliked dogs that wouldn't mind. Besides that, he didn't look like he was mean or tough enough to be a good holdup dog for bronco cattle, and a dog needed a good nose for that, too, if they were going to be real good. "Oh, I don't know, partner, I don't like shootin' dogs. Anyway, he's your dog, you deal with it."

"No, Charlie, do me a favor and take him to the pound or something, I don't want to deal with it."

Charlie looked at the cowboy as he was talking and then felt something pressing on the top of his foot. He looked down, and the dog had put one of his paws on the top of Charlie's instep, and he stared up into Charlie's eyes. "Go way, I don't want to pet you, you no good pot licker," Charlie said. The dog cocked his head sideways and tapped Charlie's foot with his right front paw. Oh crap, Charlie thought to himself. "Okay, how about just giving me the dog?"

"Alright, Charlie, he's yours."

The next day Charlie went prowling and took the dog with him. They got on a fresh lion track, and the dog took off trailing the lion like a seasoned hound. The second day they found a track and caught the lion, which made Charlie think that the dog was either really good or very lucky. As time went on, the former description proved to be a correct one. Charlie named him Gambler.

Gambler and Charlie bonded in a fairytale kind of way. The dog obviously loved and was loyal to Charlie, while Charlie appreciated and became more trusting in the dog. The bottom line was the dog just loved to work. He was not dependent on the pack but would disappear from sight, and then when Charlie was about to think the dog had gone AWOL chasing rabbits or deer, he would hear him baying at some cattle he had held up in a brush thicket or at a lion that he had run up a tree.

One time Charlie was hunting with one of America's most respected guides and lion hunters, Charlie Leeder, who lives in southern Utah. They were hunting on a high mountain on the Utah-Nevada border and were trying to find a lion for a client who had given Charlie Leeder a large sum of money for his services. They weren't having much luck and had ridden with the client in tow over a large expanse of rugged terrain. Charlie Leeder had made several subtle remarks about Gambler whom he considered to be nothing but a mediocre cow dog. Gambler had separated himself from the pack and had climbed high up on a ridge and was walking along the horizon by himself. "What the hell is your dog doing now, Charlie?" Charlie Leeder asked as he gazed upwards in disgust.

"I don't know but he's on to something."

"Yeah, I bet." Charlie Leeder answered gazing toward the dog a quarter mile above them. The client groaned in pain from the long hours in the saddle and twisted his face in an expression of extreme boredom and disappointment.

Suddenly Gambler went to howling and running and disappeared up into a large rock outcropping. "Your dog's got himself a rabbit." Charlie Leeder rode on following a trail though the rocks, and his dogs remained close by.

Charlie Gould left the trail and rode upward toward the mountain crest and the sound of Gambler's barking, and when he reached the summit he found Gambler barking at a very large tom lion who was staring downward from his perch on a large granite boulder. "Hey, Charlie, you need to bring your partner and come up here," Charlie hollered down the mountainside.

"I don't want to come all the way up there on a wild goose chase."

"No, you need to come up here, my dog's got you a very big lion.

There was no more negative comments made by anyone about Charlie's "cow dog."

Charlie continued to break horses for anyone who would pay him to do so. Down through the years the K4 Ranch was his best and most faithful customer, and he liked their horses. He broke a buckskin colt that was raised on the K4 that his friend Mark Goswick ended up buying that became one of the best head horses in Arizona. He broke another buckskin colt that ended up packing Brad Smith to a world title.

Chuck Sheppard was the head of the K4 horse program fifty years. Chuck was a world champion rodeo cowboy himself and his daughter Linda was married to John Kieckefer who owned the K4 Ranch. Chuck and the entire Kieckefer family were good to Charlie and Sharon. One time Chuck gave Charlie a dark grulla gelding to break that was very broncy acting. He was nervous and had some buck in him and acted like he might kick you if you weren't watching. The horse was a handful and very hard to start, but Charlie kept working with him and got where he loved him. He was quick on his feet and would watch a cow.

Charlie had broke several other K4 horses at the same time he broke the grulla who he named Punch, and when it was time to take them all back and get paid, he told Chuck Sheppard, "You owe me a lot of money for starting all of these colts. Why don't you give me that grulla, and you won't owe me anything for breaking the others?"

"No," Chuck replied, "we will need him on the ranch. We'll just pay you the money we owe you."

"No, just give me the grulla, because you're not going to like him anyway."

"Why not?"

"Because he's not gentle and, besides, I know how to get along with him."

"Well, we will take him home and ride him." Chuck had been a top RCA saddle bronc rider, but he was now very old, in his mid-seventies.

"No, Chuck," Charlie said, "you can't ride him."

"Well, I'll get Buster to ride him."

"Buster can't and won't ride him, Chuck. Trade him to me."

"No, Charlie, we won't trade."

"Okay, when you take him to the ranch, you better give him to Bruce Johnson because he's the only one out there that can ride him." Bruce Johnson was a good Texas cowboy who had the foreman's job at the ranch.

They did give Punch to Bruce who rode him and liked him, but a year later Bruce quit and moved back to Texas, and the horse went unridden and eventually ran into a fence, broke a leg, and had to be put down.

Mike Oden was very good to Charlie and Sharon, and the years at the 7 UP were good ones in spite of the hard work and adversity that arose in many forms, like the time Charlie and Sharon were both staying down in the canyon at the Lovelace Place and the Hualapai tigers went on the warpath. The nasty insects were always there to some degree, but on this one trip they showed up in great numbers. Sharon rigged a primitive mosquito net that hung from the ceiling and covered her bed, but Charlie laughed at her and rolled his bed out on the floor. The next morning Charlie was swelled up like the Michelin tire boy seen in advertisements, but instead of being white he was beet red, and his hide felt like a crew of men were holding him down and applying red hot branding irons all over his body. He quit laughing at Sharon's mosquito net.

Another time Sharon was helping Charlie fix the water gap in the bottom of Burro Creek between the 7 UP and the old Bob White Ranch that lay downstream. They had stretched the fence back across the creek bed and were about to put the finishing touches on the job, which was tying the fence down to some rocks at intervals in the creek bottom. Sharon proceeded to pick up a well-shaped rock and carry it over to where Charlie was working when she realized she had picked up a rattlesnake along with the rock, and the snake was a foot from her face and staring at her when she saw it. It took Charlie awhile to calm her down even after she quit crying.

Sharon made many trips packing groceries and other supplies from Halfway House to the Lovelace Place so Charlie could stay busy tending to the cattle, packing salt, and chasing mountain lions. She had several very good gentle horses to ride and a good, gentle pack mule plus a burro that was gentle and good to pack. She was quite attached to the burro.

One evening when they were both camped at Halfway, Charlie came in late, just before dark, after a long ride. He would hang morrals full of grain on all the horses and mules every evening. That night as he hung the morrals on all the mules and horses, he and Sharon both noticed Sharon's pack burro was missing. "It doesn't matter, he'll be in tomorrow night. He's just out there grazin' somewhere," Charlie assured Sharon. The next night the burro was missing again, so Charlie and Sharon saddled two horses and went looking for him. They couldn't find him anywhere and were about to give up when Charlie noticed something that looked different, and after stopping and gazing at a hillside for a moment, he realized that a very large pine tree was missing, and then he saw that the tree had fallen completely over and was laying flat on the ground. He and Sharon rode over to look at the tree and marvel at what would make a healthy tree collapse, and there they saw Sharon's burro. The tree had fallen and landed perfectly aligned with the donkey's spine; all you could see under the wreckage was two of the burro's legs sticking out on one side of the tree, and the other two legs laying flat out on the opposite side of the tree trunk. Nothing else was visible. The burro was quite dead.

In the late summer of 2000, Charlie and Sharon had moved from Halfway House to the 7 UP headquarters, but nothing had changed about the operation besides the change in residence with the exception that the 7 UP had a telephone. Late one evening the phone rang, and when Charlie answered he could hear Mike Oden on the other end, "Charlie, why don't you come into town tomorrow and rope with me? They are having a roping in Chino Valley, and we could rope together."

"No thanks, I've got stuff to do here."

"No, come on into town. I want to rope with you."

"Well thanks for askin', but I am really busy; Sharon and I are gettin' the cows bunched up because it's not long til we need to wean. I'm busy."

"Charlie, come on into town! I really want to see you. I want to talk to you and we can rope together."

Charlie loaded up and hauled his favorite horse and drove off down the mountain and met Mike at the roping arena in Chino Valley. There were lots of Charlie's friends there including Mike. He and Mike ended up winning one of the ropings, and they had a great time.

After roping most of the day and visiting numerous other people, Mike Oden suggested they go sit down in a shady spot off to the side of the arena. They sat down, and Mike handed Charlie a cold beer, and they made small talk for a few minutes. Then, out of the blue, Mike looked at Charlie and said, "Charlie, I sold the ranch."

"Oh really? What ranch?"

Mike took a drink of Coors Light and looked at Charlie and said, "Your ranch."

Charlie laughed and said, "My ranch? I don't have a ranch. What are you talkin' about?"

"I sold the 7 UP."

"You did what?"

"I sold the 7 UP. The deal closed today."

Within several months Charlie and Sharon were gone, having moved on to other pastures; as far as Charlie was concerned, there were none greener, at least to his eyes. There were a lot of places flatter with fewer mountain lions, fewer scorpions and Hualapai tigers, and places that could run more cattle; but as the saying goes, beauty is in the eye of the beholder. Charlie liked and understood that old canyon.

Getting Baptized

"Well, what do we have here? Fightin' cocks or roosters?" A big rough looking man commented as Charlie Gould and Larry Leist walked through the front door of the bar in Las Vegas, Nevada. The two cowboys had their boots shot-gunned, with Levis stuffed down into the boot tops, and their black cowboy hats were shaped in the Southwestern style in spite of the fact they were headed north to the buckaroo country of Elko County. The man's remarks about "fightin' cocks or roosters" sparked a ruckus that got the two cowboys thrown out of the place. But not before their knuckles were skinned up a little. It was 1972 and the two young men were in their prime living the dream. Their lives would be intertwined for decades to come, and the ruckus in the Las Vegas cantina would be one of many for both.

At nineteen Charlie was already a legend for being wild. He rode bucking horses and roped wild cows and could keep up with any cowboy crew that existed. Larry was a legend himself, a noted bronc rider and cowpuncher but also a veteran sniper who had served in Viet Nam where he became the leader of a platoon that took part in some very bloody action. He had spent sometime in the ring boxing with professionals. Some half-drunk smart aleck in a Las Vegas bar didn't scare either one of them. Not even a little bit.

Charlie had some close calls. He rolled a car and totaled it, walking away without a scratch. He stepped out of the back of a pickup doing 65 mph, fifteen miles west of Seligman on Route 66, just because his cowboy hat had blown off. He got the hat back. He accidently dropped a .30.30 Winchester and it went off, and the bullet ripped into two boxes of ammunition setting off multiple explosions. He lost a thumb and took alot of shrapnel in his chest as a result of that one.

Larry Leist had changed directions and became a Christian. He had even went so far as to become the pastor of a church in Seligman, and while Charlie and Sharon were working for Mike Oden at the 7 UP Ranch, Larry had baptized Sharon in a water trough in a horse corral. A water trough with clean water. "What about you, Charlie, you want me to baptize you?"

"No, I'm not ready."

Time went on and Charlie fought the call to bow his knee to God. He felt no animosity toward Christian people, and many of his friends had become professing Christians, but he was hesitant or downright resistant to taking on that identity.

He, like most of his friends, had always drunk some beer or whiskey on occasion, but he never had the reputation of having a drinking problem. He began to drink whiskey in earnest. To most people whiskey has a mellowing effect. To Charlie it was a motivator; he burned it like high octane gasoline. It made him feel like working and he liked it.

In the year 2002, Larry Leist was managing the Boquillas Ranch at Seligman, and he offered Charlie the wagon boss job and Charlie accepted. And then soon after that, Larry announced he was going to quit his position and move on to a better opportunity, so now Charlie was going to have to work for a new manager, a concept he didn't exactly relish. He inquired about whom in particular that person might be, and when he found out who it was, he was of the opinion that it would not be a good fit. The new manager had put out the word that he didn't like Arizona cowpunchers, tied ropes, rubber on saddle horns, or taco shell hats. So instead of waiting around to find out if that was right, Charlie quit the outfit.

He and Sharon had a camp trailer and a sheepherder's wagon that he had acquired plus a wall tent and alot of camping supplies,

and a friend on the 7s Ranch offered to let them camp at a place called Bishop, northeast of Seligman fifteen miles. They set up their camp there, and Charlie started calling around the country and looking for new employment. He was disgusted with the lack of job opportunities for good cowboys. He felt tired and empty.

Charlie struggled and fought the call of God that he was hearing, but then while living at the Bishop place, he bowed his knee to God and put his faith in Christ. He and Sharon started driving into Seligman and attending Larry's church, and one Sunday Charlie told his old friend, "I want to get baptized."

"Okay, we can do it today if you want," Larry replied.

"Well, I want to go out to Bishop and get baptized there."

"Go out to Bishop, why do you want to go out there?"

"I want to be baptized out in the country, out in the wide open spaces. Not in town." Charlie continued.

"Where are you going to be baptized there?" Larry questioned him. "In the Bishop Dirt Tank? Man, it's awful low, isn't it? That's going to be awfully dirty. We can use a clean trough we keep here at the church, with clean water, it'll be nice. That dirt tank is going to be filthy."

"I don't care, I want to be baptized out there. I don't care how dirty it is, that's where I want it done." Charlie insisted.

"Okay, if that's what you want, but it will be awful dirty, and we've got clean water right here."

By the time Charlie and Larry's conversation was over, everyone that had been in church that day knew about it. A bunch of the congregation loaded up and followed Larry and Charlie's vehicles out to Charlie's camp, which was about a twenty mile drive. People brought hamburgers and hot dogs and chips to have a cookout.

When they arrived at Charlie and Sharon's camp, Larry Leist changed into some work clothes and suggested to Charlie that he should do the same, but Charlie declined. "I'm going to wear what I've got on." He had on new Wranglers that had a crease ironed down the front, good handmade cowboy boots that he left on his feet, and a pressed white shirt.

Everyone walked down to the banks of the dirt stock tank to watch Charlie Gould's baptism. Arizona was in the middle of an extremely dry year and the Bishop Dirt Tank was very low. The water was the color of brown chocolate mixed with green slime. It had leeches in it, and cow manure and moss and was continually being stirred by cattle that walked out to drink; and while they drank, they defecated and urinated in the soupy, filthy water.

Larry gritted his teeth as he walked out into the slime wearing old blue jeans and a tee shirt followed by his friend Charlie Gould in expensive boots, clean pants, and an immaculate white shirt. Charlie was smiling.

"Charlie, have you put your faith in Jesus Christ to be your savior?"

"I have."

"Okay, I baptize you in the name of the Father, the Son, and the Holy Ghost." And Larry pushed Charlie Gould down into the muck deep enough that no one present could see any part of him. And then Larry lifted Charlie up and out of the filthy water, and they walked to the shore. Everyone present later testified that Larry Leist had green slime, mud and bugs all over him when he walked out of the water, but Charlie Gould's Wranglers were blue, and the crease was still running down the middle of the front and back of the legs, and his white shirt looked crisp and was white as snow.

Sometime after his baptism, Charlie started thinking about his alcohol consumption. No one had ever accused him of being a drunk or a slacker. Larry Leist nor any other preacher had ordered him to quit drinking. He had received no instructions from anyone. He took a tally of his liquor supply and found a total of six and a half gallons of whiskey in his camp, and a great deal of it was expensive whiskey. He decided he would quit drinking it. He didn't deny its existence and wasn't necessarily ashamed of owning it or of having consumed large quantities of it, he just wasn't going to drink anymore of it. He started to throw it away but then thought that seemed stupid. Instead he kept it, and slowly over a period of months, he gave it away to people who might like it.

To Charlie Gould drinking or not drinking wasn't the issue. It wasn't what went in that mattered, it was what came out of you that counted. He contemplated about the fact that all people may not kneel, but they will all die.

Not long after that, Charlie was asked to give his testimony at a church service held at the Cowpunchers' Reunion and Rodeo held in Williams ever year. He walked up to the stage and someone handed him a microphone. He looked around and recognized everyone there, probably three hundred people. He faltered momentarily and then said. "Well, they wanted me to give my testimony. The truth is I don't have all the answers! Shoot, I don't even know what the questions are. But I can tell you this, if you put your trust in Jesus, it will go a lot better for you. At least it has for me." Having said those few words, he walked down off of the stage.

On the Banks of the Owyhee

In the spring of 2014, a Nevada buckaroo whose name is Wally Blossom had a horse roundup on the Duck Valley Indian Reservation, more commonly known as the Owyhee Indian Reservation, north of Elko, Nevada. Wally, who is a well-known cowboy in those parts, is also a rodeo stock contractor and has a substantial horse program on the reservation where he raises and runs his large herd of horses. Wally prefers doing things the traditional way, the buckaroo way, or perhaps the cowboy way depending on where you are from, but the long and short of it is, when he brands his horses or castrates them, he gathers himself a good crew and ropes them. There are no chutes, dart guns with tranquilizers, or bottles of Rompun or Dormosedan; instead, a crew of men wearing hats of different shapes show up to help. The hats may vary in style, but the people who Wally asks to help him all have one thing in common: They have a passion for roping horses, and the ropes they use are usually long, sometimes made out of rawhide, and their saddlehorns are never wrapped with rubber. Besides Wally, men like his son Myles and Nathan Kelly Jr., Will Knight and even Marshall Smith will be there.

The big Petan Ranch, also known as the YP, runs adjacent to the Owyhee Reservation for many miles, and the YP cow boss, Greg Snow, is a regular at Wally's horse roundups; and he usually brings some of the YP crew.

That spring Charlie and Sharon Gould had just moved into a camp on the YP a few miles west of the Petan headquarters and a short distance from the Owyhee River. The Idaho border was only six miles away.

Greg invited Charlie to go along and take part in Wally Blossom's horse works that was going to last a couple days. There was about a dozen men on the crew, some of them being Indians and some of them not. Everyone was riding a slick fork saddle and using silver bits and conchos and Monel stirrups that flashed in the sun as a herd of wild acting horses of every color were run into a large corral.

To start things off, about ten head were cut out of the big bunch of over a hundred, although no one was counting, and put into a smaller corral. When branding irons were hot, Wally motioned for several of the cowboys to get it on one. A wild acting colt of about three years was cut away from the other nine, and a man on a fast horse jumped in behind him and took up the chase. There was room for the horses to run and the action to be fast, but the horseman in pursuit threw his line after a short sprint at a high speed and pulled the slack of his rope up tight around the loose horse's throatlatch and dallied on his saddle horn wrapped in mule hide. The three-year-old was stopped and windmilled to the horseman's right side, and then smoothly a second man riding off to the right of the newly lassoed colt swung his reata, and with great precision took aim at the colt's jumping front legs, and he caught them in midair. He took his "dally jueltas" around his mule-hide-wrapped guadalajara saddle horn, and things came tight. Smoke was seen drifting upward off of the mule hide, and about the time the colt began to tip sideways, the man who had the colt roped around the neck let two feet of his twine run around his slick horn, and the colt was busted flat on his side. As soon as the horse was laid down, two more riders quickly got their ropes around the colt's hind feet, and they both dallied up and held their ropes tight keeping the three-year-old completely immobile.

The horse, who had been subdued and laid down, was branded and whatever else Wally felt that he should deal with. Everyone was smiling. This is what these boys wearing chinks and flat hats do for fun, and they are very good at it.

The necking and forefooting of horses went on for awhile, and the expertise with which the horses were caught and handled was impressive, even to Charlie who took a back seat as far as roping went, not wanting to conduct himself like a know-it-all from Arizona. He helped on the ground running branding irons or taking ropes off of horses' necks and helped with the sorting while horseback. Finally Wally Blossom said, "Charlie—you want to show us buckaroos how you Arizona boys rope horses?"

"Yeah, sure, I like to rope."

A big stud had been held back, perhaps by accident, perhaps intentionally, Charlie couldn't say for sure, but he knew the eyes of Elko County were watching as the big horse ran down the fence going right to left, and when he was running flat out, a buckaroo with a long and fast rope reached out and roped the horse around the throatlatch. The rope stretched and cut burn marks into the buckaroo's mule-hide-wrapped horn as the good horse roper brought the horse around in an arc to his left and off the fence. The big horse was squealing and growling through his

...Charlie took dead aim at the horse's right knee...

choked esophagus as he jumped, striking into space with his front feet and lunging forward. Charlie moved his horse into position and as the mad horse fought his way past him going left to right, Charlie took aim at the horse's right knee and cast his twine, and it floated though the atmosphere for twenty feet, and then the top of the loop hit the front of the horse's legs, and then the bottom broke underneath the striking hooves and curled upwards and behind the legs and then shrank in size as Charlie held the slack up high in his right hand, and numerous coils of long rope in his left along with his rawhide reins and romal. He dallied on mule hide and a post horn and smoke rose passing through his hands, and when things got really tight, the buckaroo with the flat hat and the neck rope let several feet of his rope run, and the horse laid down on his side like it was meant to be—nice and smooth.

"Hey, the man from Arizona can dally!" Someone hollered. Someone else commented rather loudly, "Ahh—we thought you was one of those cowpunchers." Everyone laughed and Charlie Gould smiled but inside he was relieved that he had passed his initiation because that's what it all was, but by executing a perfect catch in front of some of the northwest's best hands, he has been accepted and he can relax. He can even miss a loop once in awhile because there have been some miscalculations and bad loops thrown by everyone there, but it was important to accept the challenge and come out the winner. Everyone had fun and the roping continued. There was no inner tube or tied ropes or taco-shelled hats, none of which would bother Charlie, but he knows this is the buckaroos' turf and to survive here you have to play by the rules, and he needs the job. Besides, he likes these guys, they can call theirselves buckaroos if they want to, but they are pretty handy.

Half of the crew of twelve men are part of Greg Snow's Petan Ranch crew. Greg Snow himself is widely respected among those who pack reatas and dallying on a slick horn is a religion. On two different occasions, Greg has competed and won first at the famous Californios Big Loop contest, which was one of the best traditional and fancy long rope exhibitions ever held anywhere.

The first time Greg won the Californio Big Loop, it was held in Red Bluff, California, and he was teamed up with Frank

Dominquez and Dave Weaver. The second time he was competing with Travis Graved and Ramon Cordova. Ramon, whose place of origin is unknown, ended up in Elko County and buckarooed around the big outfits. He now lives on the Owyhee Reservation where he experiences the good life and practices his artistry with a long rope, something that he is quite famous for. In a land where fancy trick and traditional buckaroo roping is much appreciated, he is known for his precision and finesse.

At Reno when Greg and his team won the Californio, the win was accomplished by doing some fancy roping in several events; the last of which was roping a large Charolais bull. Just before the team entered the arena, Ramon Cordova, whose command of the English language is unsteady, told Greg Snow, "When the toro comes out of that gate, you pusha that son of a beetchie over to the wall, and I ropa heem right in front of the peoples." When the bull entered the arena, Greg and Travis turned him toward the right fence, and Ramon who was swinging a large loop threw underhanded as the bull ran by him going right to left, and he caught him "right in front of the peoples!!" Greg forefooted the bull and Travis heeled him, and the bull went down in record time assuring the team first place.

Wally Blossom usually has two horse roundups a year where they rope as many as 150 horses in a couple days. The second roundup, usually held in the summer, is when they cut studs. Wally likes to leave his horses uncut until they are four or five years old, believing that it makes the horses stouter and stronger, and as a result they buck better. At the stud roundup, the big full-grown studs are roped around the neck and front feet just like the spring branding roundup. Charlie Gould took part in the stud roundup also and established his spot among the top hands who did the roping. Anyone who has ever forefooted a big stout stud horse in the summertime when they are at their fattest and stoutest knows that it is not child's play. Perhaps it could be compared to the days gone by when single steer ropers roped thousand pound steers instead of 450 pounders.

Charlie and Sharon went to the famous Jordan Valley Big Loop Rodeo and watched the rodeo. They had a great time but were disappointed to find out that the contestants were not allowed to dally on the front feet. They couldn't help noticing the difference watching the rodeo at Owyhee where the ropers were not required to use a large loop but were required to dally and lay the horses down. PETA hasn't made itself known at Owyhee. The Indians have an old custom: When a good Indian cowboy dies his best horse is shot and put in the grave along with the cowboy and his saddle and bridle. A rumor started that if a representative from PETA showed up at the Owyhee rodeo, a grave would be dug, and the PETA executive would be castrated and then thrown into the hole. His nuts would be tossed in on top of him and the hole filled back up with dirt. The Indians rope horses however they want to.

Charlie has become good friends with some of the Indian boys from Owyhee, and several of them have worked with the cowboy crew at the YP including Nathan Kelly Jr. Charlie admires their ability to rope and considers them to be top hands. One day he was visiting with Nathan Kelly Sr. who he particularly liked, and they discussed the history of the ranches in the area, and tales of different buckaroos that they had both known or had heard of. They talked about the art of forefooting horses and the seemingly renewed interest in it as a rodeo event. Charlie asked his friend, "Why does everyone up here want to rope horses instead of steers?"

"Well, Charlie," Nathan replied, "what does a good Corriente roping steer cost?"

"I don't know, I suppose five or six hundred dollars."

"These mustangs we rope at most of these rodeos aren't worth anything, so if you do the math, that is an easy question to answer. Besides we just like to rope horses. We think it's more fun."

Charlie could see his reasoning, and then the conversation turned to the current political issues that ranchers who graze cattle on federal lands face: issues such as the controversy about the sage grouse and other so called endangered species. They visited about the plight of Cliven Bundy and the Hammond family who were thrown in prison for clashing with federal bureaucracies. They talked about the murder of Lavoy Finicum and the difficulty ranchers have getting along with young college graduates who get management jobs with the BLM and forest service and wield tremendous power over ranch owners although they have no practical experience working on ranches or knowledge of how to survive in the private sector or any desire to help the private sector survive. After visiting about this for a long while, Charlies Indian friend looked at him and said, "You know, Charlie, 150 years ago my people had to fight the great white fathers in Washington for our land. In the end it didn't go the way we wanted it to go. Today your people are having to fight the great white fathers in Washington about the same land. It's not going too well for you either."

The men visited for a long time, and when it was time for Charlie to go, he looked at his Indian friend and said to him, in a joking way, "I would like to move onto the reservation someday and live and work with you people."

Nathan was looking at his friend and then he turned his gaze toward the Bull Run Mountains and was silent for awhile, but then finally he replied with a grin on his face. "Well, you might be one white boy that we would let that happen to."

The YP Ranch, though different in location, climate, and vegetation than ranches in Arizona like the O RO, Babbitts or the Diamond A is similar in size. It's big enough to run thousands of cows, and the buckaroo crews who ride herd on its cattle are not asked to do anything but saddle a horse and ride.

In the winter the cattle run on thousands of acres of meadows that in turn become hay fields in the summertime. The hay operation and farming is done by a crew that is separate from the buckaroo crew, and they, like the horsemen, are a capable bunch who know their jobs and understand their boundaries. There is no friction, perhaps because the setting is one of the most beautiful in North America with the Bull Run Mountains towering over the east end of the ranch at 9127 feet in elevation. The south fork of the Owyhee River runs northward from Squaw Valley and Tuscarora, flowing through the Spanish Ranch and the IL and eventually makes up the western edge of the YP. The east fork of the Owyhee River and the Owyhee Reservation are on its east side. In the summertime Greg Snow and his crew, which Charlie

Gould is now a member of, trail large herds of cattle up into the Bull Run Mountains, and on the other end of the ranch, they turn out large herds of cows and calves onto the Owyhee Desert.

If a man had a hankerin' to do so, you could get on your best circle horse and fall off into the Owyhee Canyon on the outfit's western edge and be in the state of Oregon before sundown, and on your way you could trot by the famous outlaw Claude Dallas's camp as you headed west. You can leave the ranch's eastern boundary on the same type of pony and be in Mountain City for lunch at the local café and have your horse put back in the corral eating hay before sundown. There is water everywhere with ducks and geese floating on top and trout and other game fish swimming underneath.

In the spring when the cattle are turned out of the meadows and onto the desert or up into the mountains, the buckaroo crew takes great pains to keep the cows and calves paired up correctly, sometimes working hundreds at one time and doing it day after day. As the cattle are trailed upward into the Bull Run Mountains, the calves are branded, usually several hundred at a time, and then trailed farther and higher up into the high country. The crew moves out to the desert and camps wagon style, and the thousands that are turned out onto the desert are gathered after they have located on the numerous watering places, and the calves are branded. All of the branding is done by heading and heeling the calves. There are no tied ropes and no saddle horns wrapped with rubber. Some men use rawhide reatas.

In the summertime the cattle are free to roam on hundreds of unfenced sections of desert, and the last several years, it has fell to Charlie to ride on these desert cattle and take care of them. In the late summer or early fall, depending on range conditions and the weather, these desert cows turn south and east and show up at the edge of the meadows wanting to be back in their winter home. In these meadows the hay has been cut and baled and the meadows have been irrigated, which produces a substantial amount of regrowth.

As the cows are allowed back into the meadows, they are sorted in numerous herds of equal size, and this requires a never ending amount of herd work, or rodeer work as the buckaroos say. For days on end the horsemen ride and slide and cut and slash on good horses directing cattle to one field or another as the numbers and situation requires. It is a constant barrage of cow work all done by a crew of horsemen. There are no ATVs or helicopters or two-way radios.

The same process is done as the cows come down off of the Bull Run Mountains on the east end of the ranch, and when the cow herd has been captured, the horsemen begin the long process of vaccinating the calves with a round of shots. While this is done they are sorted into bunches that are made up of all heifer calves or all steer calves and so the cow work continues day after day, and again, all done horseback without ATVs, helicopters, sirens or radios.

When it's time to wean the calves and ship, the calves are separated from their mothers by a man on a good horse ducking and dodging to one side or the other, putting cows through one gate and calves through another. When they pass through the gate they are separated by a fence but can still see each other and touch noses, and the process is smooth and easy. If a calf is missed and ends up in the cow herd, it is roped and led into its correct spot, but few mistakes are made.

In the winters, which sometimes are brutally cold, the buckaroo crew continues to ride and care for cattle which sometimes need to be doctored for some reason or another. They are roped, even if they are big bulls and the ground underneath is icy and as slick as greased lightning, so the crew shoes their horses with shoes that have had borium cleats welded onto them for increased traction. Many times the work is done when men are dressed in heavy overalls with scotch caps and hoods over their heads and felt-lined packs on their feet. Roping is done with heavy gloves or mittens on their hands.

The first summer Charlie and Sharon lived on the YP, Greg Snow sent Charlie with three young buckaroos to spend several months camped up high in the Bull Run Mountains taking care of the YP cattle running in that area. Charlie was the boss of the bunch, and they took his sheep wagon and a wall tent and made camp at about 7000 feet in elevation. They spent the summer pushing cows up high and onto good grass.

The young men liked Charlie and followed his lead concerning their work, but they turned the work into play as often as they could. One day they jumped a bunch of wild Indian horses that were running high in the mountains. When the horses took off, a young buckaroo named Jon Landa built to them and roped a two-year-old filly, and it was all done on a very steep mountainside at over 8000 feet in elevation and at a very high rate of speed. Charlie would tell the story, saying it was one of the prettiest pieces of cowboying he ever witnessed.

One night as the four men sat around the fire telling yarns, the greenest kid in the crew expulsed a great amount of gas. "What in the world is the matter with you? You don't do stuff like that right in the middle of camp. Go off there in the bushes to do your business." Charlie told him, but the kid just grinned. A few minutes later the kid repeated the process laughing at Charlie as he did it. Without saying anything Charlie got up and grabbed a pan of dirty dish water and threw it in the kid's face and ran him out of camp, and then the boy got on the fight, but Charlie just laughed at him.

The same young man was always broke, a result of going to town every time he got paid and spending all his money in the honkytonks and other establishments that make a practice of taking men's money. One day the kid asked Charlie, "How come you got all that nice stuff? I mean, heck, you've got two or three nice saddles and some nice bridles and your wife always looks nice, and I ain't got nothin'."

"Next payday you bring me your check and let me take care of it," Charlie replied.

"Heck, no, I'm not givin' you my money, I might want to go to town."

"No, you bring me your paycheck, and I'll cash it for you and give you some spendin' money, and I'll keep the rest. I'll teach you how to save some money, and you can have some nice stuff, too." The boy started giving his paychecks to Charlie, and Charlie took care of his money, at no charge, and it began to accumulate.

Around Christmas there is always a big party at the Taylor

Canyon Bar halfway between the YP and Elko. The YP crew were all there including the young kid who Charlie had taken to raise. A good number of neighboring ranchers were there also, and plenty of small children. A big Christmas tree had been set up at one end of the room, and amidst all of the Christmas cheer and laughter, the kids had gathered around the tree and were singing "Jingle Bells." Charlie stood watching the kids when the kid who he was managing money for walked up and said, "What the heck are we celebrating anyway? Is it somebody's birthday or somethin'?"

Charlie looked at him incredulously and said, "Yeah, as a matter of fact, it's Jesus Christ's birthday."

"No kiddin'. I didn't know that."

As the night wore on, the kid consumed large quantities of whiskey and became very drunk. When the party was winding down, the folks started walking toward their cars, the kid staggered toward his pickup which was a beat up old wreck that would barely run. A local ranch owner who was very wealthy and who had arrived at the party in an expensive and very shiny vehicle observed the kid who was about to get in his old wreck. The wealthy man knew the kid would never be able to keep the old pickup in the middle of the road, so he walked over and made the boy get in the passenger side of the truck, and then he drove the boy all the way to the ranch, some fifty miles, and then made sure he got in the bunkhouse where it was warm. When the kid quit the YP sometime later, Charlie gave him a large wad of money, and it was far more than he had ever had. They parted friends.

Recently someone in Arizona made a presumptuous comment, "You know I heard that old Charlie Gould is up there in Nevada working on one of those big ranches and he's wearing a flat hat!"

Well, I'm not sure what Charlie's hat looks like because I haven't seen him in four or five years, but I've never figured out why a man's hat style means anything. Maybe the truth is Arizona wasn't big enough for Charlie anymore. When Charlie was a kid he dreamed of being old enough to work for Mack Hughes who ran the IDT Association on the San Carlos Indian Reservation. When Mack ran the IDT, the reservation as a whole had somewhere over 30,000 mother cows on it. The IDT itself had around 8000, but truthfully no one knew for sure. The IDT remuda consisted of 185 horses and 30 pack mules and herds of 2500 cattle or more would be trailed for a week to reach the shipping corrals at Calva that were built to accommodate 8500 cattle at a time.

Today there are few cattle on the San Carlos and very few Apaches have any interest in cattle. Instead they sit in government housing and watch the lights of their casino flash on and off advertising the nonstop celebration of government-subsidized mammon taking place within its walls. Obesity and diabetes run rampant among the descendants of the Apache cowboys who used to work for Mack Hughes and Charlie's father, John Gould, and there are no cowboy jobs at San Carlos in this day and age. In Northern Arizona the Double O has been subdivided by real estate speculators, and Californians and other pilgrims live where steers used to graze. The Yolo Ranch where Skeet and Charlie worked in 1967 has been sold and split up in a manner that makes no sense to anyone. Many times ranch managers are hired because they possess college degrees even though they can't gather a milk cow. They are paid exorbitant salaries but never take part in the actual cow work but instead travel to the feed stores and roping events in $70,000 crew cab pickups hooked to aluminum trailers and lament the unavailability of good cowboys. The cowboy crews, when there is one, are payed wetback wages, and they come and go more often than rain; and when the cattle can't be gathered, an expensive helicopter is hired, and it is called progress. Long term Coley-Lyon's-style loyalty between real cowboys and ranch owners is a rarity. But on the banks of the Owyhee, Charlie and Sharon look out over meadows where thousands of America's best cattle graze. There is a mount of great cowponies to pick from every morning when it's time to saddle up and a good crew and cow boss to work with everyday doing things like roping, branding, doctoring; and all done without someone hollering at you on a radio or a helicopter flying overhead doing your job. At bedtime Charlie goes to sleep thinking about the cow work waiting for him the next day. Regardless of how you crease your hat, that's what all cowboys are supposed to be dreaming about.

Epilogue

One day during the '90s, Charlie was riding a colt up Horsewash Canyon a little north of Jones Mountain and a little south of Tailholt Mesa and a little northwest of a place known as Fair Oaks. The canyon, which has no historical significance, is in the foothills of the rough mountains that rise up between Williamson Valley and the chasm of Burro Creek thirty miles to the west. These mountains have been some of the last strongholds of true Arizona rough country cowboying. A place where in the old days ranches didn't run "wagons" but instead were known as pack outfits where camps were moved on the backs of mules because wagon roads didn't exist, and men like Charlie Fancher, Ed and Clifford Koontz, Travis Heckel, Yaqui Ordunez, and Whistle Mills gathered cattle as wild as deer, and through the use of learned skill, they cared for, worked and did what was necessary to get them to market. It was no easy task.

As Charlie rode up the canyon, he came to a natural waterhole that had been carved by erosion in the solid rock of the canyon bottom and was big enough to hold several thousand gallons of water when full. There was a slight seep or spring of water leaking out of the cracks in the canyon wall and ensuring the availability of a small amount of water in the bottom of the rock bowl at all times. To people of modern times who are accustomed to water that is always present at the turn of a spigot or the flip of an electric switch, the place would have no significance, and many of those types wouldn't even pause to look and wonder.

But Charlie knew what he was looking at, and he stopped the bronc he was riding and thought about all the cattle that had watered there in the old days.

In times past a place like that would have had a name because any amount of water no matter how small was precious to a cowman, but the name and significance has been lost in time. While waiting and pondering about such things, Charlie noticed something that looked like carving on the face of a vertical flat rock on the canyon face directly above the natural water hole; and when he looked closer he could make out the letters E K M and the numbers 4-23-1926 next to the letters. The letters stand for Elton K. (Whistle) Mills. And then he read the letters J W G and the numbers 4-23-1942 which stood for John W. Gould, Charlie's father.

Charlie then remembered his father telling him about finding Whistle's initials on a rock and that he had then carved his next to Whistle's on the same rock. They both had carved their initials on April 23, sixteen years apart. Charlie, who was always a lover of history and especially cowboy history, thought that surely Providence had directed him to this place, so he got off the bronc he was riding and hobbled him and with a sharp rock began carving his initials C B G next to his father's and the legendary cowboy Whistle Mills'. It was about then that he realized that it was April 23 in the year 1992, exactly sixty-six years after Whistle had been there and fifty years after his father. And then he realized that John, his father, had died on that day, April 23, one year earlier.

After finishing his carving on the rock, he climbed up onto a rock above the waterhole and the stone face containing three cowboy's initials and contemplated the echoes of the past. He thought of his father, and for some reason he thought of the smell of Prince Albert tobacco and the smoke coming out of his pipe, and that made him think of George Goswick whose self-manufactured cigarettes were rolled with Prince Albert inside, and for a moment he could smell the smoke even though it wasn't there, and he thought of days gone by when a little water in a rock hole would have meant something to somebody. He sat there for a long time and thought of cow people.

Made in United States
Troutdale, OR
11/23/2024

25163884R00146